AKIM-KOTOKU

[*Frontispiece*

Women and children took stools, wooden mortars and clothes down to the
stream to be washed. (*See* page 154.)

AKIM-KOTOKU

AN OMAN OF THE
GOLD COAST

By

M. J. FIELD, B.Sc., Ph.D. (Lond.)

Sometime Social Anthropologist to the Gold Coast Government
Author of *Religion and Medicine of the Gã People,*
Social Organization of the Gã People

NEGRO UNIVERSITIES PRESS
WESTPORT, CONNECTICUT

Originally published in 1948
by The Crown Agents for the Colonies, London

a

Reprinted in 1970 by
Negro Universities Press
A Division of Greenwood Press, Inc.
Westport, Connecticut

Library of Congress Catalogue Card Number 76-111575

SBN 8371-4600-3

Printed in the United States of America

AUTHOR'S PREFACE

In 1938 I was asked by the Gold Coast Government to go to Akim-Kotoku to investigate, firstly, the native system of state finance, and, secondly, the question of the native system of allegiance and jurisdiction.

Anthropologists are all familiar with discussion concerning tribal and territorial organization. Professor Lowie writes : 'According to Morgan's atomistic theory, primitive society differed fundamentally from civilized society in that it lacked *political* organization founded upon territorial contiguity. Primitive tribes, he contended, deal with an individual as a member of a sib, i.e., of a kinship group and accordingly, through his personal relations : the civilized state deals with him through his territorial relations as a member of a township, county or larger spatial unit. This political organization in the narrower sense is, according to Morgan, a relatively recent development at a very high cultural level. . . . Sir Henry Maine had expressed similar views : "The history of political ideas begins . . . with the assumption that kinship in blood is the sole possible ground of community in political functions, nor is there any of those subversions of feeling which we term emphatically revolutions, so startling and so complete as the change which is accomplished when some other principle—such as that, for instance, of *local contiguity*, established itself for the first time as the basis of common political action. It may be affirmed, then, of early commonwealths that their citizens considered all the groups in which they claimed membership to be founded on common lineage." '

It was therefore of great anthropological, as well as administrative, interest to find in the typical Gold Coast Native " State," which is by no means primitive in organization, not only that territorial control and political control are completely independent of one another, but that political control is based, not on local contiguity, but on military confederation.

The Pax Britannica has now removed the primary force of political cohesion. Furthermore, modern economic factors, such as mines and the cocoa industry, have given to the land-owning groups, which are mainly kinship groups, importance and power which were entirely lacking in the days when the native "states" were first formed. It is therefore obvious that the task of administering these states, each of which is now, through the action of modern economic forces, necessarily divided against itself, must be one of unique difficulty.

In these circumstances administrators, if they have not succeeded in devising at the first attempt, a completely harmonious system of indirect rule in these complicated societies, need not apologize. If in the following pages failures rather than successes appear to be emphasized, this emphasis must be taken solely as an attempt to throw into prominence their peculiar difficulties and to concentrate thought upon their knottier problems.

To anthropologists it will be obvious why the questions which the Gold Coast Government specified for investigation could not be tackled without an examination of the general anatomy, physiology, and metabolism of the 'Native State'. I have not, however, attempted a complete ethnographical account of the people and their customs, many of which are identical with those of the Ashanti and have been fully described in S. R. Rattray's classic volumes. Acquaintance with Dr. Rattray's work, on the part of the reader, is assumed throughout the present work.

Though mainly concerned with Akim-Kotoku, I have found it necessary, for reasons which will appear, I hope, in the chapters, to extend work into some of the towns of Akim-Bosome and Akim-Abuakwa.

Western Akim people do not speak 'pure' Twi. In taking down vernacular words and texts in the field, I used the modern phonetic symbols for all sounds, afterwards attempting to transcribe these in the antiquated orthography used by the earlier German missionaries and still retained by students of Twi, though all other students of African languages now use the standard symbols. It may well be that students of Twi will find shortcomings in my efforts in this direction, but, fortunately, linguistics, *per se*, are not of moment for the purposes of this work.

I am much indebted to Mr. Hugh Thomas, the Secretary for Native Affairs, not only for initiating this research and for recommending Akim-Kotoku as a typical Gold Coast Native State, but for the stimulus of his interest in the research during its progress. My findings have abundantly justified his belief that a Gold Coast Native State is a far more complicated organization than the earlier administrators assumed.

To my friends the Omanhene of Akim-Kotoku and the

Omanhene of Akim-Bosome, together with innumerable chiefs and elders of Western Akim, I am deeply in debt for their unfailing kindness, courtesy, and patient, willing help.

My African assistant, Mr. J. V. O. Darkoh, who visited with me—often on foot—about seventy different towns and villages of Western Akim, has greatly helped me by his talent for rapid friendship with strangers and has cheerfully borne much longer hours and greater discomforts than fall to the lot of most Government clerks.

M. J. FIELD.

October, 1940.

I am out of touch with any changes that have taken place in Akim between the writing and the publication of this book.

A chapter on the social and political effects of certain health-conditions which dominate much of Akim is among the omissions made at the request of the Gold Coast Government.

M. J. F.

June, 1947.

CONTENTS

CHAPTER I

INTRODUCTION

1

In Western Akim we find three of those African organizations known as '*oman*', a term which is usually translated 'Native State'. The *Oman*, however, lacks some of the characteristics implied in the normal use of the word 'State'. I propose to give, in this introductory chapter, a rough general idea of what an *oman* was, is, and is not, and the relationship in which it stands to the quite separate and independent organization for the control of land. Subsequent chapters will, I hope, not only make clearer the nature of an *oman* but show to what extent the individual person, through his linkages to various social institutions, is linked to the *oman*, and to what extent he is independent of it.

2

Western Akim is a geographical region : a district. An *oman* is not a district or a tract of territory. It is a confederation of groups of people. If we map in three different colours the distribution of the three groups of people comprising the three *oman*, we obtain, not three big areas of colour, but a patchwork of small areas splashed in all directions, some, indeed, going right off the map of Western Akim.

The units of which each *oman* is composed are sub-groups of people attached to stools. We may therefore say that an *oman* is a confederation of stools, which may or may not be contiguous. Furthermore, since the people in one town are usually united around one stool, it is also said, with tolerable accuracy, that an *oman* is a confederation of towns. Thus, the town Abenase is a member of the *oman*, Akim-Kotoku. Batabi is a member of the *oman*, Akim-Abuakwa.

Before we can grasp the peculiar nature of the union which exists between the stools of the *oman* we must follow the process whereby the *oman* came into being. For this we must go back some three hundred years.

In the seventeenth century Western Akim was uninhabited except for some lonely, widely-spaced hunters who were members of the Toa, Oreko, and Agona clans. Their descendants to-day claim that they were aborigines and have no tradition of migrating from elsewhere, but they must, at some still earlier date,

I

have belonged to the Toa, Oreko, and Agona clans of Ashanti.
They recite the same origin myths as their Ashanti clansmen
(namely, that the Toa came down a ladder from heaven, the
Oreko out of the ground, and the Agona out of a river), but
each venerates a local spot in Western Akim as its place of origin.
They probably came very early from Ashanti as adventurous
hunters seeking new hunting-grounds ; their hunters' camps
grew into villages and later, when they set up stools, into towns.
A 'town' in the Gold Coast is a place which has a chief's stool.
Even if it consists of but half-a-dozen thatched dwellings it may
still be a " town."

Other similar hunting camps were started by Akwamu hunters
of the Aduana clan. These came from the Akwamu town,
Nyanyao, near what is now Nsawam.

Each group of these early settlers owned the land it hunted
over. An enterprising hunter opened up a bigger area than an
indifferent one. Hunters of one settlement respected the boundaries of another, but the settlements were so widely spaced that
there was seldom any contact of boundaries.

Each of these hunting communities was a free, independent
unit. There was no centralized government. None of them
served any other local chief, and they had no military organization, though the Akwamu probably maintained links with their
old home, and traded their ivory artd smoked meat.

Such early immigrants, together with the still earlier ones who
claim to be aborigines, are called 'Atwia'. Atwia are defined as
'people who were alone and were not subject to anybody.'

Early in the seventeenth century a great wave of migration
from Ashanti and Denchera began. Thenceforward, almost up
to the present day, party after party of immigrants arrived. These
were of several types :

a. Remnants of forces defeated in war, fleeing before the victors.
b. Relatives of powerful chiefs who had quarrelled with their
   families and left with a party of supporters. Right up to
   the present day the principle persists that no one should
   either fight or go to law with a clansman. If relations
   become intolerably strained one side or the other packs
   and departs.
c. Subject peoples who found the yoke of the overlord
   unbearable.
d. Fugitives from justice.

To class d belongs one of the most important immigrants.
The chief of Kokobianteh, a stool in Adanse serving Denchera,

is said to have offended against the Dencherahene and, to escape
the penalty, fled with a handful of followers to Nyanyao, where
he threw himself on the protection of the king of Akwamu. The
Akwamu king said, 'There is no place for you here, but my hunters
in the Birrim district (the 'atwia' of Asamankese and Kyibi)
have plenty of land and they will give you somewhere to live.'[1]

So the Kokobianteh stool was set up in Kyibi, and, though
it became the paramount stool of the Akim-Abuakwa *oman*, it
did not own the land it settled upon.

Miscellaneous migrations continued. For example, a relative
of the chief of Ashanti-Kokofu quarrelled with his senior kinsmen and came and took up two tracts of unoccupied land on the
East bank of the Pra and founded the towns of Brenasi and
Aprade, now members of the Akim-Bosome *oman*.

At the end of the seventeenth century began the great struggle
between Ashanti and Denchera, from which struggle the newly
formed Ashanti confederacy emerged as the overlord of Denchera.
During this war various Denchera chiefs and their stools with
the few survivors of their defeated forces fled, one after the
other, over the Pra into Western Akim. These Denchera
refugees found in Akim plenty of unoccupied land and settled.
Among the first were the founders of the towns of Abenase,
Anyinase, Chia, and Ofuasi.

The stool of Denchera-Miriem (now the paramount stool of
the Akim-Kotoku *oman*) held out in Denchera for a long time
and fought with both Osei Tutu and his successor Opoku
Ware, but was finally defeated and sought refuge in a succession
of forest hiding-places on the Ashanti side of the Pra. One
hiding-place after another was discovered by the Ashanti, so the
refugees came over the Pra into Akim and settled at Akrofonso,
near what is now Prasukama, on land given by Adausena, one
of the early Akwamu settlements.

In a fit of depression the humiliated chief drowned himself in
the Pra. Thereafter that district was dubbed 'bad land' ; so his
successor left and established himself at Jyadem [2] near Osina at
the foot of the Kwaha range. Later he moved to Oda, where his
stool is now.

The stools that remained in Denchera came under the rule of
Ashanti, and among them was the stool of Bosome. Bosompinto,
the Bosome chief, found servitude to the Ashanti so galling that
he left and crossed the Pra into Akim, settling at Akim-Swedru.
His stool is now the paramount stool of the Akim-Bosome *oman*.

---

[1] This is the Akwamu version.
[2] Not to be confused with the Jyadem near Oda.

Meanwhile the Ashanti had discovered whither all the refugees
had fled and had started crossing the Pra into Akim on punitive
raids. So the immigrants allied with the aborigines and set up
three military organizations—Akim-Abuakwa, Akim-Kotoku,
and Akim-Bosome. These military unions were termed *oman*
and the head of an *oman* was termed the *omanhene*.

The three *omanhene* were chosen from among the later immigrants from Denchera, for these were the only people experienced in warfare. The three *omanhene* of Akim-Abuakwa,
Akim-Kotoku, and Akim-Bosome had their headquarters at
Kyibi, Jyadem, and Akim-Swedru respectively. Later, Akim-
Kotoku quarrelled with Akim-Abuakwa and the *omanhene* of the
former moved from Jyadem to his present site at Oda, settling
on land lent to him by Wenchi.[1] Later still he began to pay an
annual rent for this land, and, recently, bought it outright.

The earliest of the immigrants had found plenty of unoccupied
land and they hunted over it and became owners. But as the
land began to fill up, the later arrivals applied for sites on the
lands of earlier arrivals, coming to terms with them in various
ways. The influence of the clan system was strongly marked: the
immigrants always obtained the most advantageous terms
from members of their own clan, and were received by them as
'brothers.' For instance, the Oreko aborigines of Anamase and
Adekuma received the immigrant Oreko clansmen from Ashanti
and freely lent them land to farm and build the towns of Batabi
and Kokobin, demanding only an annual sheep in acknowledgement of land ownership. Clan kinship continues to the present
day not only to be an important factor in the relationship of
one part of an *oman* to another, but also transcends the political
division between *oman* and *oman*.

When the *oman* unions were set up it was entirely a matter of
military convenience, choice, or sentiment which of these any one
town chose to join. No question of land entered into the contract. Even when an Omanhene virtually forced a defenceless
town to come under his banner he never touched or attempted
to control its land, and this for a very good reason to which we
shall return later.

Of the earliest Akwamu settlers of the Aduana clan, the towns
Ochereso, Asamankese, and Akwatea joined the Akim-Abuakwa
oman. Adausena, Ntronang, and Pankese joined the Akim-

---

[1] Wenchi was and is a member of the Akim-Abuakwa *oman*. There is nothing
incongruous, in African ideas, in the head of an *oman* living on land lent by a minor
member of another *oman*, an illustration of the principle that *oman* is nothing to
do with land.

Kotoku *oman*. Ochereso, Adubease, and Odumase are Akim-Abuakwa towns in the extreme West of Western Akim and have numbers of Kotoku people and their lands between them and their Omanhene in the East. Similarly Kusi is an Akim-Kotoku town in Eastern Akim with Akim-Abuakwa peoples between it and its *omanhene*. Adubease and Brenase, which joined the Akim-Abuakwa *oman* and Akim-Bosome *oman* respectively, each have some land on the Western side of the Pra which is not Akim at all. Amentia, an aboriginal town which joined the Bosome *oman*, is also on the West bank of the Pra.

It was quite common for towns which were not an important part of an *oman* to transfer allegiance from one *oman* to another, almost holding their allegiance up to auction. Transference was just as easy as transferring an insurance policy from one insurance company to another—in fact, that is exactly what it was, for an *oman* was nothing more or less than a mutual benefit society. Money and service were paid by the members into the *oman* in return for help in time of need. Examples of transfer are Ayiribi, Apaso, and Anyinam, which are now in the Akim-Kotoku *oman* and which used to be in the Akim-Bosome *oman*. Asuom and Otumi transferred themselves from the Kotoku *oman* to the Abuakwa. Franteng, far away in the Cape Coast district, has quite recently joined the Kotoku *oman*. Brenasi, an important member of Bosome, claims that it has recently severed all allegiance and is now a member of no *oman* whatsoever. Now that there is no warfare it sees no point in belonging to any *oman*. We shall return later to consider what are the present-day inducements to continued loyalty to the *oman*, for this question is of vital interest in administration.

Amanfupong alone in Western Akim claims that it has never joined any *oman* and therefore owes no allegiance to any *omanhene*.

For two centuries warfare with the Ashanti continued, and it was only through membership of an *oman* that any one town could save itself from annihilation.

It must be borne clearly in mind that the *oman* union was military only and that each member retained its independence in all civil affairs. In the matter of land this has never been modified, and to this day land control is independent of *oman* control. But political affairs were modified by the fact that for two centuries there were virtually no political affairs other than military affairs. Warfare was the sole preoccupation. As one informant put it, 'We never lay down to sleep at night without wondering whether the Ashanti would wake us before morning.'

Wartime emergency conditions became, in these two centuries, the normal conditions. Political organization and military organization therefore became in many respects identical. In particular the financing of the incessant warfare made the *oman* a financial mutual benefit society as well as a military mutual benefit society. The financial union between the members of the *oman* and the financial organization of the *oman* survives to-day and is the most important factor in continued political union.

3

The organization of the *oman* was as follows. Every town or stool joining an *oman* was allotted a position in one or other of the five groups of battle formation—the *Benkum*, the *Nifa*, etc. (left wing, right wing, etc.). By dint of shuffling, these five 'wings' were kept, roughly, numerically equal. Each of these five 'wings' was commanded by one of the five big 'wing chiefs' (the *Benkumhene*, the *Nifahene*, etc.). To these all other chiefs were, in matters of warfare, subordinate. A subordinate chief approached the *omanhene* and was approached by him, only through that wing chief under whom the subordinate served militarily.

The financial responsibilities of each of the five wings were assessed equally. If the *omanhene* required for warfare 500 *perequans* of gold, each of the five wing chiefs had the duty of collecting 100 *perequans* from the subordinate chiefs in his 'wing'. If the *omanhene* had 500 barrels of gunpowder to distribute each wing chief received 100 barrels for further distribution. The component towns of any one wing were not equally assessed, but when a distribution took place each town received the same fraction of the whole as it contributed when a collection was made.

Not only did the *omanhene* make periodic financial demands on the whole *oman*, but he also claimed for the *oman* one-third of any extra-ordinary wealth that might chance to come to any one stool. Suppose a stool to have acquired, in any way whatsoever, 300 *perequans* of gold, then it had to send 100 *perequans* to the *omanhene* for the use of the *oman*. Of all such fortuitous wealth coming to the *omanhene* he retained one-third for the *oman* treasury and distributed the remainder equally between his five wing-chiefs, who further sub-divided their portions between the component stools of their wings.

The affairs of the *oman* were managed by an *oman* council consisting of representatives of every chief's stool in the *oman*.

This council controlled the spending of the *oman* funds and decided what taxes were to be imposed.

In addition to dealing with *oman* affairs, the *oman* council was occasionally approached by members of the *oman* and asked to act as independent arbitration court in disputes requiring a dis-interested opinion. The *oman* council thus gradually came to fulfil the function of a court of appeal.

4

With the establishment of the Pax Britannica the primary reason for the existence of the *oman* disappeared. The habits of financial and political co-operation and social intercourse were, however, firmly established. In the financial sphere there arose much new activity. This we must now consider.

A stool or town which possesses land has complete control over that land and no *oman* has any say in its land affairs. All rents accruing from lands let to strangers for normal uses (i.e. agriculture and building) belong wholly to the landowner, and are not shared by the *omanhene*. But once land is converted into cash by selling, then it is no longer land but potential gun-powder and comes under the heading of that extra-ordinary wealth of which the *omanhene* is entitled to one-third. It is only in modern times that land has become a saleable commodity, but the practice of selling it has now come to stay.

Again, in Western Akim there are now numerous and profit-able mines and many of the land-owning stools receive good unearned incomes from the mining companies who have con-cessions on their land. Of this money also the *omanhene* takes one-third. He also takes one-third of money made by timber sales. And whenever money is collected for 'pleasure', say for the festivities associated with the enstoolment of a new chief, one-third of it must be sent to the *omanhene*.

The *omanhene* in turn must distribute throughout the *oman* two-thirds of all this wealth which comes to him. Thus the *oman* is united by the circulation of money back and forth.

The new income from mines and land sales means that the land, originally valueless to the *oman* and quite independent of it, has become *linked* to the *oman*. The *oman* does not control or own it, but has acquired a very acute interest (in the non-legal sense) in it.

Another outcome of modern conditions is that it is still advan-tageous to the poor or landless stool to belong to the *oman*, but the obligation to pay one-third of all wealth to the *oman* makes *oman* membership disadvantageous to a landed or wealthy stool, since the result is to mitigate the poverty of the one at the expense of the other.

The financially costly warfare of modern litigation which goes on all over the Gold Coast does, in some slight degree, act as a cohesive force replacing the co-operation necessitated by the ancient type of warfare. For when a town of one *oman* has a land dispute involving a lawsuit with a town of another *oman*, it can sometimes persuade its *omanhene* to assist it, though he is under no direct obligation to help with land affairs. There are several instances of towns which have severed their allegiance to an *omanhene* who refused to give such help. In some cases the severed town has joined another *oman* which held out the desired aid.

5

We have seen that, although land control and *oman* control are independent, there is a certain linkage of the land, through its finances, to the *oman*, and also that every part of the *oman* is involved in this financial association. If this were the whole story, the situation would be simple and an *omanhene* might eventually come to be regarded as the ultimate owner of his subjects' land in the same sense that all land in England is owned by the Crown. But it frequently happens that *more than one oman* is financially linked to a given piece of land. Although I went to Akim intending to confine my attention to the people of the Akim-Kotoku *oman* I soon found that, as soon as I started to examine their land affairs, these led me among the members of more than one *oman*. This state of affairs can arise in several ways, but the commonest is through the *joint* ownership of a tract of land by several towns, some of which belong to one *oman* and some to another.

The best way to understand the types of situation which can exist is to examine a few concrete examples of land-and-*oman* relationships. To the stranger, who expects an *oman* to be like a small European State, the first impression is one of incredible chaos, but once he has grasped the independence of land control and *oman* control, and has furthermore learnt something of the significance of clan brotherhood, orderliness at once appears.

Our first instance concerns the towns Adekuma and Anamase. Adekuma people and Anamase people are aborigines of the Oreko clan. They say they have always been 'one' though they divided into two settlements. These were on one tract of land, jointly owned, and without any boundaries between the two owners. The members of both towns hunted over the whole tract. Also they shared equally all income and all burdens. Each one said, 'We are one. Their trouble is our trouble, their good fortune is our good fortune, their land is our land and ours is theirs.' But Anamase chose to join the Bosome *oman* : Adekuma was forced to join Abuakwa. This does not affect the land or the brotherhood. If they were to sell any land they would divide the proceeds equally. Anamase would then give one-third of its share to its *omanhene* and Adekuma one-third to its *omanhene*.

This same Adekuma-Anamase situation is further complicated. The joint *Oreko* landowners were approached on two different occasions by two batches of immigrant *Oreko* clansmen from Ashanti. Because of the clan sentiment these strangers were received and freely given sites to build their towns, Batabi and Kokobin, and permission to farm and hunt over the land without paying anything but an annual sheep. Both these towns are members of the Akim-Abuakwa *oman*. Neither of them owns any land though they have the free run of the land. If gold were found on one of their farms the proceeds would be divided equally between Adekuma and Anamase, who, after paying their respective *omanhenes*, would give Batabi and Kokobin a small gratuity. The one on whose farm the gold was found would receive a rather bigger gratuity. If a financial burden descended—say litigation—Adekuma and Anamase would have to bear the whole, but Batabi and Kokobin would probably come forward with a voluntary contribution in return for gifts received in the past.

But we have not finished with the complications of these four towns. A third batch of *Oreko* refugees appeared (from Ashanti-Bankame) looking for a home. The Akim-Kotoku *oman* received them into its military confederation, but could give them no dwelling-place, so Anamase (a member of the Bosome *oman*) gave them a part of Anamase town to dwell in and a part of Anamase land to farm. This was towards the end of the nineteenth century, and people had grown less generous about land, so Anamase demanded rent. The newcomers agreed, but payment was spasmodic and the amount variable till recently when the District Commissioner persuaded the parties to fix the amount at £55 a year. This is paid to the Anamase chief and he shares it equally with Adekuma. From his own share he gives his *omanhene* a small voluntary gratuity. (An *omanhene*, though entitled to one-third of the proceeds [1] of land sold, gets no share of either farm rents or busa-farm income. That is, he shares in

[1] See Chapter 6.

2

all fortuitous wealth, but not in income from the normal agricultural use of land.)

Thus we have Anamase, Adekuma, Kokobin, and Batabi saying, 'We are all one, we have no boundaries between us.' And yet we find them serving three different *omanhenes*, and we find half of one town paying rent to the other half of the same town, and another town sharing in that income.

Another curious situation is that of the town Akim-Swedru, the seat of the *omanhene* of the Akim-Bosome *oman*. It is partly on its own land and partly on the lands of both Awisa and Aduasa which serve the Akim-Kotoku *oman* and the Akim-Abuakwa *oman* respectively.

Again, the 'brother' towns Aprade, Amanfupong, and Nyankumasi, of one clan, are 'on one land' without boundaries between them. Aprade and Amanfupong are joint landowners, Nyankumasi pays an annual sheep. Aprade serves the Akim-Bosome *oman*, Nyankumasi serves Akim-Abuakwa and Amanfupong serves no *oman*. Attached to Amanfupong is a colony of Swedru people who used to pay £4 a year for their farms, but now pay an annual £40. This income is shared with Aprade. Achiasi, which serves the Akim-Abuakwa *oman*, is also on Aprade-Amanfupong land but pays an annual rent of about £200.

Again, the town of Apaso consists of two sets of people, both of the *Bretu* clan, but having migrated from different parts of Ashanti. One set serves the Akim-Bosome *oman* and the other the Akim-Kotoku.

Again, Abenase, Awisa, and Edubea are each on its own tract of land with other people's land between them, but they behave as 'brother' towns with Abenase as the senior brother. They share, though not equally, income and such financial burdens as litigation. This is because they are not only of the same *Agona* clan but came from Denchera as one party with one stool. For purposes of hunting and keeping a look-out for Ashanti raiders they found it convenient to scatter and settle on three different tracts, but, so far as they themselves are concerned, they treat the three tracts as one. On each tract they found some aborigines, again all *Agona* clansmen, who welcomed them, and in each of the three cases aborigines combined with immigrants to make one town under one stool. In the case of Abenase the immigrant stool was made the town's chief stool: in the cases of Awisa and Edubea the aboriginal chiefs were made the town chiefs.

It is often said by Akim people 'An *omanhene* has no land.' This is not strictly true, but it is very nearly so, for the three *omanhenes* of Akim were among the later immigrants who found

little unoccupied land. We also find that the big wing chiefs
are usually among the relatively landless, for they too were
usually chosen from among the war-lords of the later Denchera
immigration. It may sometimes happen, however, that a wing
chief or another big office-holder in the *oman* is of an aboriginal
town and is therefore a land controller, concurrently with but
independently of his office in the *oman*. These isolated instances
may convey, on a superficial glance, an illusion of correlation
between land control and *oman* control, but this is due to mere
coincidence. Consider a concrete case.

The *Benkumhene* of Akim-Kotoku is the chief of the town
of Manso. A large tract of land is *jointly* owned by Manso,
Akroso, Ashantimang, and Amentem-Nwanta, all aborigines
of the *Toa* clan who used to occupy one town. On this tract of
jointly owned land are also the towns of Esuboi-South, Esuosu,
and Eshiem. The latter town consists of recent Fanti tenants
paying an annual rent. The former two towns live rent free.
Now, if any extraordinary land income accrues to one of these
seven towns, it is taken to the Manso chief who, after deducting
the *omanhene's* one-third, divides it equally between the four
joint landowners. If, however, the Manso chief in his other
capacity, that of *Benkumhene*, receives a sum of *oman* money in
the course of one of the *omanhene's* distributions, he divides it
between Manso, Akroso, Ashantimang, Amenten-Nkwants,
Eshiem, Kusi, and Suponsa, for these are the members of the
Benkum wing of the *oman*. And if he collects money from his
wing when the *Omanhene* levies a tax he collects it from these
seven members. Esuboi-South and Esuosu, although they live
on Manso land, serve the *oman* in other wings, so they neither
receive from nor give to the *Benkumhene*.

These examples by no means exhaust the types of relationship
which exist between land and *oman*, and exist without causing
any bewilderment to the people concerned. But they are sufficient to make it clear that whatever an *oman* is, it is not an association of landowners or a machinery for the central control of
land. It is equally clear that there are formidable obstacles to
its ever becoming such a machinery.

At the present stage in the evolution of African constitutions
it would be difficult to condemn too strongly any attempt by
any ambitious *omanhene*, to subvert the constitution of his *oman*
by claiming rights over his subjects' land. He would create
difficulties and enemies in abundance, would deceive no serious
and competent student, and would forfeit the respect of the
African common man.

6

The general significance of the stool should be considered briefly in any introductory survey of the *oman*.

We have little exact information concerning the rôle of the stool before the days of the great military unions. Probably the head of a group of kinsmen, who was both judge and priest, sat upon a stool when he delivered all-important dicta. After his death his departed spirit was worshipped and his stool which, like his bath-sponge and other objects closely associated with his person, was considered to have absorbed something of the essence of his being, was venerated. On days when his spirit was worshipped his stool, normally laid upon its side, was set up on its base as a signal to his departed spirit to come and sit upon it.

The dead are believed to have it in their power to confer either blessing or misfortune on the living, and the main object of the cult of the dead is to secure the one and avert the other. The ancestor's stool thus came to be regarded as a fount of blessing and a protection from all ills. In the early agricultural and hunting days, the blessings sought were mainly good crops, good bags of game and abundant healthy offspring. But when warfare became the main preoccupation the stool was besought chiefly for the blessing of victory and deliverance from death and defeat. The stools of warlike ancestors were particularly potent. And in order that the stool might the better exert its influence and endow its followers with valour and strength it was always carried into battle on the head of a special carrier. The people who 'fought under one stool' did so almost literally.

The stool was the military rallying point, the supernatural rallying point, and the pivot of warfare organization. It was during the centuries of warfare that the stool developed to the full what is still its vital social quality—that of a *unifying agent*.

When the *oman* army went to war there were scores of stools on the battlefield, each uniting groups of warriors and many of them uniting groups of lesser stools. The *omanhene's* stool united them all into one army. The whole *oman* was united, not so much by its submission to the *omanhene's* leadership, as by its consciousness of being under the supernatural, victory-bringing power of his stool.

As we shall see later, the 'chief's stool' of a town usually began as the private stool of a kinship group. By becoming the leading stool of several such groups it united them into a town and led them to war. Usually a 'chief' is defined as a stool-holder whose

stool has an oath attached to it.   Such oaths generally com-
memorate events of warfare and are hard-earned.

7

Before going further, we should become acquainted with the
meaning of certain titles which will be used from time to time.
Asasewura.   This is a controller of land, the descendant of
the man who 'made the boundaries.'
Odikro.   The head of one town only.   An *odikro* may or may
not be the *asasewura* of the land on which his town stands : he
may also be the *asasewura* in some other town in whose other
affairs he takes no part.   For instance, the *odikro* of Abontodiase
is the *asasewura* of both his own town and Esuboi-North.   That
is, Esuboi is on Abontodiase land.   The *odikro* of the one town is
an *asasewura*; that of the other is not.
Opanyim.   A headman or caretaker who may or may not have
a small family stool of his own, deputed by an *odikro* or *ohene* to
look after a colonial settlement from a bigger town or village.
The word simply means 'an elder'.
Ohene.   In Denchera and Ashanti this title meant the military
overlord of a group of towns, and the holder had the right to
be carried in a palanquin.   In Western Akim to-day those immigrant chiefs who were *ohene* in their old homes retain their titles
still, even when they now have charge of one town only and
should properly be called *odikro*.   For instance, the *ohene* of
Anyinase was a 'very big chief indeed' in Denchera and was
second only to the 'king' of Denchera himself.   In Western
Akim he has only one town and would, but for the departed
glory which gives him a courtesy title, be called *odikro*.   Again,
the *odikro* of Ayiribe has recently been given the title of *ohene*
and the right to ride in a palanquin simply because he is a relative
of the *omanhene*.   Other than as a dignity, therefore, the title
means very little in Western Akim to-day, except that an *ohene*
pays or receives a bigger share of collected or distributed moneys
than does an *odikro*.
An *ohene*, like an *odikro*, may or may not be an *asasewura*.
Usually he is not, for most of the *ohenes* are immigrants who
arrived after the land had filled up.   Anyinase, whose *ohene* was
such a 'big man' in Denchera, pays an annual rent to Apoli, a
tiny town serving another state.   On the other hand, an *ohene*
may be an *asasewura*, though this seldom happens.   Manso, whose
ohene is the *Benkumhene* of Kotoku, is one of the aboriginal
settlements.

Omanhene. Head of the *oman*, military confederation or 'state.'

There is an interesting case in progress at present (1939) between the chief of Amanfupong and a Bosome town. Amanfupong not only is suing his adversary for trespass but protests that the *Omanhene* of Bosome has no jurisdiction over him because Amanfupong alone of all the Western Akim towns never swore fealty to either Bosome or any other *oman*.

He is further claiming, not only independence, but the rank of *omanhene*. This, I believe, is quite untenable. He is undoubtedly an *asasewura*, and if he was never sworn in he is not a member of any *oman*, but since he is not the head of a military union he is no *omanhene*.

Nifahene. Commander of the right wing of the army and political head of the towns whose warriors fought in that wing.

Benkumhene. Commander of the left wing and political head of the towns fighting in that wing.

Adontenhene. Commander of the central body of the army and political head of the towns in that section.

Krontihene. Commander of the van of the main body and political head of the towns in that section. Also head of the civil affairs of Oda town as distinct from the *oman* affairs of which the *Omanhene* is head.

Gyasehene. Commander of that section of the army which includes the *Omanhene* and his stool. Political head of the towns fighting in that section. The *Gyase* had three sections, the *Gyase* proper, the *Ankobea* or outposts guard and the *Kyidom* or rear-guard.

The above five *ohenes* are of equal rank.

Twafohene. Commander of the *Twafo*, an advance guard of scouts, forming a sub-division of the *Adonten*. Political head of those towns fighting in the *Twafo*. Those towns approach the *Adontenhene* through the *Twafohene*.

Ankobeahene. Commander of the *Ankobea*, one of three subdivisions of the *Gyase* section of the army. Political head of those towns fighting in the *Ankobea*. Those towns approach the *Gyasehene* through the *Ankobeahene*.

Kyidomhene. Commander of the *Kyidom*, one of three subdivisions of the *Gyase* section. Political head of the towns fighting in that section. Those towns approach the *Gyasehene* only through the *Kyidomhene*.

Dabenhene. Lord of the *Omanhene's* sleeping-room and leader of a sub-section of the fighting force. Political head of some of the towns serving in the *Ankobea* sub-section of the *Gyase* section. These approach the *Gyasehene* through the *Dabenhene*.

CHAPTER II

THE TOWN

Structure of the Town

A town (*krom*) is defined as a place which has at least one stool.

Most towns have nothing townish in their appearance to the stranger, and Europeans tend to call them villages. A true village, however, is a farming settlement whose inhabitants are colonists or campers from some town of which they count as citizens and whither they return for all important festivals and affairs of town and family.

The town which I have selected to describe as typical is Abenase. It consists of just over 200 adult males (i.e. taxable males), a slightly larger number of females and their children. There is also a large floating population of strangers bringing the census figures of the town up to 970. These strangers, however, take no part in town affairs and for the time being I shall ignore them.

Every citizen is a member of an extended family whose head has charge of a family stool. This stool is the family rallying-point and is virtually the family deity.

There are eight such stools in Abenase. Five of these belong to the *Agona* clan, one to the *Asuna*, one to the *Bretu*, and one to the *Koana*. That is, the town consists of four exogamous groups and eight stool groups. Theoretically all the *Agona* clan people are kinsmen, so they must marry non-*Agona* partners, but only those under one stool can trace their common ancestor or their exact relationship to one another. A brief consideration of the history of the town will make this matter clear.

After the Battle of Feyase (about 1700) a tiny group of *Agona* refugees arrived from Denchera bringing with them the stool of *Otu Ayipe Firimpong*, an *ohene* (war-lord) of the shattered Denchera Kingdom. This was the first stool of the town and is still the *ohene's* stool.

Among the *Agona* immigrants was a hunter named *Joanin* who acted as scout and explorer, discovered a site for the town, and became a 'big man'. When the immigrants settled a new stool was made for Joanin. This is now known as the Joanin stool.

The descendants of Joanin's sisters comprise the extended-family now under the Joanin stool.[1]

When the Agona immigrants arrived they came upon a party of aborigines whom they found worshipping the local river and whom they regarded as landowners. One of the principal women of this aboriginal group married the immigrant *ohene's* brother and her descendants formed a third group which made for itself a stool called the *Esu Kese* stool, after the river which the aborigines both worshipped and claimed as their first progenitor. Whether the aborigines were yet earlier immigrants from Ashanti and claimed *Agona* clanship before the arrival of the Denchera people or whether they had no clan system at all is uncertain. Some informants insist that 'they did not know either war, stools, or clans', but were adopted into the *Agona* clan because the immigrants considered it necessary for all people to belong to some clan. At any rate, they were and are regarded as an *Agona* group.[2]

This gives us three *Agona* groups with their three *Agona* stools in the new town.

Shortly after this another 'big man' of the *Agona* clan, one *Abrokwa Panyin*, came from Denchera with his sister. He made a stool known as the *Abrokwa Panyin* stool, and his sister's descendants are still under it. Another similar stool was established by an *Agona* man, *Kwabena Bosum Mpim*, which stool is now the head of another *Agona* group.

The town thus originally consisted entirely of the *Agona* clan, and therefore its members had to go outside the town to find marriage partners.

Meanwhile other immigrants had in similar fashion brought or created other stools and had made other towns. The neighbouring town, Ayiribe, was formed round a stool of the *Bretu* clan, Akokoaso round a *Koana* stool. Marriage was mainly patrilocal; therefore, when an Abenase man brought into his town a wife from Akokoase or Ayiribe, her descendants constituted a *Koana* or *Bretu* colony in Abenase. Some of these descendants would, by the nephew succession system, be called back to their mothers' towns to succeed mothers' brothers,

---

[1] Had it not happened that an *Ohene* and his stool were brought from Denchera, Joanin would have been made *odikro* of the new town and his stool would have been the *odikro's* stool. The founder of any town and creator of its first stool becomes its *odikro*. The title *ohene* depends on military rank in a military confederation of towns.

[2] Probably it is true that "they did not know clans" before the immigrants arrived, for, had they been regarded as *Agona* at the time of the arrival intermarriage would not have been allowed.

but a number would remain. When such a new group became sufficiently large it was allowed to make a stool. Thus the *Koana*, *Bretu*,[1] and *Asuna* stools were founded in Abenase.

We find then to-day in Abenase eight stools, each under its own *asafohene* :

The *Agona* stool of *Ayipe Firimpong* (*Ohene's* stool).
The *Agona Esukese* stool (*Asasewura's* stool).
The *Agona* stool of *Joanin*.
The *Agona* stool of *Kwabena Bosum Mpim*.
The *Agona* stool of *Abrokwa Panyin*.
The *Bretu* stool (*Krontihene's* stool).
The *Koana* stool.
The *Asuna* stool.

Thus in any town the *odikro* or *ohene*[2] is simply the descendant of the founder of the town and its first stool, no matter what his clan. No clan is inherently more 'royal' than another. *Agona* is royal in Abenase, *Koana* in Akokoaso, *Bretu* in Ayiribe.

---

[1] A dramatic story is connected with the establishment of the Bretu people in Abenase.

The Ayiribe chief, *Kyum-Berema*, married *Enina Egya*, the sister of *Abrokwo Panyin*, the holder of one of the *Agona* stools of Abenase. She went to live with him in Ayiribe, and quickly had two children, a boy, *Tebi*, and a girl, *Amoa*. After this she bore no more children and her people, believing this to be her husband's fault, took her away from him. In those days the children of divorced couples were often divided, so *Amoa* came with her mother to Abenase and *Tebi* stayed with his father in Ayiribe. The boy brooded over this separation and developed a bitter grievance. When the girl reached puberty her father sent a message that he would like her to visit him. This suggestion pleased her Abenase relations and they sent with her a little retinue of attendants, including three of her half-sisters, born since her re-marriage. The little party stayed eight days in Ayiribe and the father was delighted with his daughter. This increased the resentment of the boy *Tebi*, and he determined to kill his sister, his three half-sisters, and himself 'so that there should be no more family.' The girls had arranged that before going home they would collect some of the abundant local snails to take with them, so the boy said he would go to the forest with them and help in the collecting. He hid his gun by the river and then told the attendants to take the girls first to the riverside. They did this, but left behind in the house the elder girl who wanted to finish peeling some plantains for cooking. When the others had reached the river and were standing in the stream drawing water and bathing, the boy fired at them and killed the two youngest sisters. There was a great commotion and the elder girl ran to see. She found her brother, who had not had time to re-load his gun, chasing the attendants with a cutlass. She avoided him, ran back to Ayiribe, and all the townspeople set out to seize the boy. They found the bodies of the two girls, but neither the boy nor his gun was ever seen again. Abenase 'made a case' against Ayiribe, and Ayiribe readily agreed to make all possible amends. So two *Bretu* girls were given by Ayiribe to Abenase to replace the two murdered *Agona* girls.

The descendants of these two *Bretu* girls soon became sufficiently numerous to be allowed to make a stool.

[2] See Chapter I.

The Asafohene [1]

Each recognized stool[2] group of a town is under an *asafohene*. This man is the ceremonial head of the group and is responsible for the ritual for the stool. He is responsible for the discipline of the group and he is the outside representative of the group.

Although the *asafohene* is the ceremonial and active head of the group he may himself have a 'father' who is the real head and from whom he actually takes his orders. The Abenase *ohene* has such a 'father'. This 'father' is a successful business man working in another part of the Gold Coast. He was invited to be *ohene* when the post was last vacant but declined. The present *ohene* is regarded as 'acting for him'. He visits the town whenever he has time, freely spends his wealth upon it, is consulted on all important town affairs, and bears the main financial burden of his family group and its stool. The *Koana* stool group, on the other hand, is an example of a group whose ceremonial head happens to be its actual head.

The position of the *asafohene's* son is important in the stool group. He is not a member of the group, for a man belongs to the clan of his mother, but he knows, through his father's training, more than do the members themselves about the ceremonial of their own stool. He deputizes for his father in matters of stool ritual if his father is absent and when the father dies the son becomes the 'father' of the new *asafohene*. When this new *asafohene* is to be elected the electors are the heads of all the households under the stool together with the late *asafohene's* sons. The eldest of these sons convenes the election meeting and presides over it. This arrangement is a clever one, for the son, being of another clan, is himself ineligible for the post but has a keen interest in seeing that his father is worthily succeeded.

The son remains as 'father' and adviser of the new *asafohene* till he himself is called away to succeed to some position on his mother's side.

As an example of a kinship group under its *asafohene* we may take the *Koana* clansmen of Abenase. (See p. 36.) My table includes all the grown males now living in the town. A few others exist but do not live in their own town. They return, however, for important family affairs—such as funerals—and when they

---

[1] *Asafo* simply means a group or company, and, though the word very often means a military company, it does not necessarily : it does not in the word *asafohene*. The word *hene* suffixed to any title implies that the holder of the title has a stool.

[2] The word *abusua* is used both for the little town group of kinsmen under the *asafohene* and his stool, and also for the clan in the wider sense which I describe in Chapter III.

KOANA CLANSMEN OF ABENASE

People whose names are followed by the same sign ♦ ■ ● ▲ ⊗ live in the same compound

Yaa—Baram ♀

die their bodies will be brought home for burial in the family
cemetery. When the family group contributes its quota to town
taxation either messages are sent to the absentee demanding his
contribution or the *asafohene* pays it and saves up the debt against
the next visit home.

The *Koana* people of Abenase all claim descent from *Ya Baram*,
the first *Koana* woman to marry into Abenase from Akokoaso.
They know exactly how they are descended from *Ya Baram's*
'daughters', but the exact relation of these 'daughters' to *Ya
Baram* they either do not know or are unwilling to divulge.

Slave Blood

A few elderly people who came into the town as slaves or
as the children of slaves do not belong to any stool group and
when they die will be buried in a strangers' cemetery. Each of
them is, however, affiliated to some stool group, and in a few
generations their descendants' slave blood will be, if not completely forgotten, ignored. Slave blood has never been so much
despised in practice as it is in theory, and, though no one will
admit to having a drop of slave blood, most people have some
and are not the less respected in everyday life.

When the towns were first formed—about 1700—families
were greatly depleted. In particular there was a shortage of
women, for most of the refugees who survived were men of
the scattered fighting forces, cut off from their homes and their
women-folk. After settling in their new country few of them
ever again made contact with their old homes, and most families
absorbed by adoption as many strangers as they could. It was
common for a man to purchase or capture an attractive little
girl, have her brought up as his daughter or sister's daughter,
and marry her to his nephew or son. Even some of the women
who formed the central links in the chain of matrilineal succession in royal houses were adopted rather than born into their
families.

I first arrived in Abenase from a part of the Gold Coast where
I had found the people pleased and proud to tell me all they
knew of their forbears and to give me information enough to
construct long and interesting family trees. But in Akim-
Kotoku I was at first puzzled to find that nearly every informant,
after telling me cheerfully of his parents and grandparents,
suddenly relapsed into sulky silence and would give no details
of earlier ancestors. Sometimes an informant who had been
courteous and interested would suddenly flare into anger and

say 'What business is it of yours who was my grandmother's mother? I am too busy to tell you any more.' Neighbours would then hint to me the reason for this sudden reticence and I soon came to realize that few people's lineages would bear close investigation and that it would be wise to abandon all attempts to construct detailed family trees.

Again and again incidents cropped up showing that sensitiveness about slave blood was present in most people. For instance, I asked the reason for the destoolment of a bygone chief and found that his principal offence was that 'he spoke of people's origins'.

Again, a pleasant, respected and popular youth of my acquaintance was offered the hand in marriage of a chief's sister's daughter. Unaccountably he declined, though he liked the girl and was pleased with the honour done him by the offer. The real reason for his refusal was that he foresaw a day when the girl's son might be a candidate for the stool and some dissentient voice might point out that the candidate's father had slave blood in him—the risk of which just accusation he was unwilling to face.

On another occasion I attended the hearing of a dispute brought by two sisters against the *asafohene* who was the head of their family. The sisters were elderly women and were the daughters of a woman who had been purchased by the *asafohene's* maternal uncle and adopted as a member of his family. The sisters were respected persons and no one remembered their origin except the *asafohene*, who had, with old age and ill-health, become grossly disagreeable. One day this old man called at a palm-wine booth for a drink, and, sitting there in public, prefaced his drink with a small libation and prayer for blessing on all his clansmen, mentioning audibly all the members by name and adding that two of them were not true members but slaves. This came to the ears of the two women concerned, and, although he was their *asafohene* and 'father', they summoned him before the *ohene's* 'chamber court'—a private court where the *ohene*, assisted only by such elders as he invites, hears cases in private while reclining on his couch. The women brought two distinct charges. One was an old grievance about the profits of some cocoa-trees of which the old man had defrauded one of the women. She would doubtless have let this matter slide rather than sue her 'father' had not she been angered by the injury he had publicly done to her pride.

The old man lost both cases. In the cocoa case he was ordered to restore the woman's right to the cocoa and pay her a pacification fee of two shillings. He took this judgment with an ill

grace, shouting and storming. But when it came to the slave
case in which he was ordered to pacify each woman with eight
shillings, he accepted the judgment meekly and in perfect
silence, clearly ashamed of himself for having done a grievous
wrong.

I recall again the behaviour of an elder, important and
respected, but of slave birth, on an occasion when it was formally reported to the chief that a labourer from the Northern
Territories, a complete stranger, had died in the town. The
elder in question, usually a most tranquil person, wept bitterly.
I inquired whether the weeping elder had been a friend of the
dead man. 'Oh no,' was the answer, 'but he always weeps
when strangers die because that reminds him that when his own
death comes he too will be laid in the strangers' cemetery among
people who do not know their origin.'

The Elders of the Town

The town is governed, not by a 'chief', but by a body of
elders of whom the 'chief' is the chairman.

The elders of Abenase are :

The *Ohene* or 'Chief'.
The *Gyacehene*.
The *Krontihene*.
Seven *Asafohenes*, of which one is concurrently *Krontihene*.
Two *Asafoakyes*.
One *Asafosipi*.
Three *okyeames*, spokesmen or orators. (Usually translated
    'linguist'.)
One *Ohenebea* or 'queen mother'.

Some towns—such as Assene—which have an important
ancient deity (*obosum*) other than a stool, may have an *abosomfo*
or priest among the elders, but Abenase and most other places
have no such priests.

We may now sketch in roughly the position of each of these
'big men' in the town.

The Chief

Whether a chief is an *odikro* (the head of one town only) or
whether he is an *ohene* (having some seniority over certain other
chiefs in the military confederation to which all the towns
belong), his position in his own town does not vary.

The chief's headship of the town was primarily military and his stool was carried to war to bring victory. In this stool the good fortune of the town was believed to be condensed.

The manner in which a chief is installed brings out not only the military nature of his position but the fact that it is his duty to obey his people. I had the opportunity of attending the installation festivity of the chief of Ayiribe, Abenase's near neighbour : the proceedings there may be regarded as the usual ones.

The Ayiribe election and private enstooling ceremony had been completed : the swearing-in of the new chief was public. The function was held in the market-place and, besides the townsmen, representatives of all the neighbouring towns attended as a mark of neighbourly courtesy.

When everyone was assembled, one of the visitors rose and asked the elders who was their new chief, that the visitor might go home and tell his town. The *okyeame* rose and said, 'His name is *Adinkra*. He comes from Koforidua.' [1]

Then the members of the military company (*asafo*) went to fetch him from his house and, as a farewell to him as an ordinary citizen, gave him a last ceremonial flogging. Then they smeared him with white clay—the symbol of innocence and congratulation—and brought him before the assembly where they set him on a decorated chair under a coloured umbrella.

After he had risen and thanked them he distributed £21 for 'thanksgiving rum', money provided by the members of his clan stool to 'thank the town'. This money was divided into ritual shares, one-third of the whole being sent to the Omanhene.[2] He also presented the town with a case of rum.

Then oaths of fidelity were sworn. The new chief stood with his cloth slipped to his waist to signify submission, took the state sword in his hand and turned to the townspeople, saying, 'I am a small boy and succession has to-day called me to succeed my grandfathers. Everything that my grandfathers have done is what I must do. You, my elders, whom I am to-day facing, I have to obey you. If ever there is trouble between this town and any other town, and I run away, I shall have violated *ntam kese* (the 'Great Oath'). All townspeople, men, women, boys, and girls, I am to-day your "father". If there is any trouble on one of these children and I do not help, but run away, I shall have violated *ntam kese*.'

---

[1] His mother was an Ayiribe woman, but he had been brought up with his father at Koforidua.

[2] The Omanhene claims one-third of all moneys collected 'for play'.

Then he turned to the queen-mother, saying, 'You are my mother : you and I will enfold (*bu*) this town. If I do not, and I go against you or go behind you (*sunamasie*), I shall have violated *ntam kese.*'

Then the elders, one by one, stood holding the same sword and swore, 'If we, your elders, do not help you in all your undertakings, or if we run away in your trouble, we shall have violated *ntam kese.*'

Then the *asafoakye* on behalf of the military body held the sword and swore, 'I, the *asafoakye* whom this town has chosen, I who have promised to give my life for this town, to me you have come to-day in the stead of your grandfathers. If any war or trouble come and I and my children do not defend you, I shall have violated *ntam kese.*'

The election and appointment of a new chief—as distinct from his public installation—is a task performed, as it were, on a delicately balanced see-saw. The chief is the representative of a clan group : he is also the representative of a town. In selecting him his own clan group and the body of town elders must both be satisfied. This is not always easy.

The first stage in the election is a meeting of the *asafohenes* and the *gyasehene*. The latter is authorized by the meeting to ask the senior member of the royal clansmen for a chief.

This senior then convenes a meeting of his relatives and they elect, not a chief, but a candidate for chieftainship. The queen-mother's opinion is said to be of great weight, but this depends on her personality. The *gyasehene* is then told the candidate's name and he takes it to the *asafohenes* for consideration. The *gyasehene's* own opinion carries special weight, for, if he says, 'I can't serve this man', nobody can make him, and no chief can get on without the *gyasehene's* help.

If the elders accept the nomination of the royal house all is plain sailing. If they do not, they send back the *gyasehene* to ask for another nomination, and they go on till they get an offer they like.

The Krontihene

The *krontihene* (or *mankrado*), like the *ohene* or the *odikro*, has a stool which used to be taken to war. His stool went in front of the main body, and, whereas the *ohene's* stool might retreat to avoid capture, the *krontihene* was sworn never to retreat but 'to advance until his head was gone from off him'. It was the *krontihene* who was the real commander of the military operations.

The *krontihene* is the leader of the *asafohenes*. He may also be described as the town's chief citizen and the mouthpiece of the populace. As one of my informants put it, 'When the *krontihene* says, "I agree," to anything the chief says, then the chief knows that the town is with him ; but if the *krontihene* says "I disagree," then the chief had better say no more about that matter.'

It is the *krontihene* who takes the town's grumbles and suggestions to the *ohene*. For instance, in Abenase it was felt that some of the food prices in the market were unduly high, so the people complained to the *krontihene*, and he took the matter to the *ohene*, suggesting that gong-gong should be beaten through the town fixing a maximum price.

Again, a few years ago it was widely felt that the marriage fees of Akim-Kotoku were too heavy. Though no town is bound to submit its customs to *oman* dictation it is obvious that in such a matter as marriage fees uniformity of custom throughout the state is desirable. The *omanhene* therefore tackled the matter. He called together, not the chiefs of the towns, but the *krontihenes*, and asked them to find out what their people thought of the suggestion and, if the people approved, to pass it on to their respective chiefs. This was done, and, as the suggestion happened to be a popular one, the next time the chiefs met the *omanhene* they were unanimous in advising him to send his gong-gong beater throughout the state announcing the general alteration in custom.

It sometimes happens in these days that the *omanhene*, in making a suggestion, uses the channel selected by the Government, viz. his chiefs. Each chief then passes this on to his *asafohenes*. The *asafohenes* and the *krontihene* will then have a meeting which the chief does not attend, and, if they disapprove, will inform him of their opinion. He in turn will inform the *omanhene*, and if the *omanhene* still wishes to pursue the matter it is for the dissentient *krontihenes* that he will send.

The *krontihene* is the chief's deputy and the 'father' of the town in his absence. He alone may sit in the chief's chair in court when the chief is away. Neither chief nor *krontihene* may leave the town in the absence of the other and neither may leave it without permission of the elders.

If the elders wish to reprimand, admonish, or even depose their chief it is the *krontihene* who is their mouthpiece. One chief even made the sweeping generalization 'Every *krontihene* is against the chief,' meaning that whenever there is either criticism of or opposition to the chief it is expressed through the *krontihene*. The krontihene is, in fact, a most important part of the mechanism

1. A palm-wine booth. (*See* page 20.)

2. Elder without portfolio. On plate 11 he is seen at his money-table at a funeral. (*See* page 29.)

whereby the power of the chief is limited and the essentially democratic nature of the native government is preserved.

The *krontihene* is *asafohene* of the group under his own clan-stool and *krontihene* of the whole town. He is elected by his own kinsmen, but if the other elders disapprove of the choice they can demand another.

One chief, desiring to disparage the *krontihene's* position, described him to me as, 'The one who looks after the town's young men.' And though he said it to belittle the *krontihene*, it bears on an important aspect of the *krontihene*. The 'young men', or the populace in general, in so far as they are represented by the *asafohenes* of their respective clan groups, can get their opinion registered only when it is orthodox, for an *asafohene* is invariably a pillar of tradition. And being also the senior kinsman of the young men in his group, the *asafohene* has all the sanctions of kinship with which to crush their heterodoxy. In the *krontihene*, however, they have a possible champion for heresy and a possibility of representation on other than a kinship basis.

Another chief said of the *krontihene*, 'Every *krontihene* is a stranger,' and yet another, 'The *krontihene* controls the town's strangers,' both referring to the fact that the chief's war-stool was the nucleus round which the town formed and that the *krontihene* is, I think invariably, of another and later group of clansmen. At the same time there is an Akim proverb 'It is strangers that make a town', meaning that the numerical strength given by the 'strangers' was as necessary to the town as the rallying point provided by the stool.

The Gyasehene

The *gyasehene* is the head of the *gyase*. The *gyase* is 'the circle round the chief's fire'. It consists of the chief's sons and daughters, household, wives, spokesmen, stool carriers, servants, and any guests, together with the clansmen of his stool. Whenever I stayed in Abenase or Oda, or attended functions there, my official place was among the *gyase* as one of its guests, and I was included in all the courtesies usually extended to them.

The *gyasehene's* stool is kept in the same stool-room as the *ohene's* or *odikro's* ancient stool and the queen-mother's stool. The *gyasehene* is usually, though not invariably, the chief's son, and in any case he must have been brought up near the stool of which he has charge and in the circle of people of whom he is head. We saw that the chief of Ayiribe was called from his father's house at Koforidua to succeed as chief in his mother's town,

Ayiribe,[1] and this is common and normal in all successions. The *gyasehene*, however, is chosen from the circle of chief's sons, and where the chief has wives belonging to a variety of clans there is an equally wide choice of clans from which to choose the *gyasehene*. In actual practice, however, cross-cousin marriage is followed closely enough in the royal circle to ensure that the *gyasehene's* post remains in one clan. In Abenase the present *gyasehene* is the son of a chief and the husband of a chief's sister, and this is normal. Thus the ideal relationship between the *gyasehene* and the chief is as in the scheme below, where black circles and white circles represent the chief's clan and the *gyasehene's* clan respectively. In most places actual facts show a close approximation to this ideal.

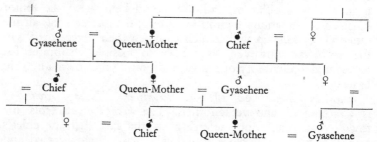

Whether the *gyasehene* be the chief's father in fact or not, he is expected to be a father to him in behaviour. In the selection of a new candidate for the chief's stool the *gyasehene's* opinion is supposed to be more valuable and impartial than if he himself belonged to the chief's own clan.

The Asafoakye

The town has two of these officers.

The word means 'father of the *asafo*', and in this connection (unlike that of the word *asafohene*) the word *asafo* has no kinship implication but means a military company.[2] The *asafoakye* is the head of the town's military force.

There is in Abenase only one *asafo* company of which the elders take any account—namely, the '*Asafo Prampram*' or '*Apesemaka*', to which all able-bodied grown males are eligible

---

[1] This system has the great advantage of creating strong ties between widely separated peoples. The Ayiribe chief will always feel a link with Koforidua. All those literate Africans who hope for the ultimate union of the whole Gold Coast and, at the same time, advocate a change to patrilineal succession on the ground that it is more 'advanced', would do well to reflect on the unifying effects of the nephew-succession system.

[2] It is somewhat misleading that *asafohene* means the head of a group of kinsmen and *asafoakye* the head of a military company.

to belong. About ten years ago the youths formed a second company, the '*kyirim*', which they modelled on Fanti lines, but the elders say that 'it is just play of the young men', and do not recognize its officers.

No affairs in the *asafo* are on matrilineal lines. A father trains his sons, provides them with magical war-medicines, weapons, and other appurtenances of war. The sons inherit the father's weapons. If the force breaks up into sub-sections on the battle-field a son stays with his father.

The *asafoakye's* position is not hereditary, that is to say, he is not, like each of the foregoing 'big men', the representative of a group of kinsmen. He is elected from any family in the town. It is the practice, however, to elect the son of the late officer if he is suitable.

Now that warfare has ceased the *asafo* is a kind of public works department. It deals with all sorts of emergencies ; for example, it would act as fire brigade. The members are summoned by the beating of the *Apesemaka* drum—a small drum with a high-pitched note of great carrying power. The commonest present-day emergency is the formation of a search party to hunt for townsmen lost in the forest, and I saw several such parties organized. On another occasion the *Omanhene*, who was having some building done in Oda, asked Abenase to supply several lorry-loads of timber, split and prepared as rafters. The *asafo* felled the trees, prepared the rafters, and loaded the lorries. I shall have more to say of the work of the *asafo*.

The Asafosipi

This official is a kind of whip in the *asafo*. When the *asafoakye* has drummed *apesemaka* to call the company together the *sipi* is responsible for rounding up defaulters. He is the mediator between the *asafoakye* and the ranks. He is also the quarter-master, treasurer, and distributor of gunpowder and other supplies. In peace-time team-work for the town he issues such things as cement and bricks. If absentees are fined he collects and takes care of the money. When land is sold a part of the proceeds is usually allocated to the *asafo* for ceremonial gun-powder and other expenses of *asafo* 'play' ; it is the *sipi* who takes care of this money. When a lost townsman was found by the *asafo* his parents presented the *asafo* with pots of palm-wine. It was the *sipi* who allocated these.

Minor disputes between members of the *asafo* at *asafo* gatherings are tried by the *sipi*. When an *asafo* company celebrates with that of another town—say, at a funeral ceremony—any dispute between members of the two bodies is settled by the two *sipi* together.

The Okyeame

The *okyeame* is the chief's spokesman and ambassador. His post is not hereditary. When a new chief is appointed he appoints for himself a new *okyeame*. Those appointed by his predecessor also remain in office till their own deaths. Thus in Abenase there are now three.

The *okyeame* appointed by the present Abenase chief is a man without pedigree. He himself had the rare honesty and character to tell me voluntarily that he was of slave origin and had attained his present respected position by his own efforts.[1] He is not only a man of eloquence and wisdom but of musical talent, and is the master of drumming at festivals.

The *okyeame's* position is quite unique, and no other single officer has such free play for his personality. Theoretically the *okyeame* is only a 'tongue', but a tongue can be an influential as well as an unruly member, and influential the *okyeame* is. He is the only person, other than the chief's wife, who may visit the chief in his sleeping-room, and is thus the only person who can confer with him without witnesses of the conference. In court and on all other occasions preserving the slightest pretence of formality no one else is supposed to address the chief directly. The visitor addresses the *okyeame*, and the *okyeame* repeats the greeting or message to the chief. Any request for audience with the chief must pass through him, and, if he is unsympathetic, the matter can go no further.

As a spokesman or ambassador the *okyeame* at best colours the message : at worst he transforms it unrecognizably.

One elder said, 'If I told you of all the things that *okyeames* have done you would fill a hundred note-books and there would be plenty still untold.'

The Queen-Mother

The queen-mother's position, like the *okyeame's*, depends on the personality of the individual. I never saw the Abenase queen-mother exerting any of that power and influence which queen-mothers are said to wield. She performed the ceremonial for her own stool and did the cooking for the *ohene's* stool and the family dead at the time of *Addae* and *Afahye* celebrations,

---

[1] In Abenase there are several indications that slave blood in that town goes with superior ability.

but she took no part in current discussion and affairs. She was a silent woman with gentle but dignified manners, and, though she attended the Tribunal and took her share of any money divided between the elders, she never opened her mouth. She had been married to the *Gyasehene* but was separated from him, and, though she said that if anyone choose to reconcile them she would be quite willing, she herself took no active steps. She lived in apparent poverty in a bare, tumbledown compound with a young unmarried daughter, an older married daughter, and some children. Unlike most of the townspeople she worked hard on her farm and spent most of the day there, returning very tired in the evening. Every day she cleared a little more forest with her cutlass, felling by burning the trees which were too large for her to cut. Her plantain farm had grown enormous, and, as she sent her plantains to Oda market, her wealth must have been much greater than her way of living proclaimed. She certainly set an example of great agricultural diligence, but no one else followed it. On one occasion I quoted her farm in refutation of an informant's assertion 'Women's farms are never large'. The retort was, 'She is not a woman, she is a man'. But in spite of this she neither had nor seemed to desire much influence in town affairs. She was said to be the head of the market, which, like all markets, is run by women, but I never saw her there. She was also said to hold a court from time to time for the judging of women's palavers, but again I never knew her to do so.

The chief's wife, on the other hand, seemed to wield much of the influence expected of the queen-mother, and was for that reason resented by the elders. This wife once said to me, joking, 'You must be friends with me, for if the chief orders you to be beheaded it is only I who can beg you off.' On this a townsman commented, somewhat resentfully, 'She was jesting, but it is true that when the elders make up the chief's mind for him she causes him to change it.' I should not be surprised to learn that many destoolments to which various causes are officially assigned are traceable to the elders' resentment of the influence of the chief's favourite wife.

Elders without Portfolio

Before leaving the subject of the elders it must be mentioned that there was one old man in Abenase who had no official status as an elder but through sheer ability had come to be accorded that status in practice.

In his early childhood he came into the town either by purchase or capture, and his face bears Northern Territory tribal marks.

One of this old man's special gifts is that of remembering financial details with unfailing accuracy. At every funeral and on all other occasions when money is either collected or distributed he sits and makes a mental note of every item, and his memory is as accurate and detailed as any account-book could be. He is co-opted by every meeting of elders and his presence at all important sittings is now a matter of course. He is a silent man and participates very sparingly in general discussion, but when he does speak he is always given the closest attention, and his opinion is sought and valued.

So long as European schemes for native administration continue to recognize that the native system is rule by elders rather than rule by chiefs, that system will not, I think, be bound by an inelastic system of hereditary succession, but will always respect and utilize outstanding merit.

Dual Rôle of the Elders

The military *asafo* officers are on the governing body of elders as executive officers, and, though they may take part in general discussion, they are not regarded as rulers and legislators. The *okyeame* is also theoretically but an eloquent mouthpiece expressing an opinion not necessarily his own. The *asafo* officers and *okyeames* further differ from the stool-holding elders in being appointed by electors other than their relatives.

The real governing voices of the town are those of the clan stool-holders. These are elected by their relatives and, together, they represent every kinship group in the town. A stool-holder is but the apex of a phalanx of kinsmen.

Two things, then, are clear about town government. First, it is democratic ; second, kinship is the basis of representation.

But the elders have another rôle in addition to that of governing the town as a body, and in this rôle they are all of equal importance whether they have stools or whether they have not. This other work of the elders is done not while they are gathered in one impressive governing body but while they are scattered and hidden in their own yards. The maintenance of all general law and order rests on their shoulders. They are not only the representatives of the populace, they are the 'fathers', controllers, guides, advisers, masters, and watchers of the populace. As we shall see when we come to examine the system of justice, the elders' private individual courts are more active and more important than the big tribunal on which they all unite. Hardly a day passes over the head of any elder without his having to settle some minor dispute, give instructions to one person and counsel to another. The administration of justice is a much more retail business than any European stranger seeking it only in formal tribunals has any idea. The elders, even when they give their wisdom and service freely so far as money goes, receive for it something which they value more—deference and prestige.

Division of Court Takings

The relative rank of the various elders is shown by the manner of dividing the takings when the tribunal has heard a case. The money is always divided in the same way.

First of all the small fixed charges are deducted. The drummer who beats the *Katamanton* drum which calls the elders together gets one shilling every time he brings out his drum. The court heralds, who are also stool-bearers and wear black monkey-skin caps, get three-and-sixpence between them for each sitting, however short or long. They keep order in the court, and when the chief or any other 'big man' speaks they interject the equivalent of 'Hear, hear !' so loudly and frequently that it is impossible to hear the speech.

Any policemen present, whether the chief's own or visiting police, get two shillings between them. Policemen are, of course, innovations.

When the fixed deductions have been made, out of every remaining twenty shillings the sum of four shillings is first taken to be divided between the *okyeames*. Of the remaining sixteen shillings the *ohene* receives one-third and the *asafohenes* [1] equal shares of the other two-thirds. If the queen-mother is present her share comes out of the *asafohenes'* amount, but it is only about half of theirs because she does not contribute to their collections.

The *ohene* divides his portion between himself, the *gyasehene*, and a few distinguished old men who may be regarded as ministers without portfolio. For instance, two of the chief's elder brothers are often present and the old account-keeping man who has no pedigree. Any distinguished visitors are always included in this group. Whenever I myself attended a court it was always insisted that I shared in the emoluments of this group even when I protested that I had taken no part in the business.

The *asafohenes* also give a gratuity out of their share to the officers of the military *asafo*. Each gives about two shillings in the pound.

The chief gives a small gratuity out of his own share to the wielders of the cow-and-elephant-tail switches.

[1] Absentees get nothing.

In the court the members occupy three sides of a square. The chief on his dais has one side, and between him and the wall behind him sit the queen-mother, the *gyasehene*, the distinguished visitors and unofficial members. Along the opposite side of the square sit the *asafohenes*, each on his decorated '*asipim*' chair. Along the third side, on the chief's right, sit the *okyeames* with small boys holding their staves for them. When an *okyeame* speaks he rises and holds his own staff.

At the chief's feet on the steps of the dais sit two small boys waving cow-tail switches and an old man with an elephant's-tail switch.

The Asafo in the Town Service

Several examples of the *asafo* in action as a search party were provided while I was in Abenase, and I may here describe one of these occasions.

A young man who was known to have been for some time suffering from fits of deep depression—the result of venereal disease—wandered off into the forest one day taking a gun and a cutlass. He was away three days and then, just as the town had decided to search for him, he turned up at a distant village, distraught and talking incoherently about feeling impulses to kill both himself and others. The villagers gave him food and a bed and sent a messenger to his parents in Abenase. But they omitted to hide his gun, and the next day another message came from them that he had disappeared in the night with the gun and four cartridges.

His parents went at once to the chief, the chief had the *Kata-manton* drum beaten to call the elders and the gong-gong to tell the populace to assemble. The *asafo* officers were asked to organize search parties. This they very competently did.

The searchers were divided into companies, some under the *asafo* officers themselves, others under capable men selected by the *asafo* officers. Each company was allotted certain forest paths to follow and certain villages in which to make enquiries. Each set off at a rapid pace.

Within a few hours one of the parties, guided by some villagers who had seen the quarry, found him, confiscated his gun, bound his wrists with vines, and brought him back on a lead, though he was perfectly docile and amenable.

Then the chief, elders, the man and his parents assembled in the chief's yard as if for the trial of a 'case'. The man himself was then quite sane, shedding a few silent tears of humiliation. The chief asked him kindly what was his trouble that he should flee into the forest. He said he had been having feelings of misery, feelings of hating company, and an urge to shoot himself and others. The chief then asked his parents whether they had known of his condition, and when they said they had he reproved them for not having looked after him and taken him to a medicine man for treatment. Had he killed either himself or another, the chief reminded them, it would have been their fault.

He then ordered the parents to provide the *asafo* officers with sufficient palm-wine to 'thank' all who had helped in the search.

Before the meeting dispersed the chief *asafokye* announced that the *Krontihene* and two other *asafohenes*—of the *Joanin* and *Esukesi* stools—had failed to attend the *asafo* rally and were therefore fined two-and-sixpence each. As the *asafokye* afterwards explained, 'At an ordinary meeting of elders, I am junior to the *asafohenes* and could not fine them, but in *asafo* affairs they are junior to me and I can fine them if they fail to obey.'

A few of the populace who had not turned up were more subtly punished by being treated as 'women' at the next gathering for communal work, and being made to join the women's gang at weeding work.

The Asafo as a Heterodox Group

The officers of the military *asafo*, alone among the town elders, are not representative of kinship groups. Furthermore, *asafo* meetings may be attended by neither chief, *krontihene*, nor clan *asafohenes*, except by special invitation. It is therefore clear that the *asafo* could be used to express any tendency to rebel against traditional authority, be it the authority of the clan *asafohene* as a tyrannical 'father' or the authority of the chief and *asafohenes* as a political body.

I am told that in pre-British days lively incidents of the kind often occurred. At a seditious meeting of the *asafo* the members would be helplessly bound to both obedience and secrecy by all-powerful oaths and supernatural sanctions, and might then be ordered to assassinate certain 'big men'. Dramatic stories are told of individuals finding themselves the prey of conflicting loyalties. A man might, for instance, be ordered to murder his own maternal grandfather, uncle, or half-brother.[1]

---

[1] Between matrilineal and patrilineal authority, as such, I do not think there has ever been any conflict more serious than the small domestic clashes that are everywhere inevitable. Though matrilineal authority appears, to the superficial glance, dominant, a closer examination shows that patrilineal claims are cleverly balanced against it. This will, I hope, be made clear in later chapters. Had the conflict been acute, I do not think the *ntro*, as a patrilineal social grouping, would have died quietly as in this district it has.

In the recent past there was, I am told, an outbreak of de-stoolments of chiefs brought about by *asafo* companies. A chief had only to make himself in the mildest degree unpopular and the *asafo* would promptly de-stool him by the simple ceremony of seizing him and bumping his buttocks three times on the ground. This practice was stopped by a Government ordinance which provided that no de-stoolment should be recognized by the Government unless it had been approved by the elders and ratified by the State Council.

I should add that I myself have never seen the *asafo* functioning as the agent of unorthodoxy. The Abenase military *asafo* officers were highly sober and orthodox elders on excellent terms with the other elders and working with them as respected equals. They also held their private courts on general matters and contributed to the preservation of law and order in exactly the same way as did the other elders. On one occasion the *asafosipi* was chosen, as a worthy representative of the town, to visit a distant town in which one of the relatives of the Abenase chief had died and was being buried.

The *asafo*, as a body, attended funerals and engaged in public works in the service of the town with every appearance of willing co-operation.

Friday as a Day of Town Service

Friday is a day on which no one is allowed to work on the land.[1] People may visit their farms to gather food but may not work there. On this day everyone is to be found in his own town. He may spend all the week in his 'village' or farming camp, but on Friday he comes home to his town, often spends the night there and returns to his village on Saturday.

On Friday everyone's services are at the disposal of his town for communal work. Friday is also market-day and the town is full of activity. It is also the day of meetings and councils of all kinds.

When I first arrived in Abenase I went at once to greet the

---

[1] It appears that several traditions combine to make Friday a non-working day on the land. Before even the Denchera immigrants appeared it was the day of worship of the local river, at that time the biggest local deity and closely bound up with the ritual for the land. No land work was ever done nor water drawn from the river on that day. The Denchera immigrants associate the day with several great military disasters which happened on a Friday and combined to make it an unlucky or 'bad day'. Several solemn 'oaths'—or rather conditional curses—are connected with Friday, and if the chief calls an elders' or general gathering on Friday and adds 'anyone who does not come will be guilty of Friday', the obligation to obey is binding.

chief, and, having explained why I wished to stay in the town, I asked that the elders might be assembled so that I could not only greet them and explain my presence, but ask their permission to roam about the town, farms, and compounds and get them to explain to their relatives that I was not bent on any mischief. I was told that nothing could be done till Friday, and that not even the chief could formally greet me till then. And till Friday I had to wait.

At the time of my arrival the District Commissioner sent the chief a message telling him to have the rest-house compound cleaned of its entanglement of woods, but this again had to wait till Friday.

Every Friday morning, as soon as the sun is well risen, the chief's gong-gong assembles the townspeople to engage in communal work of various kinds. Most of the Fridays on which I was present the people were working on the extending of the *ebem* grove—the grove in which every clan of the town serves a meal to its dead at the time of the *Afahye* festival. It had been decided to enlarge the cleared space in the forest and also to build a house in which to serve the food for the more illustrious of the dead. A bricklayer was employed for the actual building, but the populace dug and prepared the clay for the mud-bricks, felled several large trees, and cleared and burnt the thick undergrowth. Women and children did the lighter weeding.

About one-third of the townspeople, being nominally Christians, were expressly forbidden to assist in such purely heathen work as *Afahye* ceremonial, and these were allowed to substitute half-hearted weeding and sweeping of the town's thoroughfares. The work in the grove, however, was so interesting compared with the weeding, that many of the less dutiful Christians took part in it.

CHAPTER III

THE CLAN

When the social structure of a town is examined, the town is found to be composed of clan (*abusua*) groups, each under its own stool and *asafohene*. The origin of these clans is distant both in time and space. They are older than the towns, older still than the *oman* and are part of a more primitive organization.

We may liken the towns and the *oman* into which the towns have coalesced, to a system of sedimentary rocks (or 'derived' rocks). Each of these rocks is found, if examined closely, to be composed of fragments of an older igneous rock underlying the newer formations. Here and there, however, we find the sedimentary strata wearing thin and the parent archean rock cropping out on the surface in all its ancient rugged strength and making an 'unconformable junction' with the newer rocks.

So it is with the clan. We find the clan as an ingredient of the town, but we find the same clan underlying and linking towns and *oman* which have no political connections, and persistently cropping out with impressive strength.

The Ashanti clans have been described by Dr. Rattray and I need not do it again. These same Ashanti clans are the ones which we find to-day not only in the three Akim *oman* but in Kwahu, Akwamu, Akwapim and also among all the Fanti-speaking peoples. We find, in fact, the greater part of the Gold Coast inhabited by about a dozen huge clan groups. In any one of these groups every individual regards himself as the kinsman of every other individual in the same group, though the other may live hundreds of miles away or in a political union which is a bitter enemy of the one to which the first man belongs. An *Agona* man of Ashanti would no more marry an *Agona* woman of Akwapim than he would marry an *Agona* woman of his own village. Even among Christians clan exogamy is strictly observed.

And not only is clan exogamy everywhere observed but a genuine clan brotherliness, transcending all political enmities and geographical estrangements, is still practised. For instance, a man of the *Asuna* clan comes from Kumasi to work as a brick-layer in Abenase. The first thing he does on arriving is to call upon the *asafohene* of the *Asuna* stool and pay his respects. If he has no lodging the *asafohene* will direct his young kinsmen either to find him one or to take him into one of their own houses. If he is in any trouble or need the *asafohene* will be his 'father' in court. If he dies while he is in the town the *asafohene* will either arrange to send his body to Kumasi, or, if this is not practicable, will have him buried in the *Asuna* cemetery in Abenase and will send his hair and finger nails to his own people. If such a stranger should stay for years in Abenase and marry an Abenase woman, then he becomes no longer a stranger but is included in his *asafohene's* share-outs, and all town privileges.

Similarly, if a woman stranger comes to trade or as the wife of a townsman, her 'father' in Abenase is the *asafohene* of her clan, and if she chooses never to go away again her children become full members of his stool. But of a woman it is always said 'she may marry and go away but in the end she will always come back.'

Both the history of the land and the history of the *oman* are full of examples of large groups united by a clan bond, and to-day we find such bonds persisting between groups which different *oman* allegiances have divided. Wherever we find that several towns are the joint owners of a tract of territory the stools of those towns are always of the same clan.

We have seen how the *Oreko* landowners of Anamase and Adekuma received the *Oreko* immigrants from Ashanti and allowed them to farm and build the towns Batabi and Kokobin ; how the *Koana* landowners of Amanfupong and Aprade welcomed the immigrant *Koana* and let them build their town Nyankumasi. We have seen how the *Bretu* people of Apaso welcomed the *Bretu* immigrants from Ashanti and took them into their own town, even though they chose to serve another *oman*. The *Odikro* of Aberem said, 'We are of the *Toa* clan and are aborigines. When the Mamansu people came from Ashanti we let them live here because they belong to the *Agona* clan and *Toa* and *Agona* are two branches of one clan. They still live rent-free but give us £4 at *Afahye* time to buy sheep for sacrifice.'

We are told yet another impressive tale of clan brotherliness. After the war between Akim-Kotoku and Akim-Abuakwa in the middle of the last century the *Omanhene* of Akim-Kotoku left Jyadem in Eastern Akim and sought for another site. The stool of Akim-Bosome was already established at Akim-Swedru in Western Akim, where it still is. This stool, like the Kotoku stool, is of the *Agona* clan, and for clanship's sake the *Omanhene* of Bosome (who was at that time a woman) gave sanctuary to these homeless kinsmen in her own town, and then, as she had no land to give them, approached on their behalf her neighbour the *ohene* of Wenchi who had plenty of land and persuaded him to let her clansmen live on his land. The *Agona* stools of Asseni and Aboabo also found sites for their towns on Wenchi land through the kind offices of their clanswoman.

Again, when I asked the Oda *Gyasehene* why his stool ever came into this district, he said, 'We came because we heard that there were some *Toa* people here already and we knew they would welcome us. My stool is now the head of all the *Toa* stools in this district and I am the father of all the *Toa* people.' This clan brotherliness is not a thing of the past only. The *Dabenhene*, who is of the *Asuna* clan and claims that his ancestors were aborigines who came out of a local river, also claims kinship with all the *Asuna* people who subsequently entered the district. He says, 'All *Asuna* stools of the *oman* are one. We help one another at funerals. When my stool gets its money from mines I always use a part of it (one-tenth) in sending a present to every *Asuna* stool in the *oman*.'

It is still considered bad form to have a public disagreement with a clansman, and to take a case to court against him is always avoided if possible. There was an example of this sentiment exhibited in Awisa during my stay in the district. There is a disputed boundary between Akim-Swedru and Awisa. A Swedru man felled some timber on what Awisa considered to be Awisa land. Awisa elders met in great indignation and would undoubtedly have initiated the familiar long and costly land case had not the Awisa chief said, 'They are *Agona* people like our-selves. It would be disgraceful to go to law with them. Let us settle it peaceably with them if we can.'

The persistent sentiment linking the larger groups of clans-men might well be utilized by the Government more than it is in drawing up schemes involving co-operation between African and African. For instance, if it were suggested by Government that the small and not very cohesive *oman* of Akim-Bosome should amalgamate with Akim-Abuakwa, a storm of indignant fury would break, but if it were suggested that Bosome should amalgamate with Kotoku, whose *Omanhene's* stool is of the same clan as the Bosome stool, the suggestion would probably not be immediately accepted, but it would be regarded as reasonable and given consideration.

CHAPTER IV

A GATHERING OF THE *OMAN*

It is customary all over the Gold Coast to celebrate for a newly dead man a festival of farewell to his spirit. This takes place sometimes months, sometimes years after the burial. The successor of the dead man is responsible for it and makes it as grand and expensive as he is able in order to honour his predecessor and be blest by his departed spirit.

When I first arrived in Akim-Kotoku the old *Omanhene* had been dead some months and his successor had been enstooled. The *oman* was still in mourning and remained so till after the completion of the farewell festival which I had the privilege of witnessing.

The festival was held in Oda and lasted about a week. To it came, from all over the *oman*, the chiefs, 'big men', and as many ordinary citizens as were able. So must they often have gathered in time of war, feeling that their safety depended upon their unity. The unity which still persists between them was impressively manifested at this great gathering.

All the visitors were the guests of the *Omanhene*. For weeks he had been collecting hundreds of sheep and fowls and making arrangements for huge supplies of yams and plantains. Organization was a model of staff work. Thousands of guests were housed, fed, and honoured without a hitch.

Not only were members of the *oman* entertained, but distinguished representatives of other *omans* came to honour the dead *Omanhene*, and elaborate courtesies were exchanged. It then became evident that the matrilineal succession system combined with patrilocal marriage forges links of friendship between distant parts of the Gold Coast. For instance, the Queen-Mother of Bekwai in Ashanti is the daughter of an Oda father. She arrived with all her Ashanti retinue and was entertained by her kinsman, Osei Tutu Agyeman, the Ashanti-bred son of an Ashanti father and an Oda mother, who has succeeded to a stool in Oda.

The whole of the first day was spent in the reception of guests. Lorry-loads of people poured into the town from far and near. Each party consisted of a chief and his *gyase*, his *okyeames*, and *asafohenes*, together with the military captains and military companies of young men. The latter all carried muzzle-loading cap-guns, for gun-firing in honour of the dead is one of the prominent features of funeral ceremonial.[1] Nearly every military company had bought a bale of cotton cloth and had tricked out its young men in a distinctive 'uniform' which enabled the observer to follow their movements in the crowd. For instance, the young men of Adoagyire wore striking royal-blue jumpers which were easily picked out.

As each party arrived, the young men sat quietly by the road-side while the chief and elders went formally to greet the *Oman-hene* and be welcomed by him. The *Omanhene* sat in one of his courtyards surrounded by *okyeames*, heralds, and other members of the household, while party after party was ushered in bearing presents of yam, fowls, dried fish, and cases of rum. Speeches of greeting were exchanged and each party was told where it was to be billeted. Chiefs who are members of the Akim-Kotoku *oman* all have their own town quarters in Oda, where they often have to stay for several days at a time during *oman* Councils and other business of the *oman*, but their *asafo* companies at the funeral all had to be billeted. The *Omanhene* had prepared a careful list of guests and hosts. Comforts and a welcome were waiting for every visitor. The *Omanhene* sent a daily lorry-load of food to each chief's retinue throughout their stay.

After greeting the *Omanhene* each party went to greet the queen-mother and were then free to settle into their quarters.

Meanwhile various helpers had been working hard erecting palm-leaf awnings round the large open square outside the *Omanhene's* house. This square is used for various ceremonial gatherings and contains a rain-pot on a three-branched post, and a kind of ironstone altar of the sort common all over the Gold Coast. There is also a large *otutu* on which the *Omanhene's* chair is placed when he sits in public.[2]

The main business of the first night was the ceremony of 'sleeping with the dead'. The spirit of the dead *Omanhene* was supposed to have left the inside of his house and to have started on its journey. It was desired that it should not go back into its house again, so the relations and others who wished to do it honour slept outside with it, as friends may accompany a departing traveller on the first day's journey on his road.

---

[1] The firing is intended to announce to the long dead that an important new-comer is on the way to join them.

[2] Every chief's courtyard contains one of these erections for his chair. The older ones are of red clay, the modern ones are cement. Beneath each one is buried some 'strong medicine' to protect the sitter from magically projected evil. It is said that human sacrifice was involved in the making, and in the periodic renewal, of these strong medicines. Probably the victim was buried alive.

About nine o'clock in the evening parties of sleepers began to arrive with their mattresses and blankets which they spread in scores under the palm-leaf shelters.

All the ancient and famous war-drums, hung with skulls and other trophies, were brought out and beaten at intervals during the night, and throughout the whole night firing parties of about a score of guns grouped themselves round the square and at a signal fired simultaneously into the sky. Neither day nor night from now till the end of the festival were the guns silent for many minutes at a time.

The dead *Omanhene's* widows and the recently dead *Kyidomhene's* widows did not join the sleepers in the square. They already had their mattresses out of doors in a long street under the wall of the *Omanhene's* compound. There were dozens of them camped there for several days wearing widow's garb and never going indoors.

People who did not spread their mats and sleep set up their chairs and sat. One by one throughout the night the big 'Wing chiefs' arrived with their war-drums and their military retinues. They sat on their chairs while their drummers drummed and their warriors danced, sang, fired guns, and beat together their pairs of beating-sticks.

The successor of the dead *Omanhene* did not himself sleep out, but he emerged from his house once during the night surrounded by a dancing crowd of men and women and drums. He sat for a short time on the cement platform and received salutations. Then he paraded once round the square with his drummers and retinue and then went in.

All night the populace continued to pour into the town in lorries and on foot, with drums and singing. By morning the town was crammed.

The next day was a day of mourning. The *Omanhene* sat on his outdoor platform dressed in black with knotted rushes round his neck. Everyone else wore either knotted rushes or a chaplet of leaves, but most of the mourning clothes were a rich and gorgeous orange colour. Every chief with his retinue and drummers came and greeted the *Omanhene* and then sat in the square in mourning attitudes for the rest of the day. No one drank.

The *asafo* parties did not sit, but paraded one after the other in the square, firing their guns and dancing, and then retiring to parade round the town while other parties performed in the square. The younger members of the *asafo* companies wore bands of rushes round their heads, their own favoured uniform shirts, and odd articles of fantastic apparel that made them look

4

like schoolboys playing at brigands and pirates. A large pan of magically treated water and herbs stood in the square to prevent any gun accident or any injury in young men's quarrels ; not that they did quarrel : though there was hardly room to breathe, the orderliness was amazing.

Twice during the morning the *Omanhene* descended from his platform and did a mourning dance round the square. To express the greatness of his sorrow he lolled limply on the supporting arms of his attendants.

Parties of women—the widows, daughters, and other relations of the deceased—paraded before the *Omanhene* performing mourning dances with wailing and tears. The stricken army of widows, sitting on their mattresses in their own streets, all clutched staves with bunches of grass tied to the tops. This was to indicate that they no longer had a husband to whom they might cling.

The next day was much the same except that drinking began and money contributions were made by guests towards the funeral expenses. Everyone drank as much neat rum or gin as he liked, but I saw no one disorderly.

On this day—which was Sunday—most of the 'strangers' of the district, who were there for farming or trading, gathered themselves into groups in distinctive group clothing and came to add their courteous greetings. For instance, the Ga people, who mustered over a hundred, had bought a bale of boldly patterned black-and-white cloth out of which they all dressed. They came with their elected local 'chief' or 'father'—a cobbler— and sat for a couple of hours in the square. 'The *Omanhene*,' they said, 'allowed us to come and stay in his country, so we come to help to do him honour now that he is dead.'

The next day was the climax of the ceremonial. In the morning a bullock was brought to the square, thrown, bound, and left lying in the sun all day. In earlier times the many human sacrifices associated with royal funerals are said to have included a publicly sacrificed victim tortured for a whole day. For most of the human sacrifices at royal funerals an animal substitute is useless, as the sacrifices were made in order to provide the departing personage with the services of a retinue of human attendants, and, indeed, few Africans deny that human sacrifice is still secretly practised at all Akan royal funerals. I am not clear to what end the human victim in other times should have been tortured, but at any rate it is now conceded that the public torment may be received by a bullock. As the beast lay on the ground passers-by gave it savage kicks, and towards evening the three executioners, wearing distinctive executioners' hats, sat in a row on its prone body, flogged it and slapped it with the flat of their swords. Later it was slaughtered and left lying with a cut throat in a pool of blood.

Meanwhile the *Omanhene* sat nearly all day on his elevated seat while chief after chief, with retinue and military *asafo* company, came and greeted him, the 'big men' bowing at his feet, the *asafo* giving greetings of gun-fire. In the afternoon the chiefs all dressed themselves in war dress, each took a gun, and, supported on the arms of his officers in the centre of a maelstrom of shouting warriors, each chief in turn charged round the square firing his gun into the air. The military costumes of the chiefs and 'big men' were all ancient vestments that had been to war. They consisted of a knee-length tunic of the Northern Territory type, sewn all over with magical talismans, and a cap also covered with 'medicines'. A heavy harness of additional medicines was hung on waist, neck, and arms.

The whole ceremony emphasized not only that Akan 'chieftain-ship' was essentially military but also how closely bound up with magic was all preparation for war. Gold Coast religion con-forms to the generalization that all ritual is designed for the increase of life. The small amount of religion which survives in Akim from the days before Akim social organization was put on a military basis is mostly concerned with the increase of human and agricultural fertility. The warfare religion, of which the bulk of *oman* and stool ceremonial is a part, was concerned with the warding off of a special sort of death—namely, death in war. The stool which was always carried to war, was itself a magical war talisman. And into the person of the *Omanhene* was condensed the supreme magic for success in warfare.[1]

When all the chiefs in their military garb had fired their guns, the *Omanhene* himself went away and attired himself in his ancient war vestments. These included so many talismans and medicines worn under a very large tunic that he was a bulging shapeless mass, hardly able to walk and could only fire his gun at arm's length. His gun, like all the other guns that had actually seen war, was festooned with protective medicines. Upheld by supporting arms lest he should stumble and fall, he careered wildly three times round the square firing his gun into the sky amid a deafening tumult of drums and voices.

Some of the *asafo* companies carried with them war medicines in large basins-shrines on the heads of *akomfo* dancers. The

---

[1] The enstoolment ceremony, which is carried out in secret, is essentially a magic for rendering the chief supernaturally brave and invincible.

excitement caused every *akomfo* to become 'possessed by the
spirit of his medicine' and he danced in frenzied ecstasy with
rolling eyes, rolling head, and rolling gait. One *akomfo* franti-
cally tore up and devoured live fowls.

During the day several newly installed chiefs in the *oman* took
the opportunity of this full-dress occasion to swear fealty to the
Omanhene and bring their stools to be re-dedicated to the service
of the *oman*. One of these was the chief of Ayiribe, whose
installation in his own town I have already described.

In the late afternoon the *abusua kruwa* [1] of the dead *Omanhene*
was brought out in procession under an umbrella, followed by
those of the dead *Kyidomhene* and various members of the *Omanhene's* family who had died since the last big royal funeral. All
these dead people were believed to be 'travelling together'.

The ordinary *abusua kruwa* is essentially a cup-shaped vessel
in which fragments of the hair of all the surviving members of
the dead persons' local clan group are put. The vessel incor-
porates a portrait image of the dead person. In Ashanti it consists of a basin with a lid and the image forms a kind of knob on
the top of the lid. In Akim-Kotoku the *kruwa* consists of an
earthen cup standing inverted on its rim and forming a squat
pedestal for the image which is of the person's face only and is
flat and thin like a plate stood on edge and about equal in area
to a real face.

For a very eminent personage the cup and the image may be
two separate articles, and so it was for the dead *Omanhene* and
his travelling companies. The images were elaborate little
statues of glazed black earthenware, some not without artistic
merit. The maker was an elderly woman ceramist, not of Akim-
Kotoku, but of a neighbouring town, Nyakrom. She is one of
the few remaining good exponents of her craft. I called on her
while the images were in preparation and asked to see her at
work, but though she was pleased at my interest she could allow
neither me nor anyone else to see the images being made lest
the likeness or the personality of the spectator rather than that
of the dead person should accidentally get into the image.

At the *Omanhene's* funeral ceremony the images were brought
out under grand umbrellas in procession, each carried in a huge
brass pan. Each image was dressed in rich clothes and some
were represented sitting on little chairs. They were placed for
a time under palm-leaf awnings in the square and their living
friends came and saluted them and bade them farewell.

Then they were carried in procession to the *barim* or royal

[1] 'Clan bowl'.

3. Funeral images in the *barim*. (*See* page 44.)

4. Food for the dead in the *barim* grove. (*See* page 45.)

mausoleum. The crowd waved and shouted Good-bye with much emotion, but no one went to the *barim* except a few essential people. Chief of these was the old keeper of the *barim* who was carried shoulder high in a boat-shaped palanquin. The bulk of the procession consisted of widows carrying last gifts of food and drink for the dead.

Earlier in the day each widow had killed a sheep, cooked a tasty stew, and prepared a basin of yam fufu. This work was done in the street where the widows were encamped, and when they all pounded their fufu together the vertical poles of their pestles looked like the masts of a fleet of sailing-boats in harbour.

Each widow carried the food in a covered dish on the top of which was spread the sheet of white fat from the omentum of a sheep. The nose and one foot of the beast were laid on the top. The dishes of food were laid under the trees outside the *barim* and the images were set up in a little fenced enclosure. I was not allowed to enter the *barim* grove on that day, but I saw the proceedings—in a torrential downpour of rain—through a gap in the *barim* hedge. The following day the *Omanhene* himself most kindly took me into the grove—disturbing a multitude of vultures which had descended upon the food—and, after due prayers and libations, he allowed me to photograph the images, the basins of food, and the great brass pan under the great tree.

I may add at this point that the arrangements for the disposal of an *omanhene's* remains are exactly the same as those followed in Ashanti and described already by Rattray.[1] The first resting-place of the dead body is in a secret forest grove or *Aban* near Abenase, which town gets its name from this. The last resting-place of the royal brass coffins should be in the *barim* building, but, as the town with its flocks of strangers has encroached very near to the grove, the coffins are now kept more safely in a special room in the *Omanhene's* house.

As soon as the procession with the images had left for the *barim* the celebrations were over and all traces were removed as quickly as possible. The crowds melted away as if by magic and the *asafo* companies began to pile into lorries and depart. Late in the evening three specially appointed officials—the *Omanhene's okyeame*, who is also his half-brother, the *Dabenhene* and the *Odikro* of Ntronang, sat in the square and counted out the money—rice-bags full of it—that had been contributed towards the expenses.

The chiefs of the Akim-Kotoku *oman* remained an extra day

[1] *Religion and Art in Ashanti*, Chap. XI.

in Oda in order that they might have a meeting with the *Oman-hene* to discuss the financial position, and to decide whether further taxation was necessary.

When each chief went home the *Omanhene* gave him a sheep to kill for his stool to purify it and remove the effects of its worshippers' contact with death.

I should add that my description of the festival is the barest outline. A great deal of ceremonial took place which I was unable to witness, so huge were the crowds and so busy the officials who would otherwise have been courteously pleased to help me see everything and to explain every detail.

But two things I could not miss. The solidarity of the *oman* and the solidarity between the living and the dead.

CHAPTER V

FINANCES OF THE *OMAN*

The Oman *as a Financial Confederation*

I have already said that the *oman* was, until the establishment of the Pax Britannica, a military confederation of fighting stools under a paramount stool.

It must be clearly understood that there neither was nor is any correlation between land ownership and membership of the *oman*. Some towns voluntarily joined the *oman*, some towns were virtually forced to join it, but in neither circumstance did their joining mean any alteration in their relationship to the land.

The *Omanhene* was the commander of the military activities of every town which joined the *oman*. Military aid was often synonymous with financial aid, for guns and ammunition had to be purchased.

All military units of equal size had equal financial obligations towards the *oman*. Now that warfare has ceased, the organization of the *oman* as a financial confederation remains unchanged; the financial obligations of the part towards the whole are in the same proportion as were its military obligations.

As in the olden days a village which had a dozen men captured in a sudden raid by the Ashanti might count on the whole *oman* to avenge them, so to-day a small and poverty-stricken town shares in the income of the whole *oman*. And just as the village had to provide what warriors and gunpowder it was able when the whole *oman* went to war, so now it must pay what it is able into *oman* expenses. The *oman* was a military mutual benefit society : it is now a financial mutual benefit society.

Organization

The *oman* army was composed of five main divisions—*Benkum, Nifa, Adonten, Krontire,* and *Gyase* (left, right, centre, van of the body, and the *Gyase* unit respectively). The *Adonten* had an advance guard of scouts called the *Twafo* and the *Gyase* had three subdivisions, the *Ankobea*, the *Kyidom*, and the *Gyase* proper (the outposts guard, the rearguard, and the *Omanhene's* stool bodyguard).

When a town joined the confederation it was allocated to one or other of these seven units. A certain amount of shuffling took place from time to time, for towns often left one confederation and joined another, leaving inequalities in strength between the various divisions, which inequalities were removed so far as possible. For example, the towns of Ochereso, Asuom, and Otumi used to be in the Akim-Kotoku confederation and were in the *Benkum* wing. They voluntarily left the Akim-Kotoku confederation and joined Akim-Abuakwa. The depleted *Benkum* wing was therefore strengthened by the transfer of some towns from the *Gyase* division. Again, Pankese, Nkwanta, and Aboabo used to be in the *Adonten* division and are now in the *Krontire* division.

Each of the five main divisions is in charge of an *ohene*. The *Benkumhene*, the *Adontenhene*, and the *Nifahene* are the chiefs of the towns of Manso, Assene, and Apaso respectively. The *Krontihene* lives in the capital town, Oda, where also lives the *Omanhene*. The former is virtually the chief of Oda town and attends to the affairs of the populace. The business of the latter is mainly the business of the whole *oman*.

The *Gyasehene* also has his headquarters in Oda, so has the *Ankobeahene*, but he himself dwells mostly in his town, Adoagyire, which is far away beyond the boundaries of our map of Western Akim. His town Adoagyire is that part of Nsawam which lies north of the river Densu, and here one of his forbears founded a colony after a military campaign which led him into that district. The *Kyidomhene* has his headquarters and his stool in Oda and his country seat at Hwekwae, a village on Adausena land. The *Twafohene* also has his stool in Oda.

The stools of all these great war-lords, with the exception of those of the *Benkumhene* and the *Nifahene*, came with their owners, who were refugees from Denchera, with the then *Omanhene* and his stool. Because of their former military experience, they were made the leaders of the new Akim-Kotoku army. The *Benkumhene's* stool, that of the town of Manso, is the stool of the aboriginal *Toa* clan people whose towns are the joint landowners of a large tract of land. The *Benkumhene's* stool is the only one of the five big stools which has any land of its own save that of the colonizing *Ankobeahene* in his far-flung Adoagyire.

The *Nifahene* has his stool at Apaso, which is a suburb of Awisa town. This stool came, in the first place, from Adanse with followers experienced in warfare. About forty years ago most of the descendants of these Adanse warriors went away to Ashanti, and, though the *Nifahene* now has but a tiny remnant

CHART TO SHOW HOW £500 WOULD BE EITHER COLLECTED FROM OR DISTRIBUTED AMONG THE COMPONENT PARTS OF THE STATE.

CHART B

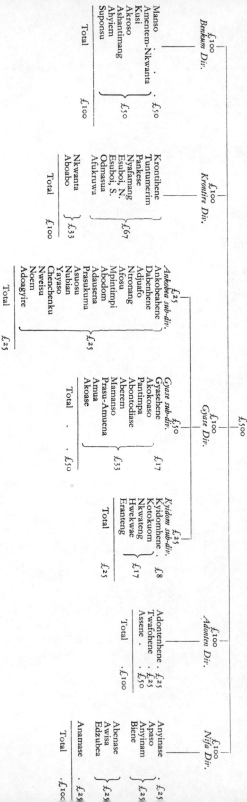

£500

Benkum Div. £100

Manso	
Amentem-Nkwanta	£50
Kusi	
Akroso	
Ashantimang	£50
Ahyiem	
Suponsu	
Total	**£100**

Krontire Div. £100

Krontihene	
Tuntumerim	£25
Pankese	
Nyafamang	
Esuboi, S.	£67
Esuboi, N.	
Odmasua	
Afukruwa	
Nkwanta	£33
Aboabo	
Total	**£100**

Gyate Div. £100

Ankobea sub-div. £25
Ankobeahene	
Dabenhene	
Adjuafo	
Ntronang	
Afosu	
Mpintimpi	£25
Abodom	
Adausena	
Prasukuma	
Asuosu	
Nubian	
Yayaso	
Chenchenku	
Nweisu	
Noem	
Adoagyire	
Total	**£25**

Gyate sub-div. £50
Gyaschene	£17
Akokoaso	
Pantimpa	
Abontodiase	
Aberem	£33
Mamanso	
Prasu-Amuena	
Amua	
Akoase	
Total	**£50**

Kyidom sub-div. £25
Kyidomhene	£8
Kotokuom	
Nkwateng	£17
Hwekwae	
Eranteng	
Total	**£25**

Adonten Div. £100

Adontenhene	£25
Twafohene	£25
Assene	£50
Total	**£100**

Nifa Div. £100

Anyinase	£25
Apaso	
Anyinam	£25
Biene	
Abenase	
Awisa	£25
Edzubea	
Anamase	£25
Total	**£100**

—two or three households [1]—of his own people left, he continues to be *Nifahene* because he still has the stool and, 'if there were war, all his people in Ashanti would come and fight again round their stool.'

Oda itself, the home of most of these big chiefs, including the *Omanhene* himself, is on land which till recently was lent to the *Omanhene* by the stool of Wenchi—a town which is not in the Kotoku *oman* at all. This land was recently bought (I believe for £700) from Wenchi. The town of Assene, the seat of the *Adontenhene*, is on the same tract of land as Oda and its site was included in the purchase from Wenchi.

Let no one therefore imagine that these great war chiefs are great landowners or ever had anything to do with land, for most of them are completely landless. They were heads of military groups pure and simple, and to-day they are heads of political groups pure and simple. The towns of these groups are geographically scattered. Some of them own their land, some do not, but in no case are their land affairs anything to do with their military and political groups. Many an informant has used the same words : 'In the days when we made the *oman*, land was of no value and we did not care who owned it. Land was not one of the things we ever even thought about.'

Distribution of Financial Burdens

The financial burden of the *oman* and the financial benefits of the *oman* are divided equally between the five main divisions just as the warfare expenses were contributed and the gunpowder distributed.

Suppose the *Omanhene* requires £500 to build a new stoolhouse. He will call a meeting of all chiefs, great and small, and will put the matter to them. If, after discussion, they support his wish, he instructs each of the five big wing-chiefs to collect £100. Each of the five will send messengers to the various chiefs in his division and request of each a certain sum. The sums demanded of the various units in the divisions I have set out in Chart B, for the compilation of which chart no little time and patience has been necessary.

Inside a division the financial responsibility of the component towns or groups does not depend upon either population or wealth but upon traditional status. A town under an *ohene* pays more than a town under an *odikro*, for an *ohene* is a 'bigger man' than an *odikro*. An *odikro* is the chief of one town only, an *ohenehene*

---

[1] The rest of Apaso consists of people who belong to the Akim-Bosome *oman*.

may or may not have some control over more than one town. For instance, Anyinase is exceptionally poverty-stricken and has a population of some eight hundred. Asuboa is much richer and has about 1,200 people. But Anyinase's chief was an *ohene* and a 'very big man indeed' in the old Denchera days, so he remains an *ohene* and pays an *ohene's* share. Neither he nor his people would have it otherwise : prestige is a thing on which money is regarded as well spent. The poorer Anyinase gets, the more tightly it clings to its ancient privilege of paying a big stool's share.

Again, take the case of Abenase, Awisa, and Edzubea. These three were one people in Denchera before they migrated and set up three separate stools in three different parts of their new country. They have remained 'brother-towns', of which Abenase, which had an *ohene* in Denchera, is senior to the other two which have *odikros* only. These three political 'brothers' pay a joint contribution, but Abenase finds half of it and the other two find a quarter each. Abenase is but half the size of Awisa and is not nearly so prosperous, but it would be the first to protest if anyone suggested that it should pay an equal or smaller share than Awisa.

When a messenger comes from one of the five big wing chiefs to any one town in his division, the elders and chief of that town assemble to hear his errand. If he has come to ask for money the elders meet again after he has gone and arrange to collect it. Suppose the *Nifahene* has asked Abenase to provide £100. (This was, in fact, the sum demanded of Abenase towards the funeral expenses of the late *Omanhene*.[1]) Messengers are sent to Awisa and Edzubea asking them to collect £25 each. The remaining £50 must be found by Abenase.

Now let us watch Abenase collecting its own £50.

There are eight clan stools in Abenase. The *asafohene* in charge of each is responsible for collecting from the individuals under his own stool and the *gyasehene* for collecting from the members of the chief's stool. The chief and his kinsmen have to find one-third of the whole £50 and the other seven find the remainder between them. That is, the chief's relatives collect £16 odd and each of the other groups collects about £5 each.

Within each individual *abusua* the members pay according to their status. The *asafohene* himself pays twice as much as anyone else and would feel insulted if anyone suggested that he should not. The *asafohene* knows the financial ability of each of his

---

[1] The town, of course, had its own expenses for ceremonial gunpowder, travelling, gifts, etc., quite apart from its contribution to the central fund.

subordinate kinsmen and no one is unfairly treated. Unmarried men pay only half a married man's share, and women, on military occasions—such as the *omanhene's* funeral—pay nothing.

Strangers, of whom there are many, contribute nothing. If any townsman is absent in another part of the country the *asafohene* or some other kinsman pays his contribution and settles up with him when he next comes home. Hosts of people all over the Gold Coast spend most of their lives as strangers far away from their homes, but they are in no doubt as to which place is their own town. A man's home is not where he lives and works, but where the stool of his kinsmen is, and where his kinsmen's funerals are held.[1] To the expenses of his own town he is pleased to contribute. No town either wishes to collect from its strangers or to have its absentees excused.

The *asafohenes* may, if they like, ask to be relieved of the trouble of collecting their family's contribution, but in such cases they cannot apply their 'means test' within their own groups. On one such occasion while I was in Abenase the town was asked for a contribution by a certain date and the elders were called together. They said there was not time to collect it in the usual way, so they advised the *ohene* to beat the gong-gong ordering contributions to be brought straight to his representatives sitting in the market-place. Unmarried men paid a shilling a head, ordinary married men two shillings, elders, other than *asafohenes*, four shillings. *Asafohenes* made what contributions they liked, but each paid more than four shillings. Men who said they had not so much as a shilling were not pressed for the money but were classified as 'women', and the next time the *asafo* turned out for manly work these 'women' were excluded and were sent to do ignominious weeding with the females and children.

On another occasion some Abenase people who had accompanied the elders to a *oman* meeting in Oda became embroiled in a political riot and some of them were arrested by the police and fined. It was decided by Abenase that it was mere chance that had caused some to be arrested and others to escape, so the whole town shouldered responsibility for their fines. Here again the money was required quickly, so the *asafohene* asked the chief to collect it. *Asafohenes* paid two shillings each and all other men, married or single, paid a shilling each. Messengers were sent to seek out absentees in their villages, and I do not think anyone was missed. The total number of grown males

---

[1] The people of Aprokumasi, who are Fanti, take their dead home to their own country for burial. So also do all the Adangme and Ga people living in the district.

represented in this collection was 203. As the census figure for the town—which figure includes strangers—is given as 790 we have an idea of what the town misses in mere money when it declines to tax its strangers, and may be certain that there are other things which it values more.

The method of collecting for the needs of the *oman* through the five wing chiefs, the town chiefs, and the *asafohenes* is the method which everyone prefers and thinks is less liable to abuse than any other. There is, however, another method sometimes used by the *Omanhene*, though I think never for strictly *oman* collections. After consulting with his chiefs he sends out his own messengers throughout the *oman* and they descend upon every household in the land, collecting direct from each individual. On the occasion of the Overseas Delegation Fund in 1934 all married men paid two shillings each, unmarried marriageable men one shilling each, boys over puberty sixpence each, married women a shilling each, and unmarried women sixpence each. The affair was not a *oman* affair, so the officers of the *oman* were not employed.

When the Queen-Mother in Oda was robbed of all her valuables and regalia in 1932 all women in the *oman* were asked to contribute towards replacement. Married women paid two shillings, unmarried but marriageable women one shilling each, and grown girls sixpence each. Men were exempt.

Financial Benefits

Of all wealth which comes to the *Omanhene* other than that collected by him for some specified purpose, he keeps only one-third. The rest is distributed all over the *oman* through the five big wing chiefs. Every individual who is a member of the *oman* receives exactly the same fraction of the total as he contributes when money is collected. The distribution is through exactly the same channels. Absentees have their shares kept for them by their *asafohenes*.

The sources of these windfalls which come to the *Omanhene*, and are shared between him and all the members of the *oman*, are various wealthy towns. When any town receives money, other than that collected to defray a definite expense, it sends the *Omanhene* one-third. Such money comes nowadays from firms taking up mining concessions, from the sale of timber, and the sale of land. Land as such is no business of the *oman* : land-owners please themselves whether they sell or not, and of income from the ordinary agricultural use of land (e.g. *busa* [1] cocoa

---
[1] See Chap. VI.

rents), the *oman* claims no share. But as soon as the land is converted into wealth, then the owner has acquired something of which the *oman* is entitled to a share.

Of all money collected 'for play' the *Omanhene* can demand one-third. For instance, at the installation of the Ayiribe chief, the town collected £21 for the celebrations. Of this £7 was sent to the *Omanhene*.

So long as a town makes its proper contributions to *oman* funds it is no concern of the *Omanhene* what it does with the rest.

Money and the Continued Cohesion of the Oman

The *Omanhene*—that is, the *oman* as a whole—is not under any obligations to assist any town which may be in financial difficulties over land litigation with a town of another *oman*, for the land is not the property of the *oman*. But the *oman* usually does find it worth its while to help when the dispute is with a town of another *oman*, for a town which loses its land in a lawsuit obviously loses its ability to make an income out of that land in the future.

For instance, there was a lawsuit between Edzubea and an Akim-Abuakwa town called Etsereso over the possession of land containing valuable gold and diamond deposits. The case was lengthy and the costs mounted into the thousands. The *Omanhene*, in the capacity of 'father', undertook to advance one-third of the cost and Abenase, as Edzubea's 'big brother', undertook to advance one-third of the remainder. But in the end the debt proved so overwhelming that the *Omanhene* paid it all off. He was not bound to do this, but, had he declined, the effect on the cohesion of the *oman* would have been serious and probably similar to that of like incidents in the neighbouring *oman* of Akim-Bosome.

In this Bosome *oman* several towns got into financial difficulty and, because their *Omanhene* refused to help them, they transferred their allegiance to Akim-Kotoku and now are part of that *oman*.

Again, the town of Brenase, also a part of Akim-Bosome, had a disagreement with its *Omanhene* over land finance, with the result that Brenase announced that it had severed all connection with the *oman* and was thenceforth an independent unit.

Another example is Franteng. This town is far away in the Cape Coast district, and used to belong to a Fanti *oman*. A few years ago it appealed to its *Omanhene* for financial aid. He refused, so it appealed to Akim-Kotoku, which gave the needed

help.   So Franteng transferred its allegiance and is now a
member of Akim-Kotoku.

In the old days of warfare a town so near to its new enemy and
so far from its new friend would have been virtually committing
suicide by withdrawing from its old alliance.   In those days
any town which quarrelled with its *oman* would simply have lost
the military guardianship of that *oman* and been thrown defenceless on the world.   This sanction was all-powerful, and the unity
and authority of the *oman* were in no danger.   The same principle
operated between a 'family' of towns and its father the *Omanhene*,
as operated between an individual and his family.   To challenge
the authority of the family or to break away from it was to lose
the only means of existence.

But to-day the most powerful force of cohesion between the
parts of the *oman* is money.   Now that the primary *raison-d'être*
of the *omans*—namely warfare—is removed there is little to keep
them from falling to pieces.[1]   The *oman* structure has been of
great convenience to administration.   But however great the
goodwill of the African to the Administrator, such considerations
would be unlikely, in themselves, to suffice to hold each *oman*
together.

I do not wish to imply that sheer greed of material gain is the
only influence by which the people are now affected.   Certain
traditional loyalties still burn with astonishing persistence within
them and the satisfactions which they seek are by no means all
material ones.   Money is valued chiefly because it enhances
prestige.   A 'big man' is always happy to pay a bigger tax than
a 'small man' pays.   Townsmen are proud that they alone contribute to expenses and share in the emoluments of the town,
and that strangers are excluded.   An *Omanhene* who helps a
smaller chief enhances thereby his own prestige : if he withholds
help he implies that the other is not worth helping and that he
does not value his friendship.

Especially should the student be warned against the hasty
condemnation of the system of distributing income and then
having to collect it again when public money is needed.   In both
town and *oman* finances it appears to the European that it would
be incomparably more efficient to pay income into a town or

---

[1] In some of the Adangme and Lower Volta districts each *oman* is so small that
it is a single town consisting of several extended families each with its own independent lands.   These families came together under a single war-stool for military
co-operation.   No financial alliance has taken the place of the military alliance and
there are no obvious advantages to the component units in remaining in the *oman*.
The result is that each *oman*, though extremely small, is rapidly breaking into its
still tinier independent components.

oman treasury (as the case may be) and save both distribution and re-collection. No doubt it would, but efficiency cuts no ice in the matter of either town or *oman* cohesion.

Though no one deplores more than I do the scramble to convert trees, land, and every other asset into money and to squander it, I am still impressed by the implications of the collection and distribution system and believe that its abolition would destroy most of the cohesion of both town and *oman*. The money circulates back and forth through the veins, arteries, and minutest capillaries of the *oman* and, even when it does not perceptibly or efficiently nourish, it keeps the channels open, and this is equally necessary to the life of the organism.

As we have seen, a town collection through the *asafohenes* approaches every ordinary member of the populace through the strongest of all natural bonds—that of kinship. It both utilizes and strengthens that bond. But the *asafohenes* are not only the heads of kinship groups, they are also the links between those groups and the central authority of the town. The importance of the *asafohenes* as the ultimate pillars of law and order among the populace and, at the same time, the pillars of town government, cannot be too strongly stressed.

An *asafohene* does his work from a variety of motives. As the representative of his kinsmen he has a genuine desire to do well by them. He also enjoys the prestige of his position as head of the family. He is proud that he will some day be worshipped as an illustrious ancestor. He enjoys even more his position as a big man in the town and his reputation for wisdom. He enjoys the club-like atmosphere of the elders' less formal meetings. He likes also to feel that his town is better than other towns and that its members have privileges and obligations which sharply distinguish them from strangers. He likes to hear the *katamanton* drum beaten in the early morning to call the elders together; he likes the chatting and gossip before business begins; he likes the excitement of hearing that £5 has arrived for distribution; and he likes the little celebration with palm-wine that the elders have after the meeting. He likes calling together his younger kinsmen to pass on the good news, and likes seeing them hanging on his words as he decides what sum each member deserves. If, in a month's time, £5 has to be collected there is at least a pleasurable feeling of importance for anyone who smacks his money on the table calling upon the assembled witnesses to take careful note of the amount. There is pleasure in appointing a special messenger to take the town's contribution to the *Adontenhene*, and there is more still in discussing the object to which the *Omanhene* is going to devote the money, which object the *Omanhene* has already discussed with the *oman* council. In all this there is much expenditure of energy in strictly unnecessary effort, but it exercises and strengthens the *asafohene's* social and political muscles. In the matter of muscle-strengthening, useless golf is as valid as useful coal-heaving. It is a labour of love to the conscientious elder.

But such abstract considerations as financial efficiency leave the average *asafohene* completely cold, and to compel him, if indeed he could be compelled, to take account of these alone would deprive him of most of his work, lose his sympathy, and lose his indispensable co-operation.

CHAPTER VI

THE TOWN AND THE LAND

Land Ownership and Land Finance

Land may be owned by either of the following :

(*a*) A town.
(*b*) A group of towns.
(*c*) A group of people who are part of a town.
(*d*) A group which is scattered both geographically and politically.

In addition to this has come the new custom whereby individuals may acquire land by purchase. Leaving out the last I shall now consider the other four types of ownership one by one.

(*a*) A town which owns its own land may be a town like Adjuafo, whose people have no tradition of ever having lived elsewhere, or it may be a town like Ayiribe founded by immigrants who discovered unoccupied land and settled on it. In both cases the town's hunters fixed the boundaries of its territory and all townsmen had equal rights to the use of that territory whether for hunting, farming, or any other purpose.

If such a town sells any of its land or timber, or lets out its land on hire to be used for any abnormal—i.e. non-agricultural—purpose (for instance, mining), the *Omanhene* is given one-third of the proceeds. If it lets out its land for rent or on the *bu'sa*[1] system, the *Omanhene* gets nothing so long as the land is used in the normal agricultural manner. That is to say, the *Omanhene* has nothing to do with the land *as such*, but as soon as his subjects acquire any extra-ordinary wealth, whether by exchanging their land for it or by any other means, then he can claim a share in this wealth for the needs of the *oman* of which the town in question is a member.

When the *Omanhene* has had his share, if any, the rest is divided between the stools of the town, the *ohene's* or *odikro's* stool receiving one-third and the other stools equal shares of the remainder.

The *asafohene* of each stool shares his portion with all the adult males under his stool, each individual receiving the same fraction of the total as he contributes when a collection is made. The

[1] See p. 74.

asafohene himself always receives and contributes more than any other member of his stool-group : the others according to their financial status—of which status the *asafohene* has always an intimate knowledge.

When a town enters into litigation concerning its own land, the *Omanhene* is not obliged to give any assistance, for the land is not his business. But he usually stands as guarantor for the town and advances any necessary sum it cannot immediately raise. Within the town the *ohene's* stool contributes one-third of the total amount raised and the other stools contribute equal amounts.

(*b*) A group of towns owns the land on which Manso (for example) stands. Several 'brother-towns' of Manso stand on the same large tract of country. These towns were originally one group of clansmen who subsequently scattered over their own land forming several settlements each setting up a new stool, and all the stools being of one clan. There are no boundaries between these towns, and all are joint owners of the whole tract.

When any part of the land is sold or extra-ordinary income accrues from it, the *Omanhene* receives one-third of the proceeds and the joint landowners divide the remainder. The towns get equal shares. Within each town the chief's stool gets one-third of the whole town's share and the rest is divided equally between the other *asafohene's* stools.

The 'brother towns' share equally in any expenses concerning the land, and within each town each stool and each individual person contributes the same proportion of the total as it or he receives when land income is distributed.

Any immigrants allowed to make a town on the land owned by the brother-towns acknowledge the earlier group as landlords. The new-comers may either live rent free or they may pay rent according to the terms they have made with the landlord. If they pay rent this is divided equally between the joint landowners. Of this the *omanhene* receives nothing, the income not being 'extra-ordinary' in the sense described above.

If income accrues from the land the new-comers have no share in the proceeds. Nor do they contribute to land expenses.

Other examples of joint landowners are Amanfupong and Aprade, on whose land Nyankumasi lives rent-free, and Anamase and Adekuma, on whose land Batabi and Kokobin live rent-free. A third batch of new-comers on Anamase-Adekuma land pay rent. Anyinam and Bieni are another pair of brother towns of one clan jointly owning the land on which both towns are built.

(c) A town may have been formed by an amalgamation of aborigines and immigrants. In such a case the aborigines are the true landowners, but all the citizens of the town have equal rights to holdings for farming and all have a share in the proceeds of land sales.

Abenase is an example of such a town. We say that 'Abenase is on its own land'. So it is, and all citizens have the same right to hunt and farm all over that land. But the descendant of the aboriginal occupant of the land is acknowledged as the *asasewura* (literally 'land-master') and is given some special privileges. If land is sold the whole town shares the proceeds, but the *asasewura's* stool has a special share. Of land expenses this stool also pays a correspondingly larger share.

Abenase has eight stools. One of this eight is the *ohene's* stool and was brought from Denchera. One of the remaining seven is known as the *Esu Kese* stool. Now, *Esu Kese* is the stream which is Abenase's water supply, and the story goes that when the Denchera travellers arrived they came upon a small party of people on the bank of this stream. On seeing the new-comers, all except one, a woman, plunged into the stream and never returned. The woman was brought before the chief and said that her people had their origin in the stream itself, worshipped it, and knew all its necessary rites and those of all the other countryside deities. She was therefore treated with great veneration, was married to an important man, her descendants were given a stool and were put in charge of the river-worship and all rites connected with the land. They were, in fact, regarded as the rightful owners of the land and the holder of the *Esu Kese* stool was called the *asasewura*.

Now, every countryside has its associated gods, and new-comers who offend either these or their servants will die. The river water will poison them, when they ford the stream they will stumble and be drowned, trees will fall on them, wild animals will devour them, blight will destroy their crops, and pestilence will kill their children. The strength of this 'supernatural sanction' can hardly be exaggerated. If it be ever asked why immigrants, strong in numbers and in military equipment, never barefacedly usurped the land and drove out the defenceless *asasewura*, the answer is not far to seek. No invader dared do this. The *asasewura* 'knew all the secrets of the land, and how to call the gods by their names'. He was in touch with all the local deities of stream, hill, grove, and forest, and was their established priest. To injure or offend him was to offend them and call down their vengeance. It may therefore be taken as

certain that no immigrant *ohene* or *omanhene*, however powerful,
ever interfered with the land or forcibly possessed himself of
any of it. It must not be thought that the immigrant 'big men'
had any compunction about destroying *people* as such, but they
would never have dared to live on their land afterwards. The
whole idea of an invader seizing territory by conquest could not
be entertained for one moment by anyone in the least familiar
with native ideas of the supernatural.[1]

It was only after long prying and keeping in close touch with
the life of Abenase that I discovered the significance of the *Esu
Kese* stool, for the *ohene* never voluntarily reveals it. The first
clue was given to me at the annual *afahye* festival when there is
a grand procession to the *Ebem* grove and the *ohene* is carried
in his palanquin. I found that one Kwesi Enim, the *asafohene* of
the *Esu Kese* stool, was also carried and, furthermore, was carried
in the place of honour in the procession, taking precedence of the
ohene. On following up this clue other interesting facts came to
light leaving no doubt who was the real *asasewura*. I found that
the *asasewura* could, if he wished, even sell land without consulting the *ohene*, and on one occasion had actually done so. The
ohene raised a protest, and the case was referred to the *Omanhene*
who ruled that the *asasewura* was within his rights though it was
discourteous of him not to have consulted the *ohene* and given
him and the other stools their usual share.

Concerning this incident the *asasewura* himself told me 'The
old *Omanhene* recognized my rights, but these days if I sold land
without the *ohene* he would send the case to Oda and the literate
clerks would send it to the Government and the Government
would say "What is '*asasewura*'? We don't know him.[2] We
only know 'chief'". So I don't do things without the *ohene* now,
but if it were not that the Government doesn't know '*asasewura*',
I should. But though the Government only knows the *ohene*,
the *ohene* knows that when anything happens about the land he
must come to me about it. So these days I don't go behind
him and he doesn't go behind me.'

Usually when Abenase land is sold, the *Omanhene* is given a third
and of the rest the *asasewura* and the *ohene* receive a third each, the
remainder being divided between the other six Abenase stools.

[1] Throughout West Africa I believe this principle holds. In the Northern
Territories the '*tendena*' is the landowner and was never dispossessed by the
invading overlords. In the Accra district of the Gold Coast the Ga-speaking
immigrants invariably retained the '*wulomo*' or priest-ruler of the aboriginal
Kpeshi tribe as both high priest and '*shitse*' or landowner, and he is still the ceremonial head of every Ga town, the *mantse* or chief being the political head and
organizer of warfare.

[2] He meant, of course 'We don't *recognize* him officially'.

The *ohene* himself held back this information from me, for he resents the equality of the *asasewura*. His version was that the *ohene* received a third and the other stools two-thirds between them. Which is true so far as it goes.

The *asasewura* has greater responsibilities as well as greater privileges. If there were a law-suit about the extent of Abenase land the town, as a whole, under the *ohene*, would be the unit taking action, but the *asasewura's* stool would make a contribution to expenses equal to the *ohene's* contribution. Also, in certain matters connected with labour on the land, the *asasewura's* relatives are responsible for doing one-third of the total work. On one occasion when the town was helping the Public Works Department in local road-making, the mystified and despairing foreman had to send his own labourers to the help of the *asasewura* before he could get the work finished within what was considered a reasonable time. No amount of appeal by the foreman to the 'chief' produced any extra helpers in the *asasewura's* gang.[1]

But for ordinary purposes it is said, and said correctly, that 'Abenase is on its own land' and no one distinguishes between the *ohene* and *asasewura*. Strangers requiring land to rent or buy approach the *ohene* and he consults the *asasewura*. Citizens of the town, no matter to which stool they belong, farm and hunt freely anywhere.

It is more than likely that many other towns situated 'on their own land' have an *asasewura's* stool other than the *odikro's* or *ohene's*, but such information comes to light only when one delves more deeply into the affairs of a town than I have been able to do in any town except Abenase. Rattray has mentioned the difficulty of extracting information about land-tenure. In his case it was the fact that the names of the dead mentioned in pouring a land libation were other than those mentioned in stool ceremonial that gave him the first inkling that the details of land tenure are usually concealed from strangers. In my own case the illuminating fact was the carrying of two people instead of one in the town procession. Such details can obviously only be observed here and there by chance or during a long stay in one place.

Another significant ceremony takes place before the festival begins. The grove on the outskirts of the town has to be cleared ready for the feast, but the *ohene* has to pay a ceremonial visit to the *asasewura* and formally ask permission to have it cleared.

---

[1] Since I left the district a diamond-mining company has taken up a concession on Abenase land and has paid money to the town. Of this the *Asasewura* received one-third, after the deduction of the *Omanhene's* share.

The *asasewura*, on this occasion, sits in his own house and the *ohene* brings him two bottles of rum, one to ask his permission to hold the ceremony and the other 'to remove the *asasewura*'. The two go together to the grove which the townsmen then begin to clear. When the work is over the *asasewura* and the *ohene* go to their respective houses and, when the former arrives, he sends a message informing the *ohene* that he 'has sat down', whereupon the *ohene* sends him more rum as thanks.

At the annual *odwira* ceremony the *ohene* kills a sheep for his stool, and, as soon as this work is finished, he sends his stool regalia—all except the stools themselves—together with the *okyeames'* staves to the *asasewura's* stool. This implies deference to the *asasewura's* stool. The same officials who kill the sheep for the *ohene's* stool must kill that for the *asasewura's*.

Under this same heading of land owned by people who are a part of a town we have to consider such a town as Anamase, which appears at first to consist of two groups of people, one of which is the landlord of the other half. Anamase is, however, two distinct towns which are closely adjacent. One (the earlier) is the landlord of the other, which is much more recent and pays rent. They have two distinct stools and are quite separate in every way except spatially. They even belong to two different *omans*, the earlier one to Akim-Bosome, the later to Akim-Kotoku.

(*d*) Land may be owned by a group that is geographically scattered. The *Dabenhene's* stool in Oda was originally the stool of a group of aborigines of the *Asuna* clan who lived on their own land on the bank of the River Petepong near Prasu-Amuena. When the immigrants arrived these people joined the *Omanhene's* household and their head became the *Dabenhene* (Lord of the sleeping-room) of the *Omanhene*, and remained with him during his subsequent migrations. Some of the descendants of the original Petepong people have now gone away to the Kyibi district and joined the Akim-Abuakwa *oman*. But they and their Oda relatives are the joint owners of the Petepong land, though none of them lives there now except a caretaker who has a tiny village called Akinkase and performs a weekly ritual for the river. Annually the *Dabenhene* himself goes there to sacrifice a sheep. The Nwiesu mine is partly on this land and some income from it comes to the *Dabenhene*. When he has given his *omanhene* one-third, the rest is divided between the *Dabenhene* personally, the elders of his clan in Oda, his kinsmen in Abuakwa and Petepong, and all the stools of the *Asuna* clan which originally branched off from the *Asuna* stool at Petepong.

These people are separated politically as well as geographically, for some of them belong to the Akim-Abuakwa *oman*.[1]

If joint landowners, politically separated, acquire money from their land they divide it equally between them and then each sends one-third of his portion to his own *Omanhene*.

For instance, the 'brother' towns Aprade, Amanfupong, and Nyankumasi, whose stools are all of one clan, are 'on one land' without boundaries between them. Aprade and Amanfupong are joint landowners. Nyankumasi pays an annual sheep. Aprade serves Akim-Bosome, Nyankumasi serves Akim-Abuakwa, and Amanfupong serves no one. Attached to Amanfupong is a colony of Swedru people who used to pay £4 a year for their farms but now pay an annual £40. This income is shared with Aprade. Achiase, which serves Abuakwa, is also on Aprade-Amanfupong land but pays an annual rent.

The complicated situation existing between the towns Adekuma, the two sections of Anamase, Kokobin, and Batabi, I have described fully in Chap. I.

Conditions of the Occupation of Land by Towns

Having considered the circumstances in which a town may be a landlord we must now consider the circumstances in which a town may be a tenant.

In former times every town living on land owned by another lived rent-free, paying simply an annual sheep in acknowledgement of ownership. To-day some landowners have begun to charge an annual money rent.

A town not on its own land may be on the land of a town which belongs to the same *oman* as itself or it may be on the land of a town which belongs to a different *oman*.

An example of a town which, till recently was on the land of a town belonging to another *oman*, is Oda. Though this town is the seat of the *Omanhene* of Akim-Kotoku it has only recently acquired its own land. Its former landlord was Wenchi, which town belongs to the Akim-Abuakwa *oman*: together with the towns of Assene and Aboabo, Oda lived rent-free on Wenchi land till it bought its site outright.

An example of a town which is on another's land and pays an annual rent is Anyinase. Its chief is an *ohene*, was one of the 'biggest men' in Denchera, and still collects from his town at

---

[1] The political separation of joint landowners also exists in other parts of the Gold Coast. For instance, the land on which Big Adda stands is owned by a tribe one part of which is a member of the Adda confederation and the other part of the Agrave confederation.

Kotoku *oman* collections as much as Abenase, Awisa, and Edzubea put together. But the town is on the land of Apoli— a member of the Akim-Abuakwa *oman*—and pays Apoli an annual rent. The last time I was in Anyinase the annual contributions towards this rent were being collected, not through the *asafohenes* but at a table in the street. Contributions were on a per-head basis and, as they concerned land affairs and not *oman* affairs (i.e. military affairs), women were included. Other people paid according to their rank :

The *Ohene* and his relatives	.. .. ..	£30
Every *asafohene* ..	.. ..	30s.
Every married man	.. ..	28s.
Every unmarried but grown man	.. ..	14s.
Every married woman ..	.. .. ..	8s.
Every grown girl	.. ..	8s.

Nkwanta, a neighbouring town, was also on Apoli land, but, as Apoli once received some financial help from Nkwanta, no rent was demanded at the time when Anyinase began to pay rent. However, Nkwanta, probably fearing that modern greed would soon prevail over ancient gratitude, arranged to buy its land outright before it began to be asked for rent. The land was therefore bought by Nkwanta for £500. Various extras brought Nkwanta's outlay up to £700. This money was collected from Nkwanta townsmen alone. Nkwanta has a partner-town, Aboabo, in matters of *oman* membership, and in all financial burdens and benefits connected with the *oman* Nkwanta and Aboabo share equally, but, as *oman* is nothing to do with land, Aboabo gave Nkwanta no help in the land purchase.

It is not yet considered seemly for a land-owning town to charge rent to a town consisting of fellow clansmen, whether belonging to a different *oman* or the same *oman*, and it is not yet usual for a land-owning town to charge rent to a town which belongs to the same *oman*, of whatever clan it may consist. Thus Mamansu is on Aberem land, Tuntumerim is on Awisa land, and no rent is charged. On the other hand it is only a matter of good will : Asuboi is on the land of Abontodiase, and, though both are in one *oman*, the tenant pays a rent of £10 a year.

The town of Akim-Swedru, the seat of the *Omanhene* of Akim-Bosome, is at a junction of lands and thus finds itself partly on its own land, partly on the land of Awisa which serves Akim-Kotoku, and partly on the land of Aduasa which serves Akim-Abuakwa. It does not, however, pay any rent to either of its landlords.

Ofuasi, of the Bosome *oman*, is partly on the land of Brenase of the same *oman* and partly on the land of Abontodiase, a Kotoku town, to whom it pays an annual sheep and 24*s*.

The Holding of Farms by Citizens

Whether a town is a landowner or whether it lives on land not its own, the citizens observe among themselves the same conventions with regard to the holding of farms.

Until recent times all the food farming was in the hands of women, the men being almost exclusively preoccupied with warfare. The land is richly fertile and receives abundant rain : once it is cleared very little work is necessary to grow ample food.

Since warfare stopped and cocoa-farming started most of the food farming has remained women's work and the men have concerned themselves chiefly with cocoa. All the men and many of the women have cocoa farms, the average size of an Akim-Kotoku man's cocoa farm being less than an acre.

The food farms are close enough to the town to be visited daily to fetch food for immediate use. The cocoa farms, especially the larger ones and those bought or rented by strangers, may be several hours' walk from the town. In these distant farms the farmer builds a 'village'[1]—that is, a compound where he and some relatives can spend most of their time, returning to the town for the Friday market and spending a night or two before coming back to their 'village'.

Dr. Rattray[2] has already described and deplored the modern tendency to leave little or nothing of the town land (or 'stool-land' as it is usually called) unallocated to individuals, and I shall not do so again. Whether Abenase land is all allocated or not I am uncertain : some elders said that it was, others that it was not.

The town land is divided into areas which all have local names. The boundaries of these areas are quite unintelligible to the stranger but are as clear to the local inhabitant as Trafalgar Square or Covent Garden are to the Londoner. Each of these areas is called a *kwae* (forest). I was given the names of twenty-six Abenase *kwaes* and have no doubt the list is incomplete. Each *Kwae* has a 'father'—one of the senior people whose own farm is within it—and he is responsible for knowing what other farms are there and all about their history, extent, and ownership.

As I shall explain later, labour on food farms is closely bound up with kinship and marriage obligations, and the economic

---

[1] 'Village' = *ekura*.
[2] *Ashanti Law and Constitution*, Chap. XXXIII.

independence of a woman usually depends on her ownership of a farm. The rules concerning the inheritance and acquiring of cleared farm land are by no means rigid, and for that reason I shall now give, as nearly as possible in their own wording, the accounts given to me by two typical people—an old man and a young man.

The old man was an *Okyeame*. He said, 'I myself have four food farms. It was I who made them all. My father was a hunter and didn't trouble himself about farms. Our fathers never did. But nowadays we have begun giving farms to our sons. I have two sons and I gave each of them a farm when he was about fifteen. My daughter too was about sixteen when I gave her a farm of her own. Before that the boys helped me and the girl helped her mother. Her mother had her own farm before I married her. It is a common cause of divorce when a wife has to use her own farm to feed her husband. She complains to her people and they call a meeting of his people and the husband is warned. After a few warnings he is divorced.

'After a farm is first cleared, if it is a food farm, it will last about twenty years before the soil gets weak. When it gets weak you leave it, but it remains the property of the man who cleared it and his heirs. Wherever your cutlass has touched is yours and your children's for ever. When you tire of clearing new forest you come back to the old. Children come back where their grandfather cleared. A man's farm goes to his nephew if his nephew succeeds to the fatherhood over his sons. Whoever becomes the father of my sons when I am dead will treat them as I did and will have my farm. But their own new farms that they themselves clear will go to their own sons if they like. I have already given farms to my sons. The farm where I am working now will go to my wife who now works with me.[1]

'When a stranger comes to the town and wants to cultivate he asks the chief and is given a strip of forest. He needn't clear it all at once and it will last him and his children for ever. But we who are townsmen can cultivate where we like without asking anyone so long as we do not encroach on another man's land. The first person to start making a farm can refuse permission to the very chief himself, should he try to encroach on his land.

'As you go forward clearing and extending your farm you never cross over a stream.

---

[1] In general, what a man inherits from an uncle he must leave to a nephew. What he acquires by himself or with the help of his sons he leaves to his sons. What he acquires for himself with the help of his wife he leaves to his wife.

'Once you have cleared land you can mortgage it, let it, or sell it outright if you like. But if you sell it you must ask the *ohene* and he will take one-third of the money. It is only when uncleared forest is sold by the town that the town sends one-third to the *Omanhene*. Land that has been cultivated is not forest, and the *Omanhene* has no share of the money that the owner gives the *ohene* of the town. The selling of cleared land to strangers is not good and we don't often allow people to sell.

'Nor is it good for a town to sell its uncleared forest, but in law-suits and troubles towns often have to do it. But to let strangers work land by *abusa* is good.[1]

'My own farm is in the *kwae* called *Ahomamu*, and so are my sons' farms. I am the father of *Ahomamu*. I have a boundary with *Yao Odonko* on my right and with *Yao Duke* on my left. The old path is behind me : I started from there. In front I am still advancing, and I can clear in front till I reach the stream Nyenesu. You always go on clearing in front of you till you reach either a river, somebody's old farm, or a path. You may cross a path if you like, but you often make a path your boundary. But you must never cross a stream.'

A young man, *Kwami Dakwa*, gave me an account of his food farm and of food farming generally.

'My farm', he said, 'is in the *Kwae* called *Kankyiso*. My father began cultivating there. He started from the path to work towards the stream Esu Kese. Three other people started abreast of him also working towards the stream. These were :

'*Kodzo Ansa*, my father's younger brother.

'*Kwesi Edin*, my father's brother-in-law.

'*Kweku Sei*, my father's brother-in-law.

'We like to work abreast, because if you have nothing but forest round your farm wild animals are always spoiling your crops.

'All four of these people worked towards Esu Kese. Later my father gave my brother *Donko* and me plots on his farm between him and the stream. *Donko* works towards the stream and I work towards *Donko*. When I meet him I shall turn West into my father's land. It is all my father's on the West until some-one else meets him there, but no one has yet come. If a new-comer came he would start farther West against the path and work towards the stream (i.e. along PQ). He could work towards the East if he liked, but if my father wanted to stop him he could do so by clearing a small farm against the path in the line of his advance (i.e. at X). The new-comer would

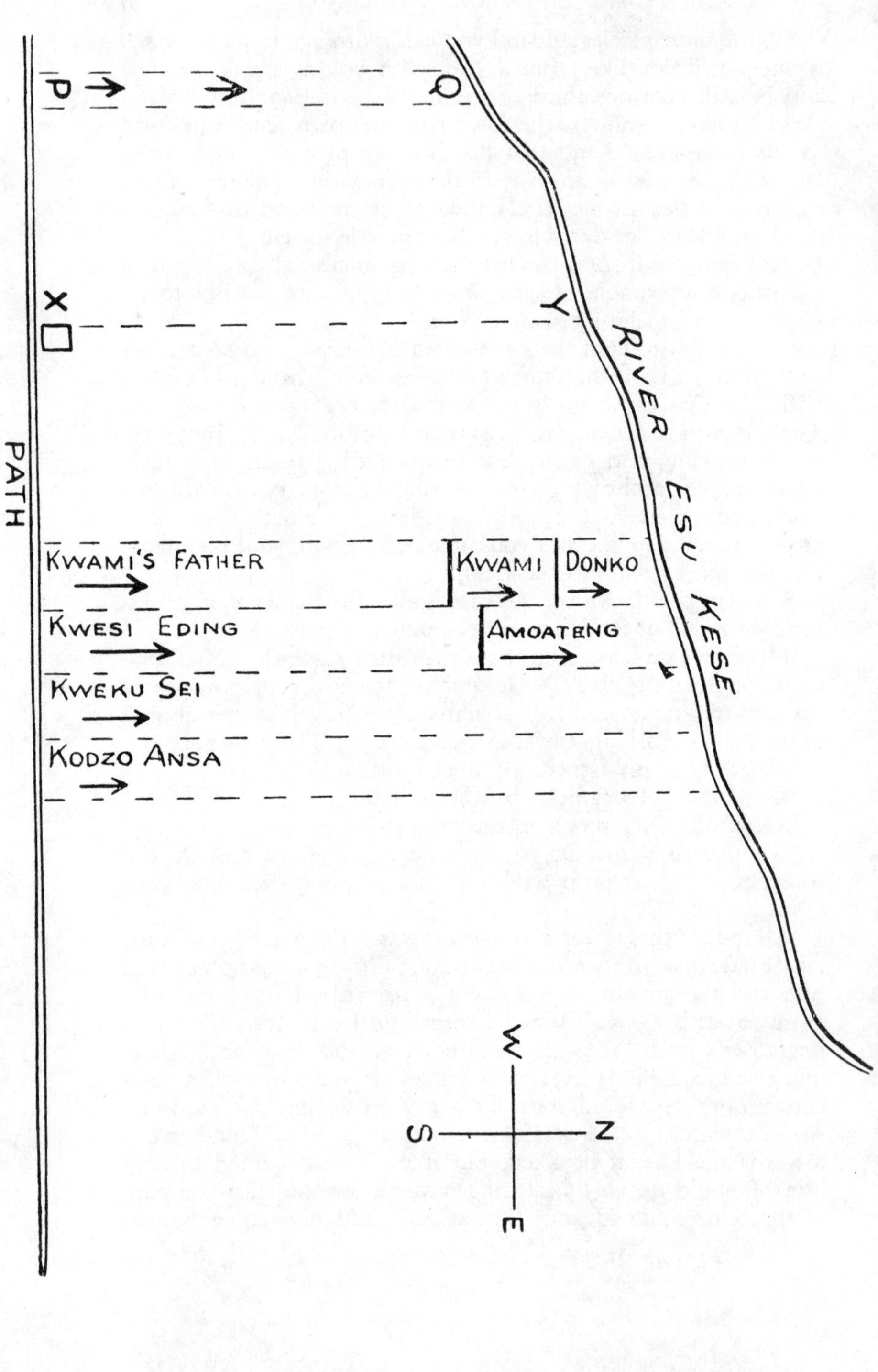

PATH

P → → → Q

X
☐ — — — — — Y

KWAMI'S FATHER
→

KWESI EDING
→

KWEKU SEI
→

KODZO ANSA
→

KWAMI │ DONKO
→ →

AMOATENG
→

RIVER ESU KESE

W
S ─┼─ N
E

never advance across the line from this small farm to the stream (i.e. across XY). If *Kwesi Edin* or *Kweku Sei* or *Kodzo Ansa* reached the stream and wanted to start new strips West of my father they would have to ask him how far to the West he intended to clear and they would have to start beyond that.

'My farm is cleared down to the boundary between me and my brother *Donko*. It is now a food farm. When it has finished growing food I shall plant cocoa there and make a new farm somewhere else for food. I think I shall clear towards the West into my father's land, but if I like I can ask my uncle to give me some of his land. Perhaps he will give me land cleared already but perhaps not cleared. Or if I liked I could start in a new *kwae* altogether. There is still some unallocated *kwae* and if you are not a stranger you can take it without asking the chief. If somebody else has already taken it he must show me, in proof, the beginning of his cultivation if he wants to keep me out.

'If I am farming abreast of someone else and I advance where there are rocks I ask my neighbour to incline his farm to one side in advancing and give me some of his fruitful land.

'If I start my farm so near to someone else's that he meets me as soon as he has advanced a little the elders may order me to turn and work backwards. If two people start near to one another they should work either abreast or back-to-back.

'My sister, who is about sixteen, has no farm of her own. She works on her mother's farm because she prefers it so. But most fathers give their daughters farms as they do their sons.

'Food farming is not often done except by women even in these days. Formerly the men went hunting and to war. Now they plant cocoa farms but they start the farm with food crops for a few years, and when these begin to get weak they plant cocoa in the same farm.

'A husband may give his wife a farm for herself and then the profits are hers entirely, but when he gives her the farm she must give him rum before witnesses as a sign that the farm is now hers. Then, even if there is a divorce, the farm remains hers. But if there is no rum put on the gift the farm is the husband's and the wife helps her husband to farm it and it stays with him if there is a divorce. A meek woman may never get anything from her husband though she work for years, but a pushful woman will ask for a farm.

'It is the same with sons as with wives. If the father gives his sons farms they must give rum in front of witnesses, other-wise the nephew may claim the farm. But if the father gives the sons farms and takes rum on the gift, then the farms are the sons' for ever.

'If a woman's own family give her a piece of their uncleared forest it needs no rum on it and, even if her husband clears it for her, it is still hers and her husband has no profit from it and gets nothing back if there is a divorce.

'If a woman marries a stranger or a slave with no relatives to come when he dies then the farm and all his other property becomes hers at his death.

'If a man gives his wife or his son an uncleared farm and they clear it, then even if he takes no rum the farm is theirs and the nephew has no claim. But if it is already cleared when it is given there must be rum upon the gift or it is no gift and will come back to the giver's family.

'Sometimes a brother will give his sister a cleared farm, but she must give rum upon it to show that it is hers for ever.'

It will be noticed that *Kwami Dakwa's* account of the holding of farm land soon tailed off into an account of the connection between farms, kinship, and marriages. Most people's accounts do the same. And in further illustration of this point I may quote another typical account given me in reply to the request 'Tell me how you acquired your farm and what is the customary way of acquiring farms.'

The informant said, 'My father gave me my farm. As soon as I was old enough to use a cutlass I worked with my father. When I was grown more he gave me a plot of forest and showed me how to fell trees. This is dangerous work if you don't do it properly. It is always from your father that you get your first farm. But sometimes if an uncle knows that a nephew will succeed him he can ask that the boy may come and work for him on his farm. If the father likes he can refuse to let his boy work for the uncle. Even if the boy works for the uncle he goes back to work for his father two or three days a week. If he works at all on the uncle's farm he will have that farm after his uncle's death. If the father gives a farm to a son who is working for an uncle the uncle and boy must go together and take rum and witnesses to thank him and set a sign upon the gift.

'A father also gives his daughters farms so that they can work and buy cloth and things for themselves. The mother comes and thanks the father with rum when he gives the daughter a farm. The daughter plants food crops in her new farm and when the food-growing power dies the father comes and plants cocoa for her and gives her a new food farm elsewhere. When she marries, her father will say to her husband, "I have given your wife this farm. When the food crops finish come and plant cocoa for her and it will be hers." If she is a hard-working girl and plants cocoa for herself before her marriage, the cocoa profits are hers though she be still unmarried. Her father will never go to that farm. If a father is a good father and his daughter is a good girl then by the time she is married she has a strong food farm and maybe cocoa, too, so that if her husband turns out bad and useless she has always food and money.

'We marry our wives with the thought that they will help us on our farms. If a woman has a bad husband she will say to him, "I am helping you to work for yourself and your nephews but you are not helping me, and I have to feed you from my farm. Therefore, go! I knew how to buy my own head-kerchiefs before I married you."

'A wife has to help her husband on his farm. Any profits she makes out of his farm-produce are his except one-third, which she keeps.[1] Perhaps a good husband will say, "Our farm is yielding. I don't want anything except to eat. See that I get my meals and you can have any profits that you can make." Last year my wife made £3 out of marketing garden eggs from my farm. She brought it all to me, but I said, "You have done well. Take it all and I will even add a little more for your annual present." My wife has green fingers (*Wo nsa ano wo kua*, Your fingers bring farming) for yam and for most things, but not for garden-eggs, and the garden-eggs she herself plants never grow: so I always plant out her garden-eggs for her as well as my own but she gathers and markets them.

'A woman must market the food from her husband's farm and get meat, salt, and other needful food in exchange. All the husband is obliged to do is to provide enough food for eating and exchange. If he has a gun he brings bush-meat so that she need not be exchanging farm produce every day.

'When a man first marries, his wife must provide cooking-pots and dishes. He must give her four outfits of clothes and a comb. Afterwards the wife provides such things as salt and eggs. The husband provides matches, kerosene, chairs, and always a stool for her to sit on. Anything else he gives her is a present, but he usually gives her one cloth a year unless times are very bad.'

---

[1] That is, the wife farms and trades for her husband on the same terms that a labourer works a farm for another man. The practice of giving the wife one-third is not, as this informant implies, universal, though she always sees that she gets something for her trouble.

To return to farm holdings, the reader will have gathered that if a man clears forest land it becomes the property of himself and his heirs. His heirs are usually nephews belonging to his own *abusua*, but he can, and is expected to, give cleared land to his sons, daughters, and wife. Such gifts must be 'sealed' with rum in the presence of witnesses, and then remain the property of the recipients and their successors or legatees.

Also it will have been gathered that uncleared land which a farmer indicates that he *intends* to clear is regarded as his and cannot be encroached upon. He indicates his intention in a manner which is clear enough to local inhabitants but not so to strangers.

Nowadays it is regarded as a useful safeguard for a townsman taking up new forest to make his boundaries before he starts. If he wishes to do this he goes first to the chief and announces his wish and asks that some responsible elders may come and witness his landmarks. The elders may accept his landmarks as sufficient or they may require him to clear a narrow path-like strip round the entire area. This both limits and protects him. He cannot extend beyond it as he might under the old system, but there is no risk of encroachment upon it.

The allocation of uncleared land to a townsman gives him no rights over the saleable timber. This remains the property of the town and must be left standing. If the town sells a tree in uncleared land which has been allocated to a townsman he receives no special share in the proceeds. If he wishes to sell a tree on his own cleared land he must ask permission of the chief and a part of the proceeds will be claimed by the town.

If he wishes to sell a cleared farm outright he may do so, but the town claims one-third of the proceeds. Such selling is not encouraged.

Group Labour on Farms

I shall describe later, in connection with kinship and matrimonial obligations, the circumstances in which a young man and his friends work for his father-in-law or prospective father-in-law.

Few farms except small food farms are ever worked by the owner alone, and the clearing of a new farm is, I believe, never done by its owner alone. A cocoa farm tends to develop a thick undergrowth of weeds, and this has to be cleared with cutlasses several times a year. Neither this work nor the harvesting is done by the owner alone.

When a young man of little standing wants, say, his cocoa farm weeded he employes the *noboa* [1] system. He collects a company of friends and relations of his own age and standing, and they all go and work together. The wife of the owner of the farm goes too and cooks a meal in the farm for the whole party. If they can afford it they have some palm-wine too. They sing and shout and chaff one another as they work, and in this light-hearted atmosphere the work quickly gets done. When only ordinary weeding is to be done the food may be mere boiled plantain, but if hard clearing is in hand a good meat stew with yam is expected.

To these working parties it is not etiquette to invite a senior. An invitation to a junior kinsman is virtually a command. Such a junior calls in as many of his equals as he likes. An invitation to an equal carries an obligation to accept a return invitation another day.

The larger food farms as well as the cocoa farms are often worked by this *noboa* method, but women's farms are not. By a kind of legal fiction, 'women's farms are never large', though they may be so in fact. Therefore a woman's farm cannot require much labour. 'It does not matter,' said my informant, 'if a woman happens to clear a patch as big as a town and a man clears a patch only as big as this room, we shall still say that women's farms are not large, and a *noboa* party will help the man but not the woman.'

Capitalist Farming

There are two other methods of getting work done when the owner of a farm either cannot or will not do it for himself. The first is used by people who have cocoa villages some distance from their towns and do not wish to live in them. A caretaker, who may be either a relative or a foreign labourer, is put into the farm and takes complete charge of it. He arranges for its clearing and for the harvesting and sale of the cocoa. For this he receives one-third of the proceeds and it is he who keeps the accounts. It is admitted that every such caretaker cheats and takes more cocoa than one-third, but the owner never argues about it so long as he receives a reasonable sum.

This method is widely employed by absentee clerks and others who have bought or inherited farms in districts other than their own.

Another method of getting work done without doing it

---

[1] Also called *doboa* and *adofo*.

oneself is to employ someone who badly needs money to arrange for the completion of a piece of work in exchange for a specified sum. For instance, a large cocoa farm needs clearing. The owner calls a younger man whom he knows to be hard up and offers him a definite sum to get the work done. An agreement is made and if the contractor is without money he is given a small advance. He then calls in his own friends and young relatives and the work is quickly done. He gives them none of the pay, but he goes to help them when they ask him.

LAND AND THE STRANGER

The Bu'sa [1] System

The dry coastal plains of the Gold Coast are not suited to cocoa growing, but as the coastal people are numerous, physically vigorous and enterprising, they are eager to participate in the country's most lucrative occupation. Much the same thing applies to the people of the Akwapim ridge, whose land, though fertile and well watered, is too small in extent to meet the needs of such numerous, energetic and able cultivators.

The Akim people, on the other hand, have much fertile land and little taste for work.[2] They have therefore found in their land a means of making money without working for it. Sometimes they sell tracts of land outright to the strangers, but more often they allow the strangers the use of the land on the system known as bu'sa.

By this system the grower pays nothing till his cocoa trees start to yield and then he gives one-third of his crops.

Here I may give an account of an actual allocation of bu'sa land at Abenase.

A Kkwapim stranger came to look round and stayed in the household of an old woman of Abenase with whom he was already acquainted. This woman happened to have a big stretch of Abenase forest allocated to her in the usual way but, as she had cleared and cultivated only a small plot of it, she told the stranger she would be willing to give it back to the town in order that the town might lend it him on the bu'sa system.

The stranger took his request to the chief and elders. They began by reprimanding him for a breach of etiquette in coming without the old woman, his hostess. She had introduced him

---

[1] Bu miensa, to divide into three.
[2] This is to be accounted for chiefly by their poor health.

to the land that he wanted and he should have brought her with
him to introduce him to the elders. For this they ordered him
to pay her 12s. pacification fee which, after due apology on his
part, they reduced to 8s. They sent for the old lady and insisted
on his handing over the money before proceeding to further
business.

The man said he required a tract of land '24 ropes' wide. A
'rope' is 24 abasam. One abasam is the length of string which
a tall man can stretch from hand to hand when he extends his
arms—that is, a fathom or 6 feet. By the arm-stretching method
'a rope' is calibrated. The concept of area is lacking in native
mathematics. The width of a strip of land is measured in ropes.
The length of the strip is never measured at all but is fixed by
agreement.

The elders acquiesced and informed the applicant that although
he would be charged nothing for the use of the land except one-
third of his cocoa crops he would have to pay £24 on the agreement for 'thanksgiving rum', one sheep, and one bottle of actual
rum. Some elders and others would go with him to show him
formally his land and to witness its size and place. These witnesses would require £5 'for getting their skins scratched in the
forest'. This £5 'for scratches' was reduced to £3 10s., but no
other reductions were made.

The applicant asked permission to introduce a literate—a
licensed surveyor—to measure out the land accurately and to
superintend the cutting of boundary strips. This was agreed
to, and the stranger was told to have the strips cut, after which
the elders would inspect them in the presence of witnesses.
Usually only methodical strangers go to the trouble of cutting
boundary strips : the older method is to say that from such and
such a tree or rock to such and such a bend in the stream is the
boundary. Sometimes gashes are cut in big trees to assist the
memory.

On the appointed day one okyeame, one asafoakye, the chief's
literate nephew who was also tribunal registrar, the old lady,
and a few other people, making a party of thirteen, went with
the stranger to inspect the boundaries and to authorize him to
start farming.

The strip 24 ropes wide had one frontage on the main road,
and the buyer was told that he might extend the strip lengthways
into the forest as far as he liked. The okyeame said, 'It is bu'sa
land, so we shall profit if you extend it : therefore extend as far
as you like. The company were then all called to witness that
this extra permission had been given.

Everybody then went home. That evening I was not a little
embarrassed to receive three messengers bringing me 6*s.* from
the chief as my share of the witnesses' money. I protested that
I had accompanied the party out of mere curiosity, not as a
helper, but they insisted that I had witnessed the proceedings
and must either accept a witness's token or imply dissatisfaction
with the proceedings.

The Akwapim man said he would not start clearing till he
had killed a sheep for 'the grandfathers of the land'. He did not
start clearing till after I had left, so I did not witness this, but
I was told that the *Asasewura* or representative would accompany
him and commend him to the care of the dead-and-gone owners
of the land and the local gods. Natives of the town do not kill
a sheep before clearing new land, as 'The spirits of the land know
them already', but they do kill a goat and ask for good crops and
prosperity.

All strangers keep the local rules about not working on Friday
and comply with any other demands of the local gods concerning
the land.

The new-comer told me that he intended to make a 'village'
on the new farm and live there for the greater part of the year,
returning to Akwapim only for his people's annual festival and
for funerals and important palavers. He said that as soon as the
land was cleared he would plant ordinary food crops—plantain,
yam, corn, etc.—and market these on as large a scale as possible
till the cropping power of the soil began to fail. Then he would
plant cocoa.

The growing of mere food is not taxed by the landlords even
when the tenant makes heavy profits, and it is not till the cocoa
begins to yield that the landlords take their one-third.

The use of *bu'sa* land gives the user no right to timber. All
big trees of any market value must be left standing and remain
the property of the town.

The Sale of Land to Strangers

We have seen an *Akwapim* stranger acquiring the use of land
on the *bu'sa* system. He might, had he wished, have bought
the land outright, and this has often been done.

I will now give a Ga stranger's account of some cocoa land
which his father bought in Akim. This informant is a Christian,
a clerk in Government service, and on the surface a highly
sophisticated and 'detribalized' literate. But his attitude towards
the land as the place of the final homecoming of wanderers into

literate bypaths [1] is, I think, fairly typical. His attitude to the
supernatural is also the usual one among literates of his class.

'My father,' he said, 'was an engine-driver on the railway, and
when he had earned his pension he retired. His sister had
married an Akwapim man who had bought some cocoa land in
Akim, so my father thought he would like to do the same with
his own savings. So his sister's husband took him to the elders
of the place and four of them showed him what land he could
have. He wanted a square of 24 ropes. He paid £130 for the
land, £7 for the witness of the elders, a bottle of rum, and one
sheep for the chief.

'On the day that he was going to put the first hoe into the
ground he asked that the *asasewura* might come. In that town the
odikro himself was the *asasewura*, so he deputed a representative
to come. There were also present my father's sister, my sister,
myself, and some old men friends of my father. It was in 1922,
and my sister was then about fourteen and I was about ten.

'The *asasewura's* representative took rum and prayed under
a very big tree and then a sheep was killed and the blood was
sprinkled on the leaves. Rum was served to all the old men.
I was asked to take a cutlass and do the first strokes of clearing
because it is I who will inherit the land. The right fore-leg of
the sheep was sent to the *asasewura* and the contents of the
stomach and intestines were sprinkled on the farm. Gifts of
meat were sent to all the big men in the town. The sheep's head
was given to me because I was going to inherit.[2]

'Then we came back to Osu and my father went away for one
more year to drive an engine again for a little more money.
Then he went to live on his farm.

'He cleared and felled all the trees except the big one under
which we killed the sheep. He planted cocoa. There was rain
and the cocoa grew well. My father started getting about
sixteen bags a season. Suddenly the trees stopped bearing.
They made good leaves but no fruit. He thought the ground
was too wet, so he diverted the brook that ran near the farm.
Then the leaves on the trees also died and the trees themselves
began to die. He cut back the branches and fresh shoots came,
but still the cocoa was poor and more trees died. He knew that
all this dying must be caused by witchcraft, so he bought a
protective medicine that cost about £8.

[1] Few Gold Coast Africans are more than superficially 'detribalized'. Their
roots are still in the land. Their attitude towards literate careers is very similar to
that of many British girls who take up a 'career' as a temporary and not very serious
adventure before turning to the ancient and unchanging haven of matrimony.
[2] The Ga follow patrilineal succession.

'There were other misfortunes too. One day my father asked his sister and her husband to let their son go with some labourers to carry thirty loads of cocoa, worth 30s. a load, to the market and bring home the money. The son went, sold the cocoa, and bought himself a gun with some of the money. On the way home he met some Hausa gamblers and played *aso* with them. At first he won and then he lost. Then he lost again till all the money was gone. Then he came home crying. My father and his sister and her son set out in the night to find the Hausa-men. They found them and there was a big fight. They were all arrested for quarrelling, and taken before the elders of the place. My father got the money back from the gamblers, but the elders charged him £5 for hearing the case. When he got home he tied his nephew up and beat him. His sister took offence and quarrelled with my father. So we all left her compound and slept in the open air on the farm. The next day we made a bamboo hut and lived there. My father took the quarrel to his father-in-law, and he and some other elders made peace, but my father and his sister have not liked one another since. Later the husband of my father's sister got leprosy, so she left him.

'I am sure that all these troubles were caused by my father's mother's sister. She spoilt the farm and caused troubles to come between us all by witchcraft. She is a very wicked old woman and I don't want to have any more to do with my father's farm while she is still alive. But when I get my pension I shall go to it. Sometimes I dream about that old woman and then I feel sick and miserable the whole of the next day.'

Another Accra man in his own 'village' near Abenase told me that he had bought outright 24 ropes of land each way and had paid for it £154. This land was all in bearing with cocoa. He had since bought another 12 ropes adjoining the big plot, and this new strip was still bearing food crops which he sent to Oda market. A small strip patch of 1 rope was full of corn. He said he had been there thirteen years and had been buying extra parcels, a rope at a time, at £7 each, ever since the cocoa was planted.

Land Companies

A very interesting new practice arising out of the sale of land to strangers is the buying of land, not by individuals, but by groups of strangers who club together.

On the land of Ayiribe, the next town to Abenase, there is a group of twelve such strangers from Kpone on the Adangme sea coast. They bought between them 69 ropes at £4 10s. a rope. The town officials and witnesses demanded £5 extra on every £10, but this was reduced to £2 10s. The sellers threw in an extra rope as a gratuity. This is usual when the sale is a large one.

The twelve members have sub-divided the land with pine-apple fences and the size of each parcel depends on the con-tribution its owner made to the whole purchase. Each one has built his own 'village' within his own area. Most of them employed labourers to help in clearing and building. Such village buildings are all of the primitive type of local materials 'without nails' and are altogether neater and more comfortable than the more pretentious but worse-built dwellings, with their sheet-iron roofs, now fashionable in all the towns.

These Kpone people have been fifteen years on their new land. Each does what he likes in his own plot, but they com-bine together to keep the main boundary clear. They have their own elected 'chief' and they keep themselves to them-selves, taking no part in the life of their Kotoku neighbours. They are hidden in the forest and approached by footpaths, and only by seeking them does one come in contact with them unless perhaps they are found in the market selling their foodstuffs. Every year they go home for a few weeks to their own country, join in their own people's annual festival, contract marriages, make contributions to the general expenses of relatives and pay the taxes of their own country.

Another large company of Krobo people, sixty-six family parties, bought a 77-rope strip of Adekuma–Amanase land and settled upon it. I believe they paid about £500 for this.

The *bu'sa* system is also used on the larger scale by groups of strangers who wish to colonize cocoa country. The village of Aprokumasi [1] is such a group of Fanti people. It was founded about ten years ago by a group of more than twenty households. It has now considerably dwindled as the cocoa has not done well, but some of the colonists are still sending food crops to Oda market. Only the farmers producing cocoa pay anything to the landlord town, but the village as a whole sends the *ohene* an annual sheep and bottle of rum as acknowledgement of their obligation. When they first started work the *ohene* killed a sheep and poured a libation on their behalf so that the gods and ghosts

[1] Aprokumasi, near the main road, has been noticed and has been put in the District Commissioner's list of Kotoku towns and villages, but it is less important than larger settlements which are buried in the forest and have not been recognized in the list.

of the land might bless their farming efforts and protect them
from accidents.

None of these land companies, of course, have any political
connection with either the town whose land they farm or have
bought or with the *oman* of which that town is a member. They
go home on all important occasions to their own distant towns,
and when they die their funeral customs are done there. They
contribute to the expenses of the stools of which they are blood
relatives just as if they still lived near to them.

Town Income from the Land

It is now the ambition of every land-owning town to make
enough income from its land to enable the townsmen to do no
work. I had not been a day in Abenase before the chief and some
elders came to ask me whether I could assist them in persuading
Europeans to come and mine their diamonds and pay them for
the privilege. They knew that Edzubea was being paid £40 a
quarter for mere *permission* to mine gold and diamonds, no
actual work having been started, and they knew that various
flourishing mines of some years' standing were bringing some
other towns large annual incomes. Their own potential wealth
was much on their minds.

They had already persuaded an African contractor to denude
their forest of most of its big trees. The contractor himself
told me that in the previous year Abenase had sold him over
eight hundred large trees of the type that take some three or four
hundred years to grow, and he was still busy felling them at
the same rate. For each tree the town received £1 1s., of which
7s. went to the *Omanhene*. Of the remainder the *ohene's* stool
received one-third and the other seven stools divided the rest.
This meant that on timber alone over £500 came into the town
and was divided up ultimately into about two hundred shares
of various sizes and was frittered away. What the town was
making from its *bu'sa* rents and from the *omanhene's* share-outs [1]
I do not know.

This prostitution of the land has a noticeably degrading effect
on the people. In towns which are not on their own land there
is a distinctly brisker and healthier atmosphere than in such
places as Abenase. In the former the people know that any

---

[1] The reader must, of course, be aware that as the Gold Coast land is not Crown
land, mining firms make their own negotiations with the native landowners without
the Government being involved. The land-owning town usually receives a
quarterly sum from the firm mining its land. The reader must go to Government
publications to learn what mines exist and to the balance-sheets of the mining
firms to learn what sums these mines pay to the landowners.

money that comes to them must be earned, and they have an air of self-respect and self-reliance. In the latter there is (with individual exceptions) an air of apathy and wretchedness, of sitting down to wait in misery for better times. The general impression is of much greater poverty, wretchedness, and shiftlessness. The *ohene* said to me once, 'This town is very poor. There are no gold mines on our land and no firm will come and work our diamonds.'

Yet the land is richly fertile and strangers from Akwapim and elsewhere swiftly get really wealthy when they apply themselves to work upon it.

CHAPTER VII

KINSHIP USAGES

Kinship Terms

The kinship terms employed in speech are the same in Akim as in Ashanti. As these have been carefully set forth by Dr. Rattray [1] I shall not give them again here.

Conventional Attitudes and Obligations between Kinsmen

Anthropologists are now tending to distinguish sharply between the conventional attitudes which are professed and the attitudes which often exist beneath the surface, sometimes breaking through. In their search for the latter they are often guided by the teachings of modern psychology. For instance, the conventional sentiment between father and son is one of strong affection, whereas psychology, emphasizing the unconscious hostility between father and son as rivals for the mother's regard, is always on the lookout for the eruption of the deeper feelings.

Such eruptions can be found. And, moreover, there are indications that the more primitive peoples are as well aware of the existence of subsocial forces as are the sophisticated, though their idiom is different. [2]

The conventional attitudes are, however, those which all social organization is designed to maintain. Therefore they are our main concern here. As Joseph Conrad has pointed out, the importance of a sentiment lies in the things people will do and suffer in order to maintain it.

A Man and his Father's Nephew

The European expects to find hostility between these two men, for the nephew is the old man's successor and might be expected to appear to the son as an interloper, especially if he comes to live in the house before the old man's death. But as a

---

[1] *Ashanti*, Chap. I.

[2] For instance, the Ga postulate as part of the individual's make-up a '*susuma*' which is wiser than the man himself, of whose wishes he is uninformed and which, if thwarted, leads the man into a life of mental conflict and worldly dissatisfaction. *Susuma*, in fact, corresponds very closely with the 'unconscious'. The 'sky family' is also invoked to explain inarticulate yearnings for personal relationships more satisfying than those available in earthly society.

rule the existence of such hostility is denied. The son says of the nephew, 'I like him because, if he had been a woman, I should have married him.' The European insists that such grounds for liking are flimsy, whereupon the son cites the more substantial compensations of the nephew's intrusion. He often stresses the nephew's usefulness as an advocate with the father. One youth said, 'When I go to my father for money he refuses me, but when I go to the nephew he asks his mother to beg my father for me. She likes me and she scolds my father, saying, "Why do you keep your son short? Do you want that nice boy to have to go and steal?"'

One man said of his father's nephew, 'If he had been a woman I should have married him, so to show his love for me he gave me his daughter to marry.' And indeed A and B (in my diagram) were man and wife.

In considering the nephew as the supplanter of the sons it must be remembered that the dead father's successor is not succeeding to property for his own use but to obligations as the trustee of a group. He is the new 'father' of the sons. When the real father dies they address him as *m'agya*—my father—and he calls them *mi ba*—my child—and it is generally agreed that they will demand more of him than they ever demanded of their real father. 'It was cunningly devised so in the beginning,' added one informant. The typical attitude of a man to his father's nephew was, I think, expressed one day by a man who was telling me about the ownership of the house in which he lived. He said, 'This was my father's house and it was inherited by his nephew when he died. My father's nephew lives elsewhere in a house he built for himself, but if I am in need of anything for this house I go to him for it.'

Nor is the position of the nephew as successor ever perfectly secure. It should not be forgotten—though by Europeans it often is—that there is strictly no such thing as a birthright to any position. Every successor to any position is elected by a family council, and if he proves an unsatisfactory trustee he can always be 'uprooted'. In any such uprooting of a nephew the sons would always be the principal witnesses. One young man said, 'We, the sons, can always say to him, "We don't like what you are doing with our father's affairs," but he cannot say anything of the sort to us. If he annoyed us too much we could always leave him. He would not like that, because the ghost of our father might say, "He has caused my sons to leave their father's house." He knows that the ghost of a father will not bless anyone who does not treat his sons well.'

When the successor is first appointed he first swears by
Anokyi [1] that all his cousins' trouble shall be his own, saying :

[2] Wekuda ne Fiada ne *Abosom Anokyi* se
Ade a ma ba di yi mi wofa mma
yi me hywewon yiye oka mu o, amanehu
mu o, me hywe won se man hywe won
yi ye a *Anokyi* nku mi.

The youths, too, swear by *Anokyi* that they will be faithful
and loyal to their new 'father'. There is seldom any fear on the
part of the sons that the nephew will deprive them of any property which their father desires them to inherit from him. Suppose the father has acquired by his own efforts property that he
desires a son to inherit, he usually calls witnesses and makes it
over, the son acknowledging the gift with ceremonial rum. Or
he may call the nephew and make him swear by *Anokyi* that his
wishes in regard to special property shall be respected.

Even in the case of property which the old man himself
inherited as a nephew and which should therefore be passed on
to the nephew, the nephew's hold is never perfectly secure.
Should he prove an unsatisfactory trustee the family elders may
even appoint one of the dead man's sons instead of him.

All these safeguards are known to both sons and nephews.

The relationship between the *gyasehene* and the chief, and the
asafohene and his predecessor's son are specially interesting cases
of the son-nephew relationship.[3]

A Man and his Wife's Father

A man and his wife's father must be stiffly polite to one another.
The father-in-law may give the other advice but may not openly
upbraid him. If the son-in-law is guilty of ill behaviour the
father-in-law does not himself reprove him but complains to
his parents or senior relatives. If the father-in-law should so
far forget himself as to revile his son-in-law as freely as he would
his son, the son-in-law approaches a few elders—any elders will
do ; they need not be kinsmen—gives them a present of drink,
and they have a private word with the father-in-law. But it must
be very delicately done.

[1] *Anokyi* is an ancient god whom I have not found to be actively worshipped by
the Akim-Kotoku beyond being invoked in oaths and curses. The succession
oath by *Anokyi* appears to be universal throughout Kotoku.
[2] Wednesday and Friday and the god *Anokyi* speak. This inheritance to which
I have come, these my uncle's sons, I will look after them well, whether in debt,
whether in affliction, I will look after them thus. If I do not look after them well,
may *Anokyi* kill me.
[3] Chap. II.

A man is expected to perform various irksome tasks for his father-in-law. Prominent among these is farm work. When the father-in-law wishes to clear a new farm he tells his daughter to inform her husband. The husband goes round collecting a company of his own male friends, and on the day appointed they all go and work. The wife and her mother both go to the farm and there cook refreshments for the workers. This food and adequate palm-wine is provided by the father-in-law. The son-in-law acts as foreman of the clearing work and 'if his friends do not work well it is his disgrace'. The father-in-law himself leaves the farm during the eating of the refreshments so that they can eat as greedily and jovially as they like. He may crack a joke or two before departing, saying perhaps, 'If you don't do the work well I shall take my daughter away from you,' to which the son-in-law replies on the same vein, 'I will do it so well that you will want to give me yet another of your daughters.' [1]

When the foreman thinks his friends have done enough work he may not dismiss them but must wait till the old man sees that they are tired and himself suggests that the day's work stop.

The day after the farm clearing the father-in-law pays a formal visit to thank his son-in-law. He in turn goes round thanking his own friends, and naturally they expect him to help them in the same way another day.

Men frequently say, 'The more daughters you have and the more friends their husbands have, the quicker your farm work gets done.'

If the father-in-law has pledged his farm or got into debt he expects his son-in-law to help him out. He makes no direct request, but he tells his daughter to drop her husband a hint. Frequently a son-in-law elect is indirectly informed that he must get his sweetheart's father out of debt before he can marry. He usually consents, for this gives him a hold over his father-in-law. 'His hand is in my mouth,' he says, 'and I can bite it if I like.' Such a gift to a prospective father-in-law is always ostensibly a loan and the young man says, 'Pay me or not, as you like.' However, should the father-in-law die, his successor—the girl's new 'father'—is bound to pay if the son demands it. The young man can explicitly demand payment and can sue his new father-in-law if he refuses—treatment which he could not offer to his real father-in-law. But if he is well disposed and wise he will let the matter slide. Usually the new 'father' will enlist his 'daughter' as advocate by giving her a good slice of cleared farm :

[1] A man may not marry two sisters.

otherwise she is in danger of suggesting to her husband that he collect the old debt.

Annually at the time of the *Afahye* feast a man must send a gift of drink to his father-in-law, but he may not invite the older man to his house.

However, if the older should invite the younger, the invitation must be accepted, but the occasion is stiffly formal. 'The young man must hang his head and never get drunk.'

Never may a son-in-law eat with his father-in-law. If either is in the act of eating when the other appears, the food must be swiftly concealed. A father may call his daughter and her husband to his farming village to stay for a month or so and work for him, but even then, however small the party, the young man may not eat with his father-in-law. If a son-in-law becomes such a favourite with his father-in-law that 'he is like a son' the old man may give him a sleeping-room in his own house as though he were indeed a son, but he must still go to his own father's house to eat.

If a man finds his father-in-law drunk he must escort him home as discreetly as possible to keep him from disgracing himself publicly. The old man will probably insult him thoroughly on their way home, but this he must regard as preferable to his father-in-law's public disgrace.

When the son-in-law goes hunting with a gun—as do most young men at times—he must always send his father-in-law a portion of any good game he kills. In return the old man sends him gifts of ammunition.

It is always the son-in-law whom an old man sends on long and difficult errands. If a debtor has run away to Kumasi the son-in-law is sent to find him and collect the debt. And he must go with a good grace. One man sent his son-in-law to bring a load of salt from the coast. Heavy rain ruined the salt, so the young man, ashamed to return without it, hired himself out as a labourer till he had earned enough to replace it.

The son-in-law submits cheerfully to exacting demands, for he can then count on his father-in-law's support should his wife go to her father with tales of an unsatisfactory husband.

Even when father-in-law and son-in-law are on the worst of terms they seldom descend to direct recriminations. When they do, the one can have the other called before a court of family elders and can demand a pacification fee. The elders, however, are always loath to deal formally with such cases, and say, 'You are in the right, but it is unwise to press it. Leave it, and we will speak to him privately.'

Even when relations become intolerable and the father-in-law and his daughter agree to dismiss the husband, there is an indirect way of delivering the dismissal. The son-in-law is asked to hew down a tree of the kind called *mase gye-wo-ba* (father-in-law, take your daughter). This tree has iron-hard wood and to fell it is a virtually impossible task, which the son-in-law abandons. The responsibility is thus lodged with him. Should the father-in-law be less circumspect, burst into open anger with his son-in-law and send him packing, he must refund the money paid to him when the marriage contract was made. If he omits to do this, he cannot forbid future communications between the severed partners. Once the son-in-law has accepted the money, the father-in-law can demand a heavy pacification fee from him if he so much as speaks to the woman again.

The permanence of marriage is said to depend largely upon the relation between a man and his father-in-law, and when the two are on specially good terms, as in *doba*[1] marriage, divorce never occurs. 'The *doba* marriage is the sign of the strong love between the two families,' said an informant.

Divorces are said always to start from the wife : she meets another man, prefers him to her husband and begins to pick quarrels with the latter. But if her father takes his son-in-law's part she has difficulty in getting rid of him.

When a father-in-law dies, his son-in-law must carry out a custom called *nsiye*. The dead man's parents send the son-in-law a pot of palm-wine and tell him of the death. He then calls his own father and uncles to a meeting and shows them the wine, saying, 'This is what I have suffered to-day.' The wine is shared and the young man, with the help, if necessary, of these guests of his, provides a 12-yard piece of new cloth called *ntama po*, on which is laid 8*s.*, called *nsawabodie*. Four more shillings are tied in another piece of cloth. These, together with two pots of palm-wine, are sent to the dead man's 'parents'. To his mother-in-law the man sends two more pots of palm-wine and 12*s.*, saying 'The wine is for your friends and the 12*s.* is to buy more wine for your friends.' Actually the 12*s.* is not for wine but for any odd expenses which may be pressing rather irksomely.

Then the young man, affecting limp prostration and clutching his gun, is taken by his male friends, anxiously supporting his nerveless form, themselves ceremonially crying, to the dead man's house. Here he and his supporters are given a pot of palm-wine and the 'parents' of the deceased come and thank

[1] See Chap. VIII.

him. After a short sitting he takes leave and goes home, but is not supposed to eat or wash till after the burial.

Eight days after the death the dead man's relatives send the son-in-law 8*s*., saying, 'This is for your wife to cook some good food for you and provide some drink.' This ends the period of fasting. The wife then sends a generous mass of food to her husband's home, and all those who helped him to 'fire his gun' come and share it with him. Those who cannot come have some sent to them.

On the fortieth day after the death, the son-in-law must send more palm-wine and go and sit in the dead man's yard. He in turn is given palm-wine and 'he can revenge the palm-wine he sent his wife's relatives by drinking plenty of theirs.'

A Man and His Wife's Brother

There is a common saying in Akim, 'If you don't like your wife's brother you will suffer.'

The wife's brother is in a specially strong position for causing suffering. Where the linkage between two people lies in their interest in a third person relationship is always more delicate than when the linkage is direct. In the case of a man and his wife's brother in a society practising both cross-cousin marriage and matrilineal succession, a man may stand to another concurrently in three such relationships, namely, wife's brother, father's heir and son's predecessor. Consider these three, one by one.

The wife's brother, as such, shares the sentiments of his and her whole *abusua* towards her husband, for the husband's children are going to be one of their group. In Europe, when the holder of some great hereditary title or estate takes a wife, the husband's relations regard her primarily as an heir-giver. If she fails in this she is a disaster. So the Akan woman's *abusua* regard her husband. Is he going to beget not only an heir for the woman's brother but a quiverful of children to swell the *abusua*? A childless man can never hold up his head before the members of his wife's *abusua*. It is said that they have only to give him to his face the epithet, '*kotekrawa*' (waxen penis), and he will certainly commit suicide.

Provided that the sister's husband begets children, the man's attitude towards him is supposed to be one of gratitude and friendship. 'Of course he is my friend,' said one man to me of his sister's husband. 'I have given him my sister and he has had children with her and so has given me something good in exchange.' And certainly between this particular speaker and his sister's husband there seemed to be much spontaneous friendship. I seldom found one of them at home without finding the other with him, sitting and smoking, playing a game of *wurri*, or helping in odd jobs. For instance, one day the brother-in-law brought to the compound some fish-traps that he was making for use in the local stream, and both men obtained much genuine enjoyment preparing together for a little sport.

The second of these three concurrent relationships—that of a man to his father's heir—we have already considered.

The third—that of man to his own heir's father—we have now to consider.

The boy is the convergence of the two men's interest. The conventional attitude between the two men is one of politeness. Each is grateful for whatever the other does for the boy up to a point, but beyond that point jealousy may set in. A father has the right to keep his son with him during his uncle's lifetime, but often the uncle offers to take the boy into his own house and the father is pleased. But disagreement on this point is not unknown. There was a case in Abenase while I was there. The uncle wanted to take charge of the nephew and send him to school. The father refused to give up his elder boy, who was his right hand on the farm, but said that the uncle might take the younger boy. The uncle said he wanted the one who would become the 'father' of his children. When I left, the matter was about to be laid before a committee of elders from both sides, and I do not know how it was settled.

I was told that this kind of case is rare and that fathers are more likely to appeal to uncles for help in sending boys to school than in resisting their efforts.

A Man and his Wife's Sisters

The younger sisters of a wife are all her husband's 'small'—or partial—wives. A man usually says of them, 'They respect and obey me more than my wife does. And they obey me before they obey their own husbands.'

The man calls these women '*mi yerekuma*'—my junior wife—and they call him '*mi kunu panyim*'—my senior husband.

The elder sister of a man's wife, however, is spoken of as his 'senior wife' (*yere panyim*), and he is her 'junior husband'.

A man can freely command occasional cooking and domestic service of the junior 'wives', but with the elder sister of his own wife he is much more diffident.

A man does not marry his dead wife's sister except in unusual

7

circumstances. When a young wife dies shortly after her marriage her family may give another unmarried daughter in her place.

A Man and His Wife's Sisters' Husbands

All these men have the same mother-in-law and they are rivals for her favour. It has been pointed out by Rattray that wives of the same man speak of one another as '*mi kura*'—my rival—implying jealousy between them. Exactly the same word is used by men with the same mother-in-law when speaking of one another. The youngest of such a group of men calls the eldest '*mi kura panyim*'—my senior rival—and the elder calls the younger '*mi kura kuma*'—my junior rival.

It is the duty of the husband of a younger sister to treat his wife no better than the husband of the elder is able to treat his. For the rivalry does not concern only the mother-in-law. A woman who is able to say to her husband, 'My sister's husband treats her better than you do me', can create bad blood between the two men.

A man is expected to be able to provide his wife with a house other than his own, and a mother-in-law has always the right to come and live with her daughter if she wishes. If the husband of a junior sister is able to give his wife a house which the mother-in-law prefers to her elder daughter's, the elder son-in-law will resent this.

A Man and His Wife's Mother

An atmosphere of stiff respect is maintained between a man and his mother-in-law. The man may not sit in her presence unless she herself is seated and invites him to be. Neither may eat in the presence of the other or even take a drink of water. The mother-in-law may, in an emergency, offer her son-in-law a meal, but she must retire while he eats it, and he must eat moderately.

The son-in-law may offer, as a courtesy, to help his mother-in-law on her farm with such heavy work as tree-felling, but she will never—as will the father-in-law—demand it of him. In such farm work the son-in-law will bring his friends to help him and the mother-in-law will send refreshments for the party. Of these the son-in-law may partake.

It is common for a married daughter to continue living in her mother's house, but if the daughter's husband goes there also he is considered disreputable. A man may give up his own room to a visitor and temporarily lodge in his mother-in-law's house without reproach, but to stay there permanently is discreditable for several reasons. First, it may mean that he has so seriously displeased both his father and his maternal uncle that they have virtually turned him out, or that he himself is too stiff-necked to apologize to them after a quarrel. Or it may mean that he is without pride and will serve the mother-in-law for the sake of material comforts. At any rate, to live in his mother-in-law's house is 'not nice' (*enye fe*).

Nor is it creditable to a man to have his mother-in-law to live with him in his own house. 'It is a disgrace to his wife's father, because every man of standing ought to be able to provide his wife with a separate house. To have your mother-in-law in your own house is as if to say 'Your father could not give your mother a house, so I have to.'' '

The mother-in-law can properly give her son-in-law advice, but usually does it through his wife. But she may not scold him to his face. When he is quarrelling, fighting, or using bad language he must desist if she appear on the scene.

Husbands all agree that the main reason for pleasing the mother-in-law is that, 'If you displease her she will help your wife to annoy you.' And she has every facility for this, since the wife usually dwells in her mother's, not her husband's, house.

When a man's mother-in-law dies, he must pay 9s. 6d. towards her funeral, but he is expected to express his esteem by giving more if he is able.

A Man and his Maternal Uncle's Wife

The attitude of a man to his maternal uncle's wife is one of several possible attitudes, depending on which of several possible circumstances exist.

If the older generation married on the cross-cousin plan, then the woman who is the wife of the uncle is concurrently the nephew's father's sister. She is then doubly his 'mother', and in both of these motherly capacities she can order him about as if he were her own son, but he must be stiffer and more polite to her than to his real mother. If, on the other hand, she is not his father's sister, he may inherit her as a wife when his uncle dies. In this case he must be especially stiff with her while his uncle is still alive, or the uncle may become suspicious and say, 'I am not dead yet,' or may even become angry and call the parents of the boy and his own family elders and say, 'I do not want this boy to succeed me when I die or to inherit my wife.'

Should the nephew and his uncle's wife actually commit adultery together during the uncle's lifetime, the nephew loses his rights of succession and may not inherit the wife. In earlier days he would have been handed over to the chief to use as a human sacrifice at the next stool *Addae* celebration, but to-day he is simply driven out of the compound and no longer regarded as having any kinship rights.

It is also common for a nephew to marry his maternal uncle's daughter. In this case he cannot also marry her mother. But he is still just as much responsible for her welfare as if he had married her. He calls her *maberewa*—my old lady—and cares for her as if she were his mother. If she is not old and wishes to marry again, it is the nephew who gives her the white clay of innocence (*ahyiri*) which has the force of permission to go away. The woman's new husband has to pay *ayifari* pacification to the dead husband's heir just as if he had seduced a wife and obtained thereby a divorce for that wife.

If the nephew has married his uncle's daughter he may marry *none* of his uncle's wives, even if some of them are much younger than his mother-in-law, for they all rank as his mother-in-law. But concurrently they rank as his 'daughters' and he is 'a father to them,' and their marriage can be arranged only through him.

A Man and his Wife's Maternal Uncle

A woman's maternal uncle is a classificatory father-in-law to the woman's husband. If such a father-in-law dies, the man must do for him exactly what he would do for his true father-in-law. In ordinary life this 'father-in-law' can order his niece's husband to work on his farm just as the true father-in-law can. The two are, however, allowed to eat together from the same dish.

A Man and his Father's Sisters

When a man's father's young sister dies husbandless the man must provide her coffin and other burial expenses.

A son must carry out any orders which his paternal aunt gives him just as he obeys his father. The paternal aunts are sometimes spoken of as the son's 'female fathers' and identify themselves with the father. As one son put it, 'If I obey my father well, these women say I am obeying *them* well and they reward me in all sorts of ways.'

When the father's sister is older than the father the son must respect her more than he does the father. The father remembers that she has in many ways acted as a 'mother' to him. Little girls of five carry their infant brothers round on their backs, and, as they grow older, see that they get their proper share of food at the children's meals, fight their battles, wash them, tend them, and generally act as mothers, the real mother being probably engrossed with a still younger child. A man never entirely loses the sentiment that his elder sister is a mother to him, and he insists that his sons shall carry on this sentiment. The son names his own eldest son with the masculinized form of his father's eldest sister's name.

A Woman and her Brother's Wives

The motherly attitude of a woman to her brother is extended to that brother's wife. The husband's sister is the protector and controller of his wife. She calls her brother's wife, not 'my sister' but *'my wife'*, saying in explanation, 'If I had been a man I should have married her.'

If a man marries before he has worked enough to give his wife a farm from which she can feed him, it is his elder sister who takes the wife to her own farm or her own husband's farm, and gives her all the produce she needs for wifely cookery. If the husband is unable to supply his wife with plates and dishes for his meals, his sister will lend them, 'so that the husband shall not be disgraced by his wife's lack.'

If the husband has a quarrel with his wife, it is his sister's duty to take the wife's part, even when the husband is in the right. If it comes to blows the sister says, 'I will not have you flog my wife.'

The powers of the husband's sister as a 'husband' include the right to order her brother's wife to cook, pound fufu, or go to the farm for her.

It is to the advantage of both women to keep on good terms. If the wife needs money from her husband, his sister may help her to get it, for 'he pays more respect to his sister than to his wife.' A woman who quarrels with her husband's sister is said to be no good : she may be in the right, but she should have more sense than to insist upon it.

If a wife is a bad wife, it is the husband's sister who advises him whether to divorce her or not, and a man who did not consult his sister in this matter would be accounted highly unwise. If the sister advises divorce, saying, 'If you keep this woman here I can be no longer your sister,' the man had better take the advice, for the sister probably has her mother behind her. The old lady never openly enters such disputes, 'for she is a big woman'. Moreover, the sister's judgment of her brother is considered sounder than the mother's of her son, because the mother's affection blinds her to his faults.

A Woman and her Husband's Brother's Wife

Women married to brothers are called 'rivals' (*Kurafo*), just as are men married to sisters. They are rivals not only for the favour of the mother-in-law but that of the husband's sister.

A Woman and her Husband's Brothers

A woman calls her husband's brothers 'my senior husband' or 'my junior husband', according as they are older or younger than her real husband. The men in turn speak of her as 'my junior wife' or 'my senior wife', according to their own position in the series of brothers. The ages of the wives have nothing to do with it. The girl-wife of an elder brother is senior to the elderly wife of a younger brother.

When a man dies, his eldest surviving brother succeeds him until all the brothers are dead : only then does the nephew succeed. The successor also inherits the wife or wives of the dead man. Therefore, between a woman and any one of her husband's brothers, is always the thought that they may some day be mates.

Adultery with a brother's wife is worse than ordinary adultery ; therefore the convention of stiff behaviour exists between a woman and her husband's brothers.

Each of the wives is bound, in certain circumstances, to cook for or serve in a secondary wifely capacity, all the brothers. If a man's own wife is away, he can give a direct order to any wife of a younger brother, or to his own wife's youngest sister, but if he wants service from an elder brother's wife he must ask her through that brother.

Wives of One Man

Between these, as between the husbands of sisters, open rivalry exists. It is greatest when a new, young wife supplants one who is getting old. Here, of course, it is all the greater because it is not neck-and-neck rivalry but is also a special case of the jealousy with which the elderly and failing of both sexes always regard the young and rising, when the young are not directly dependant on the old.

The wives speak of one another as 'my senior rival' or 'my junior rival', not according to age but length of wifehood. If a man inherits his elder brother's wives these are senior to his own, whatever their age. If he inherits a younger brother's wives these are junior to his own, whatever their age.

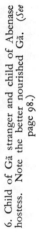

5. Gä stranger (right) with her Abenase hostess. Note the better physique of the stranger. (*See* page 98.)

6. Child of Gä stranger and child of Abenase hostess. Note the better nourished Gä. (*See* page 98.)

Other Funeral Obligations

When a married woman dies, her husband must provide her coffin, and the cloth, money, and other things which are put in with the body. The dead woman lies in state in a house of her mother's family, and this family does the entertainment before the burial. The eight-day ceremony is done in two separate houses and each house is responsible for its own guests.

If the woman has married daughters, her sons-in-law are sent a pot of palm-wine apiece and each contributes a pillow, a mat, and a cloth or 9s. 6d. The woman's husband, or his successor, does the rest.

If the woman is young and unmarried, her father provides her coffin and her 'travelling equipment'. Her mother's people share the entertainment expenses with the father's.

When a man dies his sons and daughters provide the coffin. If they are young children, some substantial man on the mother's side—usually her brother—pays the money for them, but the debt is remembered against them and they must repay it when they reach marriageable age. In the case of a girl, the debt must be paid by her husband when he marries her.

HOUSEHOLDS

Nowhere in the Gold Coast—except occasionally among Christians—have I met a household consisting only of a man, his wife, and their children. Here and there a household is found which superficially presents this appearance, but usually the husband and wife are old people who have only in their old age joined the household of a son or daughter, or the wife has joined her husband later in life.

The chief reason for this state of affairs is that a woman may neither cook for her husband, enter his room, nor (in stricter households) penetrate beyond the entrance porch of his compound while she is ceremonially unclean—that is, while she is menstruating.

A more accurate phrase than ceremonially unclean would be 'destructive of the spiritual', for her influence at such times is held to destroy every supernatural force, good or bad. No ghost, no bad medicines, no witchcraft, can harm a menstruating woman ; equally are all good medicines and influences killed by her proximity. The essence of her influence is *earthiness* : she reduces a magical object to a mere earthy shell wherein no quickening spirit can dwell.

Every man has about him, or his house, various supernatural influences. The house itself was probably blessed and medicined when it was built. It may be supernaturally protected against lightning. There may be an ancestor's stool, ancestor's weapons, a bowl for washing the *ntro*, a talisman hanging over the door, a medicine attached to the gun, or worn round the man's neck. All the tools of a man's craft, including even his hoe, are blessed, medicined, and thanked, for there is a spirit in them. All these would instantly lose their virtue for ever if a woman in her contagiously earthy state came near them. Even ordinary food, which is believed not to nourish in an impersonal, physiological way, but to act on the *kra* of the eater, either pleasing and enlivening it or displeasing and depressing it, would, if cooked by a woman in her destructive condition, lose its beneficial effect on the eater's *kra*. It would also destroy any blessed influence which prayer, sacrifices, or medicine had implanted in the eater.

Nor must the fireplace at which the woman normally cooks her husband's food be used by her when she is in her spiritually destructive state. A fireplace is always treated as a sacred thing, and the influence of fire upon food is to give it additional spiritual virtue. Nor must the unclean woman touch the pots, pans, and plates used for her husband's food.

Returning now to housing, we do not find that a man never shares a house with his wife, but until she has passed the menopause there must always be other women who can relieve her of cooking from time to time, and there must always be an arrangement whereby she can avoid her husband's room.

There is no regular pattern of association of kinsmen in houses. I made careful notes of the occupants of every house in Abenase (over a hundred in all) and found that there were no two alike. To give an idea of the variety I will briefly sketch the constitution of a few households, not selected, but taken straight from my notebook in the order of noting. The first in each list of occupants is the head of the household.

Household No. 1

(1) Head of the house, a man about 50, with paralysed legs.
(2) Wife of (1), aged about 40.
(3) Sister of (2), aged about 30.
(4) Daughter of another sister of (2), with her four children.
(5) Boy of about 14, the son of (1).
(6) A young woman—a stranger—with her infant.

Household No. 2

(1) Wife of an *Asafohene*. (He lives elsewhere in the same town.)
(2) Grown-up daughter of (1), with her infant.
(3) Daughter of the *Asafohene's* elder brother, with her child.
(4) Another grown-up daughter (1), with her two children.
(5) Daughter of (1), aged about 12.

Household No. 3

(1) Woman, aged about 60.
(2) Grown-up daughter of (1), aged about 18, married but childless.
(3) Grown-up daughter of (1), aged about 25, with her two children.
(4) Grown-up son about 26, divorced from wife ; childless.

Household No. 4

(1) Man, aged about 70.
(2) Wife of (1), aged about 60.
(3) Daughter of (1), with her three children.
(4) Daughter of (1), with her five children.
(5) Daughter of (1), aged about 35, with two young children and (6).
(6) Daughter of (5), aged about 16.
(7) Son, aged about 35, wife elsewhere.

Household No. 5

(1) Man, aged about 60 (two sons elsewhere).
(2) Son of sister of (1), aged about 30, unmarried.
(3) Son of sister of (1), wife elsewhere, no children.
(4) Son of sister of (1), two wives elsewhere.
(5) Son of sister of (1).
(6) Son of sister of (1), wife elsewhere.
(7) An Ewe stranger.
(8) Wife of (5), with two children.

Household No. 6

(1) Man aged about 60, wife elsewhere.
(2) 'Sister' of (1), aged about 30, with three children, including (4).
(3) Stranger.
(4) Son of (2), aged about 12.

Household No. 7 (small house, building unfinished)
   (1) Woman with five children (wife of (1) in Household No. 5).

Household No. 8
   (1) Man, aged about 60.
   (2) Wife of (1), with six children, including (4) and including one infant.
   (3) Wife of (1), with two children.
   (4) Grown-up daughter of (2), with her infant.
   (5) Woman stranger with her five children.

Household No. 9
   (1) Man, aged about 40. Seldom at home, but in village.
   (2) Brother of (1).
   (3) Wife of (2) and two children.

Household No. 10
   (1) Man.
   (2) Wife of (1), with two children, including (4).
   (3) Sister of (1).
   (4) Daughter of (1), aged about 12.

Household No. 11
   (1) Man, aged about 70.
   (2) Daughter of (1), with one child.
   (3) Stepson of (1), aged about 25.
   (4) Son of (1), aged about 23, unmarried.
   (5) Daughter of (1), aged about 22, with one child.
   (6) Daughter of (1), aged about 8.

Household No. 12
   (1) An *Asafoakye*, aged about 50.
   (2) Sister of (1).
   (3) Husband of (2).
   (4) Daughter of (2), with two children.
   (5) Daughter of (2), with two children.
   (6) Wife of (1).

Household No. 13
   (1) Man aged about 50, ex-soldier, never married because of 'sickness'.
   (2) Sister of (1), aged about 30. No surviving children.
   (3) Husband of (2), aged about 35.

7. A room in the older type of compound. The newer type is seen in plate 12. (*See* plate 96.)

8. The midwife washes the child. (*See* page 136.)

Household No. 14

   (1) Man, aged about 35. Two wives, one elsewhere.
   (2) Wife of (1), with four children.
   (3) Sister of (1), with one child.
   (4) Sister of (1), with one child.
   (5) Sister of (1), with two children.

Household No. 15

   (1) Man, aged about 55.
   (2) Grown-up daughter of (1), with her two children.
   (3) Grown-up daughter of (1), with her child.
   (4) Grown-up daughter of (1), with her child.
   (5) Daughter of a friend of (1), whose husband ran away.

Household No. 16

   (1) Man, aged about 50.
   (2) Wife of (1).
   (3) Daughter of (1), aged about 25, with her two children.

Household No. 17

   (1) Man, aged about 65.
   (2) Son-in-law of (1).
   (3) Wife of (1).
   (4) Daughter of (1), wife of (2), with two children.
   (5) Some grand-children whose parents are elsewhere.
   (6) Daughter of (1), married to (7), with two children.
   (7) Nephew of (1).
   (8) Daughter of (1), with her four children, husband elsewhere.

Household No. 18

   (1) Woman with husband elsewhere, with her child.
   (2) Mother of (1).
   (3) Father of (1).
   (4) Son of (2) and (3), aged about 14.
   (5) Daughter of (2) and (3), aged about 12.

N.B.—This house belongs to the husband of (1), who built it for his wife and lives elsewhere himself. His wife's parents and their younger children came to join her.

Household No. 19

   (1) An aged *asafohene*, widower, four other wives divorced.
   (2) Son of (1), aged 3.
   (3) Daughter of (1), aged about 11.

N.B.—The old man does his own cooking and cares for his young son.

Household No. 20

   (1) Man, aged about 40, wife divorced.
   (2) Sister of (1), with one child.
   (3) Husband of (2), Chief's son.
   (4) Brother of (1), aged about 30.
   (5) Wife of (4), with her three children.
   (6) Boy of about 12, attendant to (3).
   (7) Four lodgers, labourers from the Northern Territories.

Household No. 21

   (1) Woman, aged about 50.
   (2) Daughter of (1), aged about 30, with her two children.
   (3) Daughter of (1), with her two children.
   (4) Daughter of (1), with her two children.
   (5) Daughter of (2), aged about 15, married, husband elsewhere.
   (6) Husband of (3).

Household No. 22

   (1) Woman, aged about 80.
   (2) Son of (1), aged about 40, widower.
   (3) Daughter of (1), wife of an *asafokye*.
   (4) Daughter of (3), with her child.

Household No. 23

   (1) Man, aged about 70, wife divorced.
   (2) Daughter of (1), aged about 15, married, husband elsewhere.
   (3) Daughter of (1), husband elsewhere.
   (4) Son of (1), aged about 28, unmarried.[1]
   (5) Son of (1), aged about 26, unmarried.
   (6) Son of (1), aged about 18, unmarried.
   (7) Four children of (1), ages 12–6.

N.B.—The old man says of (4), (5), and (6), 'They have bad characters, so I won't help them to marry.'

---

[1] When men of marriageable age are unmarried it is usually 'because of sickness.'

Household No. 24

(1) Man, aged about 60, wife divorced.
(2) Paternal nephew of (1), wife elsewhere.
(3) Paternal nephew of (1), wife elsewhere.
(4) Paternal nephew of (1), wife elsewhere.
(5) Paternal nephew of (1), wife elsewhere.

Household No. 25

(1) Man, aged about 50.
(2) Wife of (1), aged about 50.
(3) Daughter of (1), with her two children.
(4) Daughter of (1), with her infant.
(5) Son, aged about 15.

Household No. 26

(1) Woman, aged about 30, with her four children.
(2) Mother of (1).

N.B.—The house was built by the husband of (1), who is elsewhere.

Household No. 27

(1) Woman, aged about 60.
(2) Grown-up son of (1), wife elsewhere.
(3) Grown-up son of (1), wife elsewhere.
(4) Grown-up daughter of (1) and her five children, including an infant and (6).
(5) Grown-up daughter of (1).
(6) Grown-up daughter of (4).
(7) Daughter of (5), aged about 12.

Household No. 28

(1) Woman badly afflicted with scrofula, living alone except for three children, one an infant.

Household No. 29

(1) An *asafohene*, aged about 80.
(2) Daughter of sister of (1).
(3) Daughter of sister of (1).
(4) Son of sister of (1).
(5) Wife of (4) and her three children.

Household No. 30

    (1) Woman, aged about 50.

    (2) Daughter of (1), married for several years, marriage dissolved because unfruitful.

    (3) Daughter of (1), aged about 14.

    (4) Daughter of son of (1).

Household No. 31

    (1) Woman, aged about 80.

    (2) Daughter of (1), aged about 60.

Household No. 32

    (1) Woman, aged about 30, with her child. Husband in another town.

    (2) Sister of (1), aged about 35.

    (3) Sister of (1), aged about 35.

Household No. 33

    (1) Woman, aged about 45.

    (2) Daughter of (1), aged about 25, with her child.

Household No. 34

    (1) Man, aged about 60, an *okyeame*.

    (2) Wife of (1), aged about 45.

    (3) Wife of (1), aged about 20, and her child.

    (4) Grown-up son of (1), unmarried.

Household No. 35

    (1) Woman, aged about 50, owner of the house.

    (2) Husband of (1).

    (3) Grown-up son, aged about 22, wife elsewhere.

    (4) Grown-up son, aged about 21, unmarried.

    (5) Grown-up daughter, aged about 20, with her three children.

    (6) Grown-up daughter, aged about 19, with one child.

    (7) Grown-up daughter, aged about 18, with one child.

    (8) Grown-up daughter, aged about 15, unmarried.

    (9) Grown-up daughter, aged about 13, unmarried.

Household No. 36

(1) Man, aged about 30, two wives elsewhere.
(2) Sister of (1), with her child.
(3) Wife of deceased maternal uncle of (1), aged about 70.
(4) Maternal grandmother of (1).

Household No. 37

(1) Man, aged about 40.
(2) Wife of (1).
(3) Daughter of (1), with her infant.

Household No. 38

(1) Woman, aged about 40, with her infant. She is also a grandmother, but lives alone in a house provided by her husband.

Household No. 39

(1) Head of the house absent at the mines with his wife.
(2) A stranger from Nzima, a goldsmith.
(3) A stranger from Bontuku, a goldsmith.
(4) A sister of (2), married to a man of this town, with her infant.

Household No. 40

(1) Woman, aged about 45, owner of the house.
(2) Husband of (1).
(3) Daughter of (1), aged about 18, husband elsewhere.

Household No. 41

(1) Man, aged about 30, wife elsewhere.
(2) Sister of (1), with her two children.
(3) Sister of (1), with her three children.
(4) Mother of (1), (2), and (3).

Household No. 42

(1) Man, aged 65, widower.
(2) Son of (1), wife elsewhere.
(3) Daughter of (1), aged about 18, husband elsewhere.
(4) Son of (1).
(5) Wife of (4).

CHAPTER VIII

MARRIAGE

Prohibited and Enjoined Marriages

Dr. Rattray has explained how every Ashanti person is a member of two kinship groups : the *abusua* or clan of his mother, and the *ntro* or ceremonial-washing group of his father.[1] In Ashanti and in some other parts of the Gold Coast both the clan and the *ntro* are strictly exogamous. In Akim-Kotoku, however, only the clan is now exogamous. This exogamy is as strict as it has ever been, but the *ntro*, as an exogamous group, is now extinct. A great many of the Kotoku people—even some of the old—do not even know to what *ntro* they belong. Some of the *ntro* ceremonial lore still survives fragmentarily, but as a social group the *ntro* no longer exists in Akim-Kotoku.

The same prohibitions between *near* relatives still exist as exist in Ashanti, and as Dr. Rattray has given a list of them I need not do so again.

Marriages between cross-cousins are still enjoined and to-day about half the married people of all ages are married to their cross-cousins.

Marriage between different generations of relatives is quite common. For instance, an *asafokye* in Abenase is married to his cousin's daughter thus :

ACQUIRING A WIFE

There are three common kinds of marriage contract, namely, *Wofase* marriage, *Awari* marriage, and *Doba* marriage.

Wofase marriage is cross-cousin marriage. This union, though not compulsory, is regarded as the natural [2] one, and there are no formalities and no fee beyond the payment of a

---

[1] *Ashanti*, Chap. II.
[2] It is sometimes spoken of as 'God's marriage', meaning 'natural marriage', as 'God's death' means 'natural death'.

bottle of rum or a pot of palm-wine by the husband to the wife's parents as a sign on the contract (*odisiso*).

Awari is the set of formalities associated with the ordinary marriage of non-cousins. I will now transcribe two separate accounts of *Awari* marriage given to me by two young men of Abenase who had recently taken wives by that method. The first had very little money and made only the minimum cere-monial gifts. The other, being comparatively opulent, was more lavish.

The first young man said, 'I knew the girl I wanted to marry, so I waited till one day when I met her alone, and I told her and offered her a penny. She agreed, so she took the penny. She went home and showed her mother the penny, and the mother agreed, so the girl told me to go to her father. Her father that begat her was dead and his elder brother was her father instead. My own father then sent my elder brother with a bottle of door-knocking wine (*abobosnsa*) to the girl's father. My uncle (maternal uncle) did not help my father in these expenses though uncles sometimes do if they are generous. If my uncle had objected to my marriage, I should have hesitated, because he might have disinherited me. He could not have kept me from being elected to his place after his death because that is decided by the elders, but he might have kept me from getting any of his own things.

'Then my father sent my brother with another bottle to the girl's mother's people. They said, "Have you asked her father?" The people there were the girl's mother, the mother's elder brother, the mother's mother, and the mother's sister. There was a lot of argument before they accepted the bottle. It is always so : they always talk as if they are unwilling. If they are really unwilling they send back the bottle and all is finished.

'Then my father had to *thank the girl's head* [1] with a pot of palm-wine and eight shillings. The girl's father's family gathered together and each side received four shillings, and they all shared the wine. I had to be there and hear them tell me the rules of marriage. Any good speaker from either side can be chosen to make this speech. The speaker said that if my wife got into trouble, such as debt, stealing in the market, quarrelling, or any case in court, without my consent, her parents would be responsible,

---

[1] The word 'head' is often used idiomatically, meaning spirit. For instance, of a child born in response to a request to the god Nangro at Afosu (see p. 191), it was said, 'Its head is in Nangro'. A man sometimes thanks his wife's head when she bears him a child. In marriage contracts the associated 'head-wine' and 'head-money' have reference to the bride's 'head' in this sense.

8

but if she got into debt or trouble because of something I had
ordered her to do or something I had consented to, then
I and my family would have to pay. I had to promise that I
would not ill-treat her and they said that if she disobeyed me I
must tell her father. She had to promise to obey me and they
told her to report me to her father if I ill-treated her.

'After that I bought her a wooden box, a mirror, some clothes
and things to make herself beautiful. Then a day was appointed
and her sisters brought her to me in the evening. I have heard
that in olden days these things were done with dancing and
playing, but I myself have never seen any.'

The other young man, wealthier and apparently more bashful,
said, 'When a man wants to get married, first he looks till he
sees a girl he likes. Then he gets someone—either a man or a
woman—who is familiar with the girl's household to find out
if she likes him. If he sends a man, he gives him a drink. I sent
another girl whom I know and who was a friend of the girl I
wanted. She came back and said that her friend liked me. Then
I sent my mother to the girl's *abusua* to ask if they would agree
to begin negotiations. They said "Yes." Then my mother
took four shillings to the girl's mother to give to the girl as
food-money (*didi sika*). This is to bind the girl and you must
give the money through some sober elder person so that you
have a witness in case she should turn to some other man and
deny that she ever agreed to marry you. I gave the girl I wanted
to marry, four shillings every three days for nine days. Then I
gave her two shillings a day till I had given her three pounds
thirteen shillings altogether. Then her parents said, "It is time
you came and completed the custom, for you are feeding her
and she is not cooking for you in return." So I did the rest of
the custom.

'First there was the door-knocking fee (*abobonsa*). This was
two bottles of rum, which cost nine-and-sixpence each. One
was for the girl's father and one for her mother. My father
sent one of his friends with the bottles, and he witnessed that the
girl's parents drank of the rum. This drinking is the sign of
their assent. Then my father sent sixteen shillings to each parent
for *tri nsa* (head wine). Only four shillings is compulsory.
Anything beyond that is as you wish. If there is a divorce
afterwards, you can only claim back four shillings.

'Next my father sent his friend with praising-money (*ayeyodi*).
He sent one pound to praise the father and ten shillings to praise
the mother and ten shillings to praise the girl. This is for themselves alone, and they do not share it with their *abusua*.

'When the praising-money is sent you also send the girl's father *tamoba* money because his daughter often soiled his cloth when she was a baby and sat on his knee. You send whatever sum you like for *tamoba*. If there is a divorce afterwards the *tamoba* is refunded. If the girl's father can't refund it her *abusua* pay it for him, and then in any future marriage he cannot claim *tamoba* again.

'Next I did the *kobia ayemf'ro* custom to make the girl a woman. This means that you give her the things a woman needs—a new box, a mat, a mirror, a comb, soap, talcum-powder, and any adornments you think she would like. You also give her sandals and an even number of cloths. My mother and my sister took these to the girl's house and they were spread out for everyone to see. All my friends who like me, helped me in buying them.

'The praising-money that the man sends to the girl she uses to praise him again. She buys firewood, rice, fowls, a towel, sponge, soap, bread, groundnuts, and a walking-stick. The husband shares them with his friends. If you want to omit the praising-money you can, but then the girl sends no gifts in return.

'The day the girl sends the praising-gifts is the day of kindling the fire (*gya bo*), and on that day the girl must make a new fire for her new cooking. She comes and makes a fire wherever you are going to put her—it may be in your own mother's compound, in her mother's compound, or in your own. She need not make a new fireplace, but she must make a new fire, and she must have the use of a fireplace so that she may never be late in cooking. The day of lighting the new fire is the day that she becomes your wife. In the evening, two or three people from her household bring her to her husband's house.

'The first thing she cooks on her new fire is a fine feast, and this is carried by her friends to her husband. Her husband shares this with his father, housemates, and all his friends, who will help him to clear his father-in-law's farm. When the dirty dishes are sent back to the wife's house the husband puts either four shillings or eight shillings in them for the messengers who carried the food. I put four shillings in my dishes, but when the *ohene* married his last wife he put in sixteen shillings.

'If there is a debt in the girl's family, the young man is invited to pay it, and he usually borrows from his own friends to do this. It is counted as his wife's debt that he is paying because, if she had been still working for her parents, she would have helped to pay it, but marriage has prevented her. This payment is called *trika*. I paid £2 as *trika* for my wife. If a divorce follows the *trika* is refunded.

'The time when the girl's family tell the man what are his obligations is when the *tri nsa* is paid. They tell him that her trouble is now his trouble but her good fortune is not. Suppose she finds some gold, it belongs to her family, but if she gets into debt, her husband is responsible. If she spoils anything of her husband's he must not demand compensation.'

The essentials of any 'big man's' marriage are the same as those of the lowliest marriage. But marriage negotiations are one of the ways in which a rich man is expected to display his wealth. Many a Gold Coast illiterate who makes money has few ideas about spending it, and a lavish expenditure on marriage is one of them. As a typical 'big man's' marriage I may describe that of the *ohene* of a town in which I stayed. He already had an elderly wife with grandchildren, a middle-aged wife with grown children, and two 'small' or young wives. The middle-aged wife was not only clearly his favourite but was said to dominate him and arrange his marriages to 'small wives', choosing for him young, meek girls whom she could manage.

The girl whose marriage was being arranged was one such. The wife had introduced her to the husband and suggested the marriage : he acquiesced. As his people put it, 'His eyes are the eyes of his wife.'

The girl's parents lived in another town, so the royal suitor, after asking his elders' consent to his marriage, sent the *kronti-hene* of his own town to her parents with his request and a bottle of whisky. They accepted the whisky, thereby expressing consent. They asked their daughter if she knew anything of her suitor's desire : she said that his wife had taken her and shown her to him. The *krontihene* returned home and was despatched again with a bottle of rum for each parent, £7 for the mother's *abusua*, £2 for the father, and £2 for the girl 'to thank her for consenting'. Then an additional bottle of thanks was sent to each parent. The *krontihene* took a sip of each to set his seal as a witness.

Then another £6 were sent to the girl for her trousseau, and she in return brought with her, when she came to be married, a dozen fowls (which should have been sheep), firewood, a bag of rice, fifty eggs, and a bag of salt. When she arrived with a company of attendants they were all welcomed with a grand meal and the attendants were given fifteen shillings. On each day of their stay in the town the chief sent them fowls and meat : when they left he gave them their lorry-fare home.

In conducting the negotiations for the *ohene* the *krontihene* took each sum of money first to the *ohene* of the bride's town and showed it to him. This was to ensure that this *ohene*, if asked at any time in the future to deal with a case of unfaithfulness on the part of the young wife, should be unable to reply, 'I did not know this girl was the *ohene's* wife.'

Doba marriage almost amounts to the adoption of a youth as nephew by a man who has a marriageable daughter. Only the older man can take the initiative in these cases. If he knows a young man of excellent character and would like him as a son-in-law he sends to tell the youth's father that he has a 'very strong love' for the boy and is willing to give him a daughter in marriage, accepting no payment beyond the drink associated with cross-cousin marriage.

It is said that *Doba* marriages are usually happier than most and very seldom end in divorce. 'It is because the father-in-law loves his son-in-law and chose him because he was of good character.'

BETROTHAL OF YOUNG CHILDREN

Until a few years ago a custom called *Esiwa* was common. This enabled a wealthy man to become betrothed to an infant girl. He was then responsible for providing her with food, clothing, and all expenses throughout her childhood just as if she was his wife or daughter. On her reaching puberty he took her to wife. But parents seldom wish a girl to marry unwillingly, knowing that such a marriage will be followed by trouble and divorce ; therefore, if an *'Esiwa'* girl, on reaching marriageable age, disliked her fiancé, the parents felt bound to release her by refunding everything he had spent on her. If he had been generous and lavish—as was usually the case—the parents were in great financial difficulty. In 1927 the *Omanhene's* council decided that 'parents suffered too much from *Esiwa*' and the practice should be stopped, so the *Omanhene* sent his gong-gong beaters throughout the *oman* forbidding *'Esiwa'*.

The practice of allowing an elderly man to betroth a very young girl, even an unborn one, on behalf of his young son or nephew, was not forbidden, still persists, and seldom causes any trouble, as it is understood that, although the boy's guardian pays the girl's expenses throughout childhood, the whole arrangement will be cancelled and all refund of expenses waived if either boy or girl dislikes the proposed partner when the time for marriage arrives.

Girls usually marry as soon as they reach puberty, boys as soon as they can support a wife.

. All parents watch their children's preferences for other children from their earliest childhood. When a small boy or girl, 'not knowing what is marriage', shows a marked liking for another, the parents assert that they will make good partners and hasten to arrange a marriage. Such marriages, they declare, are always satisfactory and never end in divorce. If either of the children thus betrothed dies before the age of marriage, the parents of the survivor give the same presents to the parents of the other as if the survivor had lost a husband or wife.

SOME IMPLICATIONS OF THE CROSS-COUSIN MARRIAGE AND NEPHEW SUCCESSION

It has already been necessary for me to mention some of the implications of the cross-cousin marriage system, for these crop up wherever one turns. A few more of these may now be mentioned. Non-anthropologists will better understand these implications by sketching out a genealogical tree, not on a flat sheet but on a cylinder. The accompanying diagram should be curved backwards so that X coincides with X' and Y coincides with Y'. Several things then become apparent.

(1) Whereas people who never marry relatives have each four grandparents, eight great-grandparents, sixteen great-great-grandparents, etc., people who follow strictly the cross-cousin system have each four grandparents, four great-grandparents, and four great-great-grandparents, etc.

(2) A pair of cross-cousins have all four grandparents, great-grandparents, etc., in common.

(3) The man B of the 'black' clan of the diagram succeeds his mother's brother A of the black clan. B is succeeded in the same way by his sister's son C. But C is also the *paternal grandson* of A, who held the same position two generations back. That is to say, a man succeeds to the position, not of his father, but of his father's father.

One man thus expressed a result of the cross-cousin system. 'I like my daughters to marry my sisters' sons because then, though my son goes away to succeed, his son (my grandson) comes back to my house.[1] Also my daughter, if she marries my nephew, will stay with him in my house. Her daughter too will marry my grandson who comes back to succeed in my house. The younger sons will very likely stay with their fathers, so my

---

[1] This does not necessarily mean the same building.

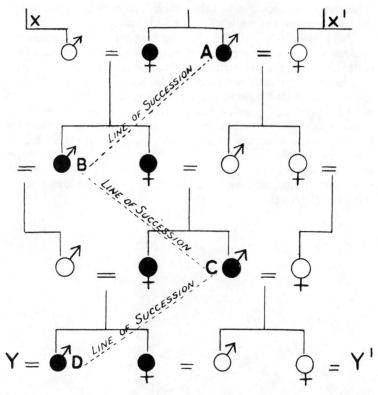

other daughters who marry younger sons will go away. But always when someone is trying to go away someone else is trying to come back.'

An aspect of this 'going away' and 'coming back' was shown to me one morning when I set out to visit Apoli, some 10 miles beyond Aduasa. I stopped at Aduasa to greet the chief and to ask for a guide for the walk through the forest to Apoli. I was told 'It is no use going to Apoli to-day: you won't find anybody of importance there. Apoli people are all here to-day for a big funeral.' And, indeed, it was so. In an interval between the various funeral rites the Apoli elders all gathered to receive me and to give me some preliminary information about their town and its relations with Aduasa. They said that there was only one clan in Apoli, namely, the *Asuna* clan to which the *Odikro's* stool belonged. The people had therefore to marry outside their own towns and had always married Aduasa people. They were therefore as much at home in Aduasa as in Apoli.

'The son of an Apoli man,' they said, 'succeeds in Aduasa, but the grandson comes back to succeed in Apoli.'

I have already mentioned the way that relations between the *gyasehene* and the chief are reinforced by the cross-cousin marriage system between the two clans. I have also mentioned the relationship between an *asafohene's* son and an *asafohene's* heir, and here too it is clear that though the *asafohene* is not succeeded on the stool by his son, he usually is, by the operations of the cross-cousin marriage system, succeeded in the second generation by his son's son. The same thing applies to any man succeeded by a nephew and, in general, it is clear that the nephew succession system is cleverly designed to operate in conjunction with the cross-cousin marriage system, and that these two institutions stand or fall together.

CHAPTER IX

INHERITANCE AND SUCCESSION

Introduction

A great deal of work has been done, mainly by trained lawyers,[1] in enunciating the native customary law of the Akan peoples. I shall not go over this again, but shall select for consideration a few points which appear to me to have received less emphasis than they deserve.

Election versus Birthright

When a man dies, the elders of his father's family and the elders of his mother's family meet to decide who shall succeed to his office—if he was an office holder—be the new 'father' of his children and other dependants, succeed to his trusteeship of family property, inherit his own property, and marry or care for his widows.

There is not, as in Europe, a law of automatic succession. There are only very usual lines to follow in electing inheritors and successors. The elders *elect* the successor according to their ideas of wisdom and justice. Nobody's position in a family tree gives him any inherent right to succeed or inherit.

Furthermore, if a successor or inheritor does not treat his position, his property, or his dependants well, he can, by a subsequent assembly of elders, be deposed, deprived, or, as the people express it, 'uprooted' (*tu ade so*). There is no law of '*semel heres, semper heres*'.

I have attended numerous post-funeral meetings for the settlement of dead men's affairs, but never have I met a single instance of property and position being allocated strictly according to the 'normal' system. For instance, at the last such meeting I attended in Abenase, the old man who had died should, according to the common pattern, have been succeeded by either his own brother or his sister's son. Both these people existed, but one was incompetent through ill-health and the other was considered irresponsible, so the position of 'father' of both property and children was given to the dead man's mother's sister's son. Again, at another meeting, the nephew of the dead man (who had no sons) expected to inherit his uncle's

---

[1] E.g. Sarbah's *Fanti Customary Law*.

cocoa farm. The elders, however, decided that the widow—a Fanti stranger—had given her husband more than the usual amount of help in planting and working those farms, and that it would be fair and decent to give her one farm for herself. The nephew—a literate—attempted to argue, and then, when told, 'Nothing is yours unless you are chosen to receive it,' relapsed into sulks.

Property is of two kinds : firstly, that held on behalf of a group of clansmen, of which the holder is the elected head, and secondly, self-acquired property. The former includes land cleared by predecessors of the same group, the majority of houses, ancestors' stools, and other *agyapade* (heirlooms). Of such property the inheritor is usually only a trustee and cannot sell or alienate anything without the consent of the whole group. Such property is always accompanied by obligations. For example, the man who inherits a brother's or uncle's house becomes the 'father' of its inmates and has the same responsibilities towards them as had his predecessor.

In the ordinary way a man is succeeded by his brother or half-brother of the same clan, and only when the last brother is dead does the next generation succeed. But such is the elasticity of inheritance and succession that it is not always felt necessary that the successor should be even of the same clan as the predecessor. A man's son may not only be appointed as controller and 'father' of the property and heir (nephew), if the latter be young, but if the sons can prove that the nephew is not doing his duty he may be 'uprooted' and one of the sons put in his place.

The other kind of property is *ahunyade*. This is property created by an individual through his own effort, for example, a cocoa farm or food farm, cleared and planted by the owner or a house built with the owner's earnings. Such property may be willed by the owner to his own sons, daughters, wives, or to anyone else he wishes. If the owner dies without expressing any wish concerning the property, the united elders of his own *abusua* and his children's *abusua* dispose of it as seems to them just. If his nieces and nephews have given him as much help in acquiring or caring for the property as have his own children and his wife, or more than they, they will receive what the elders deem to be just. Codified law, however, awards all this property to the maternal nephew.

Inheritance of Widows

The inheritance of widows is always a matter for careful consideration. The property allocated to anyone on the death of a relative is proportionate to the obligations which he undertakes to shoulder : widows are among these obligations.

A brother or maternal nephew who inherits his brother's or uncle's property inherits all the uncle's wives. It is not customary (as it is among the Gã) to distribute the widows among several eligible relatives. Who takes one, takes all.

If a succeeding nephew has married the uncle's daughter, he may not marry her mother, but he still has to support her and be her 'husband' in all secondary matters. If the man who inherits the widows does not want them as wives, he may publicly release them—just as a man may dismiss a wife who has *not* been unfaithful—by giving them 'road money'. In such a case he is usually made to give them portions of the farms that they have helped his uncle or brother to make. The children of such wives are still his responsibility, but if he does not wish to support them and allows them to be supported by their mother's people, he cannot claim a father's privilege of sending for them to come and work for him unless he refunds to their mother's relatives everything spent on them from childhood.

If the widow herself objects to becoming the wife of her husband's successor, she is not forced to it, but while she remains dependent on him she must perform a wife's secondary duties, such as cooking and working on the farm. If she wishes to leave him altogether and go to another town or marry some other man, she can do so only on the terms on which any marriage is dissolved by the wife, that is, her people must return marriage fees paid by her husband.

The Position of Women

The position of women in inheritance and succession is one of great flexibility. An exceptionally able woman seldom fails to receive the recognition she deserves, not in order to reward her for her personal qualities, but because it is felt that she will do well by others. As one informant put it, 'a woman who shows that she can look after property well will be given a big share when somebody dies, because she will guard it well for the children that come afterwards.'

If the deceased has no nephew but has nieces, one of these may, at the discretion of the elders, be given the post or property on behalf of her son or sister's son. In some cases, a woman may inherit and administer property in trust for her son, and in other cases the son may do so in trust for his mother.

Even so, the theoretical position of women is such that it is usually necessary, when electing a woman to an inheritance or succession, to invoke a kind of 'legal fiction' whereby a woman can become a man. Such a woman is called an *obeaberema*—or man-woman. In theory a woman cannot succeed to a stool, but we find that Akim-Swedru has even had a woman *Omanhene* and that the *Krontihene* of Oda has five times been a woman. The present *Odikro* of Nyafamang is a woman. Her elders say, 'We made her chief because we knew she was wise and would be a good chief. She is not a woman : she is a man.'

Some General Speculation on the Maternal Succession System

As I have indicated elsewhere in this volume it seems that the river worship which survived in the ritual of the *ntro*, which ritual was vested in the paternal line, was the aboriginal worship of the greater part of the Gold Coast, and that the whole aboriginal system of succession was in the paternal line. The clan system appears to have been introduced later. It was a maternal succession system and was connected with government on a military basis, with war-stools as both family and religio-military rallying points. For some time the two systems (river or *ntro* worship and clan-stool or ancestor worship) probably ran concurrently, the newer steadily gaining in importance. In Ashanti the *ntro* as a paternal social group still survives : in Akim-Kotoku it is extinct.

It is not difficult to see why the maternal succession system should flourish in times of incessant warfare. When the men are all away fighting, home affairs are run by women, and the conserving of the social system devolves upon them. As one informant put it, 'In war-time the fathers may all be killed and never come home, or they may come home for such a short time that a child may not even know who his father is. But he always knows who his mother is. In war-time it is only through the women that we can keep our line of succession unbroken.'

Another informant said that 'The queen-mother was the big woman who was left in charge when all the big men had gone to war.'[1]

Some writers on Gold Coast sociology have expressed surprise that the Gã-Adangme people, who are stated to be

[1] It is certain that the war years 1914–1918 gave British women a status in the community which they would never have attained in peace. It is also noticeable that in such countries as China and India, where warfare has had little status as an activity, the position of women is noticeably lower than elsewhere. Even in modern Germany, where the theory of the warlike community insists on the relegation of women to the purely domestic callings, when war is actually in progress German factories employ as much female labour as do those of other nations, and women are allowed to do most things that they are able to do.

far less 'advanced' than the Ashanti, should follow the 'more advanced' paternal succession system. It is doubtful whether 'advancement' has anything to do with it, but it is probable that warfare has a great deal. The Gã-Adangme peoples took up organized warfare and stools very much later than the Akan and never put their social organization on a military basis.

Some Significant Modern Movements

Anthropologists have often stressed the greater importance of establishing the underlying principles of any system of native custom rather than of codifying its detail. The latter is comparatively easy, but its danger is that of missing or even outraging the former.

A case in point is the custom of maternal nephew inheritance and succession, which was codified for use in the recognized courts of the Gold Coast some sixty years ago. Thereafter, any maternal nephew, wholly or partially disinherited by family council, could appeal to one of these courts and receive the whole inheritance, disclaiming at the same time the burden of obligation which, under the old system, was an inseparable accompaniment.

At the present day there is a widespread clamour in the Gold Coast to have this codified law amended in such a way that the wife and children of the dead man who, under the codified law, are left destitute, should receive one-third of his self-acquired property. Missionaries have for some time past made this a rule for their church members. Many Akan chiefs are now urging the further establishment of this principle, and the Government is receiving their representations with ready sympathy.

They are perfectly right in stressing the 'unfairness' of the codified law. It is often, however, forgotten that, under the old uncodified system, the principle of justice to the dead man's wife and children was always kept in mind. The inheritor of the property also inherited obligations towards these dependants. Furthermore, no award to the successor was irrevocable; if he neglected his responsibilities he was 'uprooted' from his position. Moreover, special awards of self-acquired property were always made to any sons, daughters, or wives who had taken special parts in helping the deceased to acquire the property.

It should also be remembered, though usually it is not, that the nephew inheritance system was closely bound up with the cross-cousin marriage system, within which, as I have pointed

out, the son of the deceased became the social 'father' or super-
vizor of the inheriting nephew. This son's son, after the death
of the nephew, succeeded to his grandfather's position. The
system was therefore much more patrilineal than appeared to
the superficial glance. The new clamour is merely seeking to
re-establish a principle which was lost sight of in codification.

Now that people's interests are farther flung and less parochial,
cross-cousin marriage tends to become less general. The patrilineal principle, implicitly recognized in this system, is now
tending to demand more explicit recognition.

In addition to this, there is little doubt that modern conditions favour a spontaneous general change from the matrilineal
to the patrilineal system. Quite apart from Christianity and
education, the non-Christian family councils are tending to make
more important awards to sons and fewer to nephews. Left
to itself, the matrilineal system would probably die a natural
death. The encouragement by administrators of out-of-court
settlements of inheritance and succession cases is among their
wisest habits, for it is to such informal settlements that one must
always go in order to discern the true level and trend of general
'progress'.

The moral of all this is obvious. Uncodified custom is plastic
and changes spontaneously with changing conditions. Immediately it is codified, it is hardened and can no longer change of
its own accord. Codified native custom may therefore prove a
serious drag on progress and change; the problem of avoiding
premature codification with its attendant retardation, and at
the same time providing an orderly modern system of justice,
must always be one of profound difficulty.

CHAPTER X

JUSTICE

Some Fundamental Characteristics

I

The most important point to be kept in mind by anyone who would understand pre-British native law, is that there does not exist a body of rigid law, either written or unwritten, which judges and magistrates are bound to administer. Nor are there permanently constituted courts standing ready to be called into action.

We find, in the first place, that judges and councils administer not law, but what they deem to be justice. Though in similar situations they tend to make similar judgments, they are not bound to do so. Changing needs are met, not by alterations in, and additions to, the rigid laws but by new applications of a plastic justice. Where law wields, as it were, a series of metal dies which may or may not cover the case neatly, justice wields a flexible paint-brush which can cope with every irregularity in the shape of the case.

In the second place, the administration of justice is not a separate department with permanent or professional officials and permanent courts.[1] No court of justice, as such, has either separate or perpetual existence, though there are several permanent bodies designed for other purposes, which may from time to time be asked to judge cases, just as individual elders, whose primary seniority lies in other fields, are often asked to act as judges.

The whole system of justice is merely an elaboration of the system of calling upon a senior and asking him to decide upon the right and wrongs of a dispute. Two young brothers call in their father. If they have different fathers they call in both. If the quarrel is more serious, the fathers call in grandfathers and uncles to assist. If a man quarrels with his wife, they call in elders from both families. If a man quarrels with his neighbour, *any* distinguished elders may be called in : it matters not who

---

[1] In some other parts of the Gold Coast we find societies hardly at all removed from the basic type from which probably all Gold Coast societies were developed. In that society no professional differentiation of leadership has taken place. The same elder was concurrently priest, ruler, military commander, judge, and elected head of a group of relatives.

they are so long as they are disinterested. Every court is constituted *ad hoc*. Sometimes an old man gets a reputation as a
wise, just judge, and people will bring their disputes to him from
far and wide, often creating great mystification in the minds of
strangers as to why he should have what appears to them to be
'jurisdiction over' the people who call him in.

Where bodies of elders and 'big men' are in the habit of
meeting together, the groups may be approached and may be
asked to hear and judge a case. The *asafohenes* of a town are
naturally the 'biggest' existing body that can be approached in
any one town. If a chief has a dispute with another he can
approach any third chief—provided that the latter is as 'big' as
or 'bigger' than himself, for no man can be judged by a junior.
A body of 'very big men' who are often to be found already
gathered is the *Oman* Council. Its primary business used to be
warfare, but it was often asked to judge cases, simply because its
members were 'big men' and were on the spot already assembled.

An example of the calling in of a stranger to hear a 'very big
case' occurred while I was in Akim-Kotoku. The young
Omanhene offended his people in a manner which they considered
serious and which they would not like me to describe. The
uninitiated student, acquainted only with the Native Administration Ordinance, would almost certainly have said, 'this case comes
under the jurisdiction of the *Oman* Council. That body must
hear the case and, if it deems the offence unpardonable, destool
the chief. If appeal to a higher court is desired, the case must
be taken before the Provincial Council of Paramount Chiefs.' [1]
What was actually done was very different. An impartial 'big
man', namely, the *Omanhene* of Asin Adandoso, was invited to
come and 'judge the case and set peace'.

Now, Akim-Kotoku had only a sentimental attachment to
Asin Adandoso. During one of its military campaigns, the
Kotoku force found itself in difficulty and Asin Adandoso sent
a force to its aid. Thereafter the Akim-Kotoku *Oman* became
known as the 'wife' of Asin Adandoso. [2] There was no political
association between the two, no permanent military alliance and
no specific obligations, but there was a sentiment of friendship
as between two families united by marriage. This sentiment
persists to-day though it seldom finds any expression save in the
exchange of funeral courtesies. As the present *Omanhene* of
Asin Adandoso happens to be a very able councillor, the idea of
asking him to come and act as judge was gratefully seized. He

---

[1] The Provincial Council of Chiefs was created by the Government about 1928.
[2] Obo and Abome in Kwabu, are similarly 'wives' of Akim-Kotoku.

readily came, bringing two or three of his own elders, and in a few days had 'set peace'.

The experienced administrators of to-day welcome and encourage such settlements out of court, but from the official records it would appear that some of their predecessors took such invitations, given by one chief to another to settle a dispute, as implying either 'some sort of loose allegiance' or interference.

Another story, interesting in this connection, was told to me by the people of Anamase, who now belong to the Akim-Bosome *Oman*. At the time of which the tale tells, Anamase had not joined any military confederation, though its 'brother town' and joint landowner, Adekuma, had been bullied into joining Akim-Abuakwa. The Abuakwa *Omanhene*, intending in like manner to bully Anamase, sent some messengers to order the Anamase chief to go and see him at Kyibi. This chief, knowing the greater strength of the other, unwillingly set off with the escort. In the course of the journey they met another party of travellers—an Ashanti *okyeame* named Nentwi and his retinue. The Anamase chief, though no political associate of Ashanti, 'swore an oath on Nentwi'[1], so that Nentwi had to 'hear his case' against the Abuakwa *Omanhene*. An elder named Kwao Gyampo, who later became the Akim-Bosome *Omanhene*, acted during the case as the 'father' of the Anamase chief. The verdict was that Abuakwa had no right to order Anamase about, and Abuakwa did, in fact, thereafter desist. Later, when Kwao Gyampo came into Western Akim as *Omanhene* of the Akim-Bosome *Oman*, Anamase at once joined his *oman* out of gratitude for his kindly 'fathering'.

2

Although the justice which pre-British courts administer cannot be regarded as a body of laws, there are certain laws of *procedure* which, if broken, render the awards of the court invalid. For instance, the committee of elders who decide who is to succeed a certain dead man may, if they deem it wise, appoint, say, his son or his sister instead of his nephew, but if the convener of the meeting fails to invite any elder who has the right to attend, the proceedings can be challenged as unconstitutional. Again, suppose a father wishes to leave his own personal farm to his daughter, his wife, or his adopted son, rather than to his own son, he may do so, but if he omits to call witnesses to the ceremony of 'thanking with rum', then the legacy will not be valid and may be set aside. Though legally-minded persons may *not* ask the question, 'Had this successor the inherent right to

[1] That is, he laid a conditional curse on Nentwi.

9

succeed ?' they may ask the question, 'Was he constitutionally elected ?'

An example of a court's awards being set aside on the ground of unconstitutional procedure arose during a case which I attended at the Abenase *ohene's* court. The *odikro* of Edzubea brought a private grievance of his own to be judged by the Abenase court. The previous history of the dispute was this.

The plaintiff succeeded his uncle as *odikro*. There was another eligible nephew, one John, but the late *odikro* had regarded John as irresponsible and incapable and had said he did not wish him to be either his successor on the stool or heir to his private property. The former matter was not, of course, his affair, but the latter was. He omitted, however, to have this wish sealed with rum, so after his death the elders, though they elected the other nephew as *odikro*, awarded John all his uncle's cocoa farms except one, which was assigned to the new *odikro*. The *odikro*, in the light of his uncle's oft-expressed wishes concerning the property, challenged the decision of the elders, and another meeting was called. At this meeting it was decided that the wishes of the deceased were unwitnessed and therefore not valid, but it was decided that John's ownership of the cocoa farms should be under the supervision of the new *odikro*. John in turn appealed against this, calling in the *Abenasehene* and his elders. This court ruled that the *odikro* should have the one farm originally awarded to him, John should have the others, and the *odikro* should have one-third of John's profits from John's cocoa.

At this stage each party should have given ten shillings' worth of rum to the court as a sign of their acceptance of the ruling. But John said he had no money. Had the *odikro* been wise he would have lent John ten shillings to make sure of payment. Instead, he said he knew John had sold thirty shillings' worth of cocoa and sent him to fetch ten shillings of the proceeds for the *odikro* (his due under the new ruling) and ten shillings for John himself to pay the acceptance rum. John failed to come back to the court, could not be found, and the court at last broke up without any acceptance rum having been paid. When the next cocoa season arrived John sent the *odikro* no share of profits. The *odikro* demanded it, was refused, so took the matter to the *Abenasehene's* court. This hearing was the one which I attended.

The court ruled that as no ratifying rum had been paid on the last court's award to the *odikro*, it was not valid and could not be claimed.

3

In every case the plaintiff and the defendant, unless they are themselves seniors, must each be accompanied by a 'father'. Even in the registered Tribunal I have known the elders refuse to begin a case till the 'fathers' have been produced. If at the close of the case the chairman of the bench sees fit to deliver a homily (for Gold Coast elders share this habit with magistrates and coroners the world over), he always addresses his lecture to the offender's father and then adds a rider pointing the moral to all parents.

This insistence on the presence of 'fathers' is partly because parents are still regarded as responsible and punishable for their children's wrong-doings and partly because someone must stand as guarantor of any fine or fee incurred by the junior.[1] In earlier days the parents' liability extended, so I am told, to the criminal offences of the son, and parents were put to death when their sons committed murder. 'They should have brought them up better.'

A Twi-speaking stranger is usually under the fatherhood of the local *asafohene* of his clan, a Lagos, Gã, or Northern Territory stranger under the headman of his own local group. The Lagos youth whom I mention elsewhere [2] was accompanied in the court by the old Lagos trader whom all the Abenase Lagocians call their 'chief'. This old man paid the lad's fine, 'because every one despises a father who lets a son go to prison.'

Such a 'son' would be under a private obligation to repay or work off his debt to the 'father'.

Finding out the Truth

The method used for finding out the truth is that of questioning and cross-questioning the witnesses. These are not allowed to hear one another's evidence. The skill and thoroughness with which the questioners make the witnesses fill in every minute detail of their stories and supply much other apparently irrelevant information brings to light discrepancies which would escape anyone else but the detective hero of popular mystery fiction. If the defendant and a witness, or if two witnesses, pre-arrange a false tale, they have little hope of sustaining much agreement. One elder broke down a seemingly watertight but false alibi so

---

[1] In land disputes between stools of different states the *Omanhene* of each chief usually acts as 'father' and advances the expenses of litigation, but the litigating stool has to refund this loan as soon as it is able.

[2] See p. 126.

skilfully that he acquired the nickname 'You-know-more-than-God'.

Supernatural means of revealing the truth are employed only as a last resort, and, though I have seen them used in other districts, I have never seen them in Akim. But I am told that here, as elsewhere, the encroachment of foreign medicine is conspicuous and stranger-diviners are usually called in. The actual manipulation of their divining apparatus is done, so far as possible, by local small boys chosen at random, small boys being assumed free from guile and corruption.

Some Typical Courts and Typical Cases

Here I may give a few samples of cases, of varying size and formality, from among those which I saw tried in Abenase.

A very typical elders' court was called together one day to hear a case between an old woman defendant and her grand-daughter plaintiff. The plaintiff's mother (the defendant's daughter) was dead and, when dying, had called together her children. To her son she gave back a hand-woven kente-cloth which he had pledged to her for a loan : this indicated that his debt was cancelled. To each of her two daughters she gave a cocoa farm. One of the daughters (the plaintiff) continued to live with the grandmother. Later the old woman, probably encouraged by the grandson who had received no cocoa farm, declared that her granddaughter must go no more to the farm, for her mother had left it to the grandmother. She stuck to this assertion till the granddaughter decided to make a case against her.

The young woman consulted her 'father'—the nephew who had succeeded her real father. This 'father' collected a bench to hear the case in the grandmother's yard. The bench con-sisted of the *asafohene* of one of the *Agona* stools in the chair, one of the chairman's brothers and one of his nephews, the *asafohene* of the *Asuna* stool and one of his nephews, the *asafohene* of the *Bretu* stool, the elder brother of the plaintiff's 'father', a cocoa buyer visiting the town and co-opted as an impartial out-sider, and the old elder without pedigree or portfolio whom I have mentioned before as renowned for his mathematics and his wisdom. The latter old man was appointed as *okyeame* of the court.

The witnesses included another daughter of the old lady, two granddaughters, two grandsons, and two other people.

The 'father' of the plaintiff was sworn in as the guarantor of any payments due from her as the result of the case ; a grandson similarly stood for the old lady.

Another case was that of an *asafohene's* daughter, who complained to her father that her husband had given her no food, money, or clothes for some months, and that she was feeding both him and the children from her own farm. She declared that she wished to leave him, as he was not fulfilling a husband's obligations. The *asafohene* sent for another old man to help him in judging, and sent for the husband and wife together. The husband admitted the offence. Had he denied it the woman's housemates and others would have been called to give evidence. The husband was told that he must pay his wife the overdue money. He promised to do this, and the elders made the couple shake hands. The old men also lectured the woman, saying, 'If you leave your husband for such a small offence there is something wrong,' implying that she was wanting an excuse to go to another man.

The woman made the elders a small present 'for rum', which sum the man was expected to refund to her.

The woman, no doubt, felt that the tables had been somewhat turned upon her, but, having shaken hands on the matter, she could not take it to any other elders till her husband had committed some further offence. She would then probably choose new elders : these would call her parents and the husband's parents, and the inquiry would be on a bigger and more formal scale.

Another case was that of a boy who had been sent by his parents from another town to act as servant in an Abenase household. One day a woman of the household boxed his ears with her left hand. This was a great insult, for the ears are noble members of the body, and the left hand is reserved for filthy and unpleasant tasks. Had the ears been boxed with the right hand or had the left given a blow on the back or the seat, there would have been no great offence.

The boy chose two elders and asked them to deal with his grievance. They sent for the woman and she admitted the offence. The elders asked the boy if he would be satisfied with an apology. He said he would, and it was given. The boy thanked the elders with a pot of palm-wine,[1] but had he said he had nothing to give, I do not think they would have complained.

In contrast to the handling of this case, another Abenase case, in itself similar, may be cited. Here the plaintiff did not wish simply that honour should be satisfied. He wished to penalize

---

[1] At the present day worth perhaps 1s. 6d.

the defendant, so he took his complaint, not to elders for redress, but to the registered town Tribunal for punishment.

This case was between the literate agent of a European trading firm and a Lagos stranger, an illiterate youth trading on his own account. The Lagocian had made some purchases from the other, and when he went to settle his account the literate made an error in stating the total. The illiterate pointed this out and added a taunt to the effect that a literate who needed an illiterate to teach him arithmetic was a poor thing. The bystanders laughed and the literate lost his temper and vowed to make the other suffer. He summoned him before the chief's Tribunal, bringing a charge of defamation of character. Lagocians are unpopular in Akim, and the court's sympathy was clearly with the plaintiff. The defendant was fined the maximum sum allowed by the Native Administration Ordinance, together with costs. He ended several pounds out of pocket.

Another example of the way in which cantankerous or grasping people tend to misuse the registered Tribunal in ways that they would never dream of using with unofficial elders' courts, occurred during my stay in Abenase.

A girl brought a head-load of plantains from her farm to the lorry-road where she wished to catch a public lorry to market. A bulky or heavy head-load needs more than one person to place it on or remove it from the head, though, once there, it is manageable by the carrier, so when the girl reached the road she asked two boys, who were passing, to help her lift down her load, a common courtesy which no one ever refuses. She then said, 'The lorry will be here in a few minutes : will you wait and help me lift my load on to the lorry ?' They readily agreed, and sat by the roadside to await the lorry. The lorry was very late and the boys sat on with the girl, neglecting some errand of their uncle's. When at last the lorry had come and gone and the boys went home to their uncle, he was annoyed by their lateness and said the girl ought to pay him for the loss of their time. He took the 'case' to the *ohene's* tribunal, and the *ohene* actually accepted it and issued a summons against the girl. However, one of the elders happened to be the girl's step-father, and insisted that children's naughtiness was 'no case', and that the summons should be withdrawn. Not till the boys' uncle had been appeased with eight shillings, and the *ohene* and elders had received some slight private compensation for the loss of their emoluments, was the case withdrawn.

The tendency to improvize special courts to meet special cases was well illustrated one day while I was in Abenase. A

youth of that town promised a young girl six shillings if she
would sleep with him in his own room. She was an Edzubea
girl but was staying in Abenase with some relatives in order to
trade in farm produce. Her parents were respectable, and the
risk to her own and their reputation was considerable : hence
the generous sum of six shillings. She duly carried out her part
of the bargain, but the youth afterwards refused to pay her.
She could not take her grievance to elders without exposing
herself and her parents to public scorn, so she took it to four
other young men of Abenase. My clerk was sharing a lodging
with one of the four, so they co-opted him as an impartial out-
sider. He said the defaulter should be made to pay, but could
not see how. Then they all came one evening to ask me if I
would give advice. They sent the clerk in first to explain their
business while the other four waited outside. I refused to advise,
but hinted what I thought.

'If the youth does not pay the girl will she approach the
elders ?'

'No, she would be too ashamed.'

'If the four young men were to give the defaulter a good
hiding, would he report *that* to the elders ? '

'No, he would be too ashamed.'

'If he had to choose between paying and being thrashed by
four men would he pay ?'

'Yes, he would.'

'Tell them it is a hard palaver and I have no advice to give.'

He went out, and I heard the party chuckling as he reported
the conversation. The hiding was, of course, exactly what they
had intended, from the very first, to offer the defaulter, but the
enjoyment of this natural impulse had to be augmented by the
additional enjoyment of behaving like a bench of self-important
elders. The trying of cases, big and small, is, in fact, one of the
elders' greatest pleasures in life. Their material rewards—except
in the Government Tribunal—are negligible. The elders' sense
of responsibility for law and order is closely bound up with the
gratification of their own innocent vanity.

Curtailed Hearings

When two people with a dispute take it to a big man, it is
necessary, in the ordinary way, to call in enough additional
elders to make a considerable bench. These have to receive
thanking-rum for their trouble, witnesses have to be called and
compensated for their time and trouble, and there is always fuss
and a certain amount of publicity. Meanwhile the plaintiff has

perhaps relented. He may desire only the formal vindication of his honour, or his friends may persuade the two parties that conciliation is the better part of litigation. An abbreviated form of hearing is then available; in fact, there are five different kinds of curtailed hearing to choose from.

These, in descending order of length, are :

(1) The Late Evening Hearing (*Anadwosem di*). The whole case must be heard and judgment delivered before retiring to rest that same night.

(2) The Sun Hearing (*Wai sem di*). The whole case must be heard and judgment delivered before sunset.

(3) The Eating Hearing (*Didi ase asem*). The whole case must be heard and judgment delivered within the time taken to eat a meal.

(4) The Bathroom Hearing (*Edwaree sem di*). The whole case must be heard and judgment delivered within the time necessary for taking a bath.

(5) The Latrine Hearing (*Tiefi asem di*). The whole case must be heard and judgment delivered within the time taken to go to the latrine and return.

Before the end of the time assigned for the hearing, the big man, who is usually a chief but sometimes an *okyeame* or *asafohene*, dictates the peace terms, as it were, between the disputants, and the two shake hands, each swearing an oath that he has now no dispute with the other.

Problems of Justice and Administration

I

The 'Indirect' administration of justice is a part of a great and difficult general problem—perhaps the most difficult of all the problems of indirect rule.

When the Government decides to give official recognition to any native institution, immediately this recognition is given the institution suffers a rapid degradation. This is not, of course, because there is anything degrading or unwholesome in Government influence as such, but simply because the institution is no longer dependent for its existence and prestige on the support of the people whom it serves, which support in turn depends on the quality of the service rendered. The institution, under European patronage, is immediately regarded as a European one and its officers as agents of the Europeans. As such agents, they are removed from the reach of all the natural native sanctions, and can say to themselves,'The Government is behind us : we can do what we like with impunity.'

For example, I recollect a town whose chief, for eight years after his appointment, was not recognized by the Government : nor had the town any registered tribunal. During that time the unrecognized chief did his work conscientiously and well, giving his people complete satisfaction. But as soon as he obtained Government recognition his whole outlook changed and his whole behaviour changed. His people now say of him 'He doesn't respect us any more, so we don't respect him.'

And nowhere in native life is the deterioration of native institutions under Government patronage so noticeable as in the administration of justice. Many District Officers are aware of the ingeniously legal miscarriages of justice that occur in the registered Tribunals, and can produce preposterous examples. They are shocked and indignant and anxious to see instituted a more knave-proof system ; but they are not always aware of the vast superiority of most of the unrecognized courts in both mental and moral quality. Among all the private courts I have attended I have never heard a case either handled in a manner I could not admire or judged unjustly or harshly. But in the registered tribunals I have frequently been ashamed to reflect that the proceedings could claim British sponsorship.

A well-known administrator writes :

'Government is fully aware of the fact that evils and abuses exist in Native Tribunals constituted under the Native Administration Ordinance, but, in any attempt to eradicate such ills, care must be taken to discriminate as to whether their initiation is the cause or whether they are symptomatic of the people's character.'

Probably neither the Ordinance nor the people's character is to blame. The problem is only a special case of the greatest difficulty of all indirect rule everywhere, namely, the difficulty of using a native institution without the native sanctions. In the unrecognized courts—as in all courts before the coming of the European—any authority which the court possesses is balanced by a corresponding burden of responsibility and obligation. The African had not only authority but the *ultimate responsibility* for justice, law, and order. To-day the ultimate responsibility rests on the European. The 'unrecognized' African court has cases brought to it only so long as it deals justly. The 'recognized' court feels itself secure, irresponsible, and privileged. It is in human nature, not specifically African nature, that its behaviour should deteriorate.

In judicial affairs, as in others, the deterioration under foreign patronage comes, as I have indicated, mainly from the removal, by the introduction of a third party, of that mutual dependence which existed between the 'big man' and the 'small man' and kept them both well behaved. But there is one tangible point on which to put the finger. The registered tribunal is, which no native court ever was, a source of income. Both chief and elders make a profit on it. It is unlikely that the average tribunal will ever compare with the old native court in decency till the elders revert to the old system of working for nothing. There seems no reason why they should not—like English magistrates, town councillors, parish councillors, and other participators in local government who still retain certain primitive traits—continue to be proud to do public work solely for the feeling of importance and the interest of a sociable hobby. We have seen the Abenase chief's rich uncle whom, if we saw him at his work of cocoa buying, we should perhaps label 'detribalized', returning at *Afahye* time and spending his money on his town. When he retires from cocoa buying he will be equally happy to spend his time on his town. There are plenty of others fundamentally like him, though most of them are less wealthy.

2

The elders' private courts show no sign of disappearing. This is well, for they are the backbone of law and order. Probably the Government owes more to them than to any other native institution. But they have to contend with some new and undeserved troubles which might possibly be lightened.

The elders' courts, the chief's chamber court, and the five courts of curtailed hearing, differ in several essentials from the registered tribunal. In the first place, the defendant is not summoned. He pleases himself about submitting to this form of settlement. He is usually glad to do so, for the expenses are slight compared with those of the registered tribunal. The elders give their services, receiving only a small *ntra dwom* (sitting-fee) and *aseda* (thanking-rum) from the winner, whom the loser is expected to reimburse. Furthermore, no fine or punishment is imposed, but the offender pays customary *pata* (pacification) to the injured party.

But it sometimes happens that a literate who has gladly accepted a hearing in a chief's private chamber-court or in a curtailed-hearing court, gets disgruntled if the judgment goes against him and then, although he has shaken hands and sworn that his quarrel is ended, he sneaks off to the District Commissioner and complains that 'his case was not recorded in the register.' I have heard both the *Omanhene* and the *Kyidomhene* bitterly complain that after consenting to hear cases privately and less profitably to themselves, accepting nothing but the usual pacification (*pata*) of the injured party by the offender, they have been subsequently 'disgraced' by reprimand from the District Commissioner before whom the loser of the case has whined that his 'case was not legally recorded'.

Sometimes, when a hearing is not before a chief but before some privately convened elders, the disgruntled loser has another trick. He goes to the District Commissioner saying that he was summoned before an 'unauthorized tribunal' and that his case was heard by a self-appointed official who had 'no jurisdiction under the Native Administration Ordinance'.

Some of the literate chiefs who have strangers in their district have themselves learnt the trick of exploiting the idea of an 'unauthorized tribunal'. They would never, of course, try it with their own elders, but many of the Gã and Adangme strangers complain bitterly that some literate chiefs have a spy system by means of which they come to hear of the pettiest household cases which the strangers' own elders have settled. The chief then insists that the elders have usurped his right of territorial jurisdiction by holding illegal tribunals. The illiterate strangers themselves seldom realize how illegally they are being bullied. From the point of view of the Ordinance they have simply settled *out of court* a case which possibly, but not probably, would have gone to the chief's tribunal. One elder said to me, 'If I spank my child for disobedience he will go to the local chief and complain that I had no jurisdiction to try his case.'

3

Although by native usage case-judging is a matter of private contract between judge and judged, and though two disputants may call in a 'big man' from the North Pole if they wish, it is more usual to call in political associates. In the past, when big disputes between town and town or between a chief and his people made it necessary to look outside for a competent judge, it was usual to choose the *Omanhene* of the *oman* and his body of chiefs. This was not because that body had any primary judicial function or any right to dictate concerning the internal affairs of the towns in the confederation (the primary function of which was military), but simply because the chiefs were constantly meeting to consult with the *Omanhene* on *oman* (i.e. military) affairs and were therefore a convenient body to approach. Like most other judges, they were so by invitation, not by inherent or professional right.

To select judges from among one's superiors in the same *oman* has thus come to be regarded as the ordinary procedure, and an intensely personal system of jurisdiction has grown up. And upon this the *oman* itself now depends, to a great extent, for its existence. As its 'big men' ceased to be its generals they became its judges. The *oman*, which was a military confederation, became, in addition to becoming a financial confederation, a judicial confederation. And if it is to continue existence as an *oman* both its financial and its judicial intactness must be preserved.

However, destruction rather than preservation of judicial customs has been the result of the earlier British policy. On the assumption that chiefs and *Omanhenes* ruled over tracts of country rather than confederations of scattered peoples, it was decreed by Government ordinance that people should be under the jurisdiction of the chief in whose 'area' they resided.

The disintegration of the *oman* resulting from this ordinance has been slower than might be supposed, for custom has a stubborn vitality which has sturdily resisted the enforcement of the order. Had it not been resisted it might well have been the death blow of the *omans*.

That a new system of jurisdiction based on efficiency, geographical accessibility, financial economy, and logical simplicity should be less acceptable to African people compared with an old system based on traditional association and group-consciousness is difficult for most Britons to grasp, though they are not surprised when they see how readily an ancient group-sentiment rallies to Britain's side colonies which cold economic and logical considerations would have kept aloof. That two Akwapim men living in Akim-Kotoku should prefer taking their case on a long journey to taking it to a conveniently situated stranger; that a town should wish to collect no taxes from strangers within its gates and prefer to send messengers hieing across country to collect from its own scattered absentees; that the absentees should be actually proud to contribute to the expenses of a town in which they no longer reside; that all this inconvenience should be preferred to the simple efficacy of paying taxes and taking cases to the nearest chief is incredible to many Europeans. But so it is, and by such incredible facts is an *oman* sustained. We may now look at a few examples of resistance to the territorial jurisdiction order.

There is a large colony of Juaben strangers [1] settled on land owned by Akim-Kotoku towns. They have several considerable towns there, but they came only because of shortage of land round Koforidua, where their brethren live, and they maintain close links with their Juaben brethren in Koforidua. The chief of Prasu-Amuena, one of their towns, is a 'big man' in the Koforidua fraternity, an integral part of that *oman*, and has to be present at all its important cases and ceremonies. Yet he must refer his own cases to Akim-Kotoku. Aboase, a town of some 1,300 people, is another of this Juaben group. Having no tribunal recognized by Government it has to take all tribunal cases to Pankese, a Kotoku town, when its own 'big brother', Prasu-Amuena, is not much farther geographically and infinitely nearer psychologically.

Prasu-Amuena is constantly disobeying the law about taking cases to the Kotoku *Omanhene* at Oda instead of to its own at Koforidua, and there are recriminations and fines whenever Oda finds it out. Kotoku has no desire whatever to handle Juaben cases for their own sake : sometimes, indeed, its *Omanhene* is confessedly incapable of tackling them, for they may concern Juaben affairs that he knows nothing about, or they may be 'oath cases' sworn on a Juaben stool, and then he has to compromise by sending them on to Koforidua and halving the court proceeds. It is only since the Native Administration Ordinance has made case-hearing a paying business that there has been any competition to hear cases. The first time I ever met the Prasu-Amuena chief he was being reprimanded and heavily fined by the Kotoku *Omanhene* for sending a case to Koforidua.

Again, there is the example of Amentia. This little town consists of aborigines on their own land, and is a member of the Bosome *oman*. It served Bosome even before Bosome left Denchera, and is of the same Agona clan. But it is situated on the west bank of the Pra, and, though its ferry connects it conveniently with its Bosome confrères, administration now decrees that it is in Ashanti. Properly, Ashanti itself is a military confederation, not a tract of territory, and Bosome has never been anything to Ashanti but a bitter enemy. Amentia therefore flatly refuses to take its cases to any Ashanti tribunal.

---

[1] These Juaben people have been settled since the end of the last century. They are in a curious position politically, as they settled during the days of warfare and on condition that they assisted Kotoku in warfare if necessary. They therefore have a position in the military divisions and pay military taxation. But they are a part of the Koforidua confederation and pay taxes to it. They and the Juaben of Koforidua were one in Ashanti before their migration and they are still united in their voluntary political activities.

It is not, fortunately for the anthropologist, any part of his task to decide whether it is desirable to preserve such an institution as the *oman*. But he cannot, in *describing* the *oman*, neglect to point out which of its ancient cohesive forces still remain to it. Undoubtedly one of these is its associated system of jurisdiction which is a personal, not a territorial, one.

CHAPTER XI

TRANSITION RITES

When a person reaches the end of one of the major phases of life, crosses the boundary and starts upon the new phase, various rites are performed in order to promote his welfare in his new state of being, and to start him off, as it were, on the right road.

These major transition points are three. At birth the person leaves the world of ghosts and comes to live in this world. At puberty the person passes from the state of childhood and becomes a man or woman. At death he leaves this world for the world of ghosts.

The ceremonial connected with these three stages still follows the traditional lines, and indeed, so long as it is performed at all it is not likely to alter much except in amount, for, as someone has said, 'To die is a very old-fashioned thing to do.' But, as we shall see in the chapter [1] on the Nangro festival, the new shrines are usurping a certain amount of responsibility for the welfare of the unborn and newly born child.

The main feature of transition rites in the Gold Coast is that they are not carried out by professionals but by the immediate circle of the person concerned and mostly in his own home.

Except in connection with funeral ceremonial, the elaboration of this individual welfare ceremonial in Akim is very slight compared with that in some other parts of the Gold Coast. In particular there is in Akim no puberty ceremony for boys and very little antenatal ceremonial. [2]

Oyiniedi Ceremony

This is the ceremony of taking a newborn child out of the world of ghosts and introducing it into this world. It is still carefully performed by the old midwives.

The child is shut up indoors for its first seven days on earth.

---

[1] Chap. XIII.

[2] By Africans speaking English, all puberty rites are usually called 'marriage custom'. When Europeans talk to such literates about 'marriage' they should beware of talking at cross-purposes. Africans call puberty rites 'marriage custom' even when not so much as a prospective bridegroom has materialized. The word 'marriage' is also used by literates as a euphemism for sexual intercourse and has not necessarily anything to do with the business of taking a wife. Africans also often say 'my wife' when they mean 'my cross cousin' and when they mean 'my betrothed'.

During this time its friends believe that it may, in mere childish mischief, be paying but a flying visit to this world and may slip away at any moment. Nothing special is done for its welfare during this week except the tying of raffia on all its joints to keep them temporarily strong. If it dies during this week, it is whipped and given only gestures of disapproval, so that it may understand clearly that it has played a low-down trick which it must on no account repeat.

At the end of the week the child is assumed to have a serious intention of staying in this world, and it is accordingly brought out and formally set upon its road.

The mother sits in the yard with the babe on her knee. Its father, or some male relative appointed to represent him, takes scissors and cuts a little bunch of hair from its head. Then the midwife washes the child and afterwards smears its body with clay and perfumed paste. She puts beads on its neck, wrists, and ankles ; round its waist she ties two strings of beads, one to keep it free from sickness and the other to make it 'sit down'— that is, to settle permanently. These beads have all been worn by some other infant that has thrived. If a child does not thrive its beads are never given to another.

Then the midwife takes the hair cut off by the man and, holding it in her fingers, chars it in the fire. While it is still smoking she holds it in the child's growing hair, saying three times :

> ' Mi yi wo fi asamade,
> En yare, trase, ne ye dwuma ma wose.'

(*I take you out of the world of the ghosts. Do not be sick, settle down, and may you have work.*)

Then she takes a new cloth given by the father and lays it folded upon the child's body, saying :

> ' Wo se de ntama yi ma wo ene sumi
> ene kete odi yi wo fi samade. Trase, ne
> ye dwuma ma wose.'

(*Here is this cloth for you, and now a pillow and now a bed : receive these to take you out of the world of the ghosts. Settle down, and may you have work.*)

At the ceremony which I witnessed, the midwife did not give the child a ceremonial drink of water, though some people possess a special spoon called a *sawa* for this purpose. Some 'big people'—for example, the queen-mother in Oda—have among their treasures a silver *sawa* used on high-born children, and the phrase 'born with a silver spoon in his mouth' is one which would really convey a meaning. It is still said in railing at stupid children, 'Have you not drunk of the *sawa* of your fathers ?'

Ogobra or Bradwu Custom

These are the puberty rites done for a girl menstruating for the first time.

I happened to see the rites performed for a girl who was betrothed to the Abenase chief, and he sent one of his 'big wives' to be one of her 'mothers'. On this occasion the real mother was the other officiator.

First the girl was ceremonially turned out of the house in which she had been living. Then two women, chosen for having lost none of their own children, took her, together with a crowd of little girls who, I was assured, had no idea what the occasion was really about, down to the river. They set her on a whitened stool on the bank and washed her with river water. An egg was flung into the river and the river was asked to bless and make her fruitful. Then basins of water were taken from the river and all available little children were seized and their heads ducked in the basins. The basins were then emptied into the stream and it was asked to take note of the children just immersed in its water and to send the girl plenty of others like them.

The girl herself, like all menstruating women, was not allowed to enter the stream. Such women may take their water-pots to the stream, but they must get some other woman to wade in and fill them.

Then the girl was brought back and seated in the street while her 'mothers' painted her body with patterns in white clay and decorated her with beads. Her own mother had prepared a big basin of *oto*[1] and some hard-boiled eggs. Before anything was done with this food some of it was put on a piece of old broken crockery 'for the old lady', the server saying three times 'Old lady, take this food and let this girl bear thirty children'. The potsherd of food was then taken away and flung on the town rubbish heap.

Nobody has any clear idea about this old lady [2] of the rubbish heap. Some informants said, 'The rubbish heap takes everything that comes to it, both filthy and clean. An old lady, too, accepts the good and bad of life alike : the bad does not shock her

---

[1] Yam, egg, and palm-oil mash.

[2] In Gã country when the elders are judging a case and retire to consider their verdict they say they 'go to consult the old lady'.

10

or trouble her, the good does not make her over-pleased. When the mother rails and scolds, the grandmother silently forgives.'

When the 'old lady' had been served the girl was given three mouthfuls of *oto*, each of which she spat out. Then she was handed a hard-boiled egg and told to swallow it whole. A girl who cannot achieve this feat is assumed to be no virgin, but as she is allowed to cover her head with a cloth while she performs it—or not, as the case may be—nobody's curiosity on the point is really satisfied.

After swallowing—or presumably swallowing—the whole egg, the girl was given a drink of water, a basin of *oto*, and three more eggs to eat in the normal manner. The rest of the food was shared among the spectators, but none was given to any grown man.

For six days after this, the girl had to stay in seclusion and not to enter any man's house. At the end of that time she was decked out in grand clothes, her skin was smeared with a mixture of oil and imitation gold-dust—in former days it would have been real—and she paraded the town in a procession of other girls, visiting all her friends and exhibiting her charms. Within a few weeks she was taken, without further ceremony, to the chief as his wife.

Ordinary Funerals

At no time in a person's life is he so sociable as at his death.

The disposal of his corpse, the send-off of his spirit to its new home, the allocation of his earthly responsibilities to new shoulders, and the disposal of his property, all bring together groups of people whose movements in his lifetime he would have had no power to command.

We have seen that the funeral of a paramount chief flings its net far into many a distant *oman*, and also that it enmeshes, in some way or other, every person in the *oman*.

Let us now look at the funeral of a very poor and insignificant person, a funeral shorn of all but its barest essentials. Even here we find an astonishingly wide circle of people co-operating.

The funeral I shall now describe was that of a young man of Abenase. Not only were his parents very poor and humble but he himself was especially insignificant. He was unmarried, for reasons of health, though well above marriageable age. Such an unmarried man is accounted almost worthless, for he has not even the potential worth of a healthy child.

This young man, like most with his affliction, had long been

10. Drumming at Bosum Pra's forest festival.
(*See* page 153.)

9. She was decked out in fine clothes.
(*See* page 138.)

lean and miserable, going about his daily work in a desultory, apathetic way. One day, on returning from the farm with a load of wood, he said he felt tired and weak, lay down, and in a few hours died.

In the house were his elderly parents, his two grown-up sisters, and their children. His brothers lived elsewhere.

The first thing that was done when he died was to send for his brothers. The head of his *abusua* (*asafohene*) and all other members of the *abusua* were informed. The *asafohene* despatched someone to represent himself, and this representative and as many other responsible members of the *abusua* who could be found, came and witnessed that he was dead.

The women of the *abusua*, under the directions of the senior old lady, came and washed the body, 'for his body is theirs'. Having washed it, they dressed and adorned it far more grandly than it had ever been in life, put cigarettes between its lips and fingers, and laid it on several layers of good, coloured, hand-woven cloths spread on a narrow borrowed bedstead in one of the three-walled rooms opening into the yard of the compound. The cloths and bedstead should have been provided by the father and brothers, but these, being poor, borrowed from their friends.

As soon as the body was prepared, two members of the *abusua* were sent with a gift of drink to say to the Chief of the town, 'To-day we have lost somebody.' The chief sent a representative to go and view the body. Even if the dead man had been important the chief himself would not have attended the funeral. A chief who goes to a funeral must be purified a week later and a sheep must be slaughtered to propitiate his stool.

Meanwhile the father and brothers—whose responsibility it always is to provide a coffin—had sought out the local carpenter and set him to work. Before starting, the carpenter stood by his bench with some rum and prayed that his own *kra* might not go into the coffin during its fashioning, and that he might have no accident with his tools. 'Nobody likes a coffin, and a carpenter's *kra* does not, so it might wound him with his own tools during the work.' When the coffin was completed except for the lid, the carpenter took more rum and prayed again, first that the dead man might sleep soundly in his new 'house', and second, that God might save the carpenter from having to make more coffins.

While the carpenter was at work, the young men of the father's family dug the grave. Any young friends of the dead man can help in this if they wish, but the responsibility is the father's.

Meanwhile, at the house, friends and relations were gathered, the men sitting outside the yard in the street, the women inside. The mother and sisters of the dead man sat beside the body fanning it and crying aloud.

All visitors on arriving at such a gathering greet the parents of the dead man and then the dead man himself. The visitor pats the corpse gently with the left hand, saying softly, 'Due, due' (I am sorry for you). The men are brief and quiet but the women bellow heartily. Their wailings, however, if noted carefully, are found to be more than mere noisy lamentations. They are nearly all requests to the dead person to greet So-and-so, who died last year, to ask So-and-so not to forget the old home but to send a blessing, to ask the old people to send back a dead child or send a child to some hitherto barren woman. Above all, the dead man is begged to return again, reborn, before long.[1]

The other visitors all sat quietly, drinking only a little palm-wine provided by the dead man's brothers. No food is cooked or eaten while the corpse lies unburied, but kola-nuts are chewed [2] to keep people going.

When important people die, they lie in state so long as is bearable, and relations arrive often from great distances, but when there is no important visitor to await, the burial takes place as soon as the coffin is ready.

When the carpenter had finished, the brothers brought the coffin. Various young men elbowed forward and started a loud quarrel about the right to assist in putting the body into the coffin. This struck me as unseemly till I learnt that it was a ceremonial quarrel, staged to do honour to the dead man. It is said that 'A man who is always quarrelling in his lifetime will not be quarrelled over at his death.'

When this matter was settled, some three or four men took the coffin into the room where was the corpse. Two others held a large cloth over the entrance to screen the proceedings from view, but we in the yard heard all that was said. Before the coffin was closed one elder poured out rum and addressed the dead man in a loud voice. First he enumerated all the articles placed in the coffin, mentioning the name of the giver of each.

[1] The greetings are, in fact, strongly reminiscent of messages round the railway carriage window after a day excursion in England. 'Give my love to Charlie. Tell Aunt Maggie to write. Thank Granny for the lovely gooseberries. Ask Cousin May to let the children come and stay. Sorry you have to go so soon ; come again as soon as ever you can'.

[2] Kola-nuts deaden the sensations of hunger and thirst and also remove feelings of fatigue.

Next he asked the dead man to remember in his new life all his friends of the old, and to send to them a share of all good things that might come to him. Next, the elderly orator, speaking no doubt as much *at* his living juniors as to his dead one, advised him to respect and obey the elders in his new home, for there as here no happiness or prosperity could come to any young man who failed to honour the old. Then he sternly charged him with the duty of avenging his own death should this have been caused by any living person. Such a person he must swiftly make to die, but if no man's malice was to blame, then must the dead sleep in peace. Finally he begged the departing kinsman to come again.

The things put into the coffin were a pillow, a sleeping-mat, a blanket, the dead man's old farming clothes, his head-pad for carrying loads, six shillings in money for his 'ferry fare' and other travelling expenses, several new cloths—one from the father, the others from the brothers—a handkerchief and cigarettes. Each cloth had a strip torn from it, for nothing given to the dead must be quite equal to that given to the living. The relatives quarrelled ceremonially for the possession of the torn strips as souvenirs. No matches were given to the dead to light the cigarettes. 'If he wants a light he can come unseen to the house and get it from the fire.' Nor might he have a cutlass, hoe, or any other potential weapon, for 'he would use it in killing someone. If he wants a cutlass or hoe he can come and take the spirit of someone else's.' But he must have enough money, or he might trouble the living with sleeplessness or minor mishaps. When the living find themselves so troubled, they consult an *akomfo* and if she reveals that the dead relative is short of cash she tells them to fling it or place it where he may come and find it.

'When the dead man arrives in his new town in the world of the dead,' an elder told me, 'he will go and pay his respects to the elders just as if he were arriving at a new town on earth, and they will tell him where he may live and will give him a plot of land to farm. Then, if he sees with his new clear eyes that someone has spitefully killed him, he will tell the elders, and they will judge his case and will send a summons (i.e. death) to those who did him wrong.'

After a little more ceremonial quarrelling about the right to carry the coffin, it was taken by a few young men through a hole broken in the fence of the yard and rushed rapidly to the cemetery. The few moments when the coffin is leaving the yard are always the most genuinely emotional, and real friends struggle

with real tears. All hands wave in farewell and everyone calls
'Good-bye', 'Good night', or 'Sleep well'.

If the coffin goes quickly and quietly to the grave, this is a
good sign ; the dead man is content. But if the coffin bucks
and shies, sends the bearers staggering and lurching, or bolts
round the town, then the dead man is dissatisfied and will not
rest in peace.

The day after the burial, relatives and friends gathered for
more mourning and no one in the town went to farm. Whether
general land work is actually forbidden on these occasions I am
uncertain, but no one ever does any. The women sat in the yard,
the men brought their chairs and sat in the street.

I was told that if the *Omanhene's* funeral had not been still
'unfinished' there would have been wailing and dancing but, as
it was, there was no noise. Palm-wine, provided by the father
and his sons and brothers, was passed round. No food except
kola and secret snacks was taken till the party broke up in the
evening.

Seven days after the death was another little informal reception. The father provided a pot of palm-wine to thank his
particular cronies for their sympathy. The brothers provided
another pot for theirs. Relatives who had heard of the death
too late to come before the burial, came on the seventh day to
be in time for the important meeting which always takes place
on the eighth day. They sat in or outside the yard quietly
'eating sorrow' and chatting. The bed on which the body had
lain was still in position, the cloth which it had worn was on the
head of the bed. When another sister arrived from her distant
village she went straight to the head of the bed and stood there
lamenting loudly. Every fresh female arrival did the same. All
visitors brought money contributions and these were given into
the charge of a treasurer—a non-relative chosen for his reliability
—who sat by a little table on which the money was spread.

In the late afternoon the 'big men' of the town began to arrive,
each bringing a money contribution. They all sat outside with
the father and other males. The father did not appear pleased
to see them and, from time to time, burst into tirades of abuse.
The young men also bickered at intervals. This ill-humour was,
however, of a ceremonial nature and expressive of sorrow. 'If
you abuse other people it relieves your own sorrow.'

On this day everyone in the town must send or bring his
townsman's contributions to the *Nsuabode* fund. This is an
official levy ordered by the chief and elders : everyone must
pay it or be fined for disobedience to the chief. Actually no one

ever objects to it, for he knows that when death comes to his own household, he and his relatives will be similarly relieved of the bulk of the financial burden. This payment is, in fact, a premium on his own funeral insurance and everyone in the town is a member of this mutual benefit society.

For an ordinary humble funeral every married man pays sixpence and every *asafohene* one or two shillings. When the time comes for an *asafohene* himself to die the populace will all make slightly bigger contributions to his grander ceremonial.

Women need not contribute under this scheme. 'A woman's part is to shed tears.' But most of them bring voluntary contributions and many of the men make freewill additions to the compulsory sum.

At the end of the day, when the visitors have gone, the father's *abusua* and the mother's *abusua* each have a private meeting convened by the father and the maternal uncle respectively. The outlay of each group is calculated at its own meeting, but the convener does not announce his receipts.

The eighth day is always the day of public financial reckoning, and announcements concerning succession to the dead man's responsibilities and inheritance of his property. The young man whose funeral I have been describing had few responsibilities and fewer goods to leave, but there was still much to be done.

The men sat, as before, outside the yard while the women inside cooked a last meal to take to the grave. The treasurer at the little table announced that the total expenses of the funeral were three pounds and that the public had contributed thirty shillings.

Had the deceased been a 'big man' the town would have claimed a death duty from his successor. This amount is announced by the *okyeame* in the presence of the town elders at the eighth-day meeting. Usually the relatives see the *okyeame* privately before the meeting and—no doubt with some tangible inducement—arrange with him what amount he shall demand. His word is always final for 'no one can make an *okyeame* be silent.' The amount paid over is supposed to be 'for rum', and its acceptance by the *okyeame* on behalf of the town is a token that the successor is officially recognized in place of the predecessor.

As the dead young man's brothers had not all come from their villages the disposal of his few belongings was postponed.

There was nothing more to be done publicly, so the women dished up the food to take to the grave. The plantain-stalks and any other vegetable refuse that could possibly take root again were thoroughly charred in the fire and the refuse was carefully swept up and ceremonially flung out of the town.

Five women and one man went to the grave, the women carrying the basins of food and such oddments as are always left on the grave, the man carrying gun and cutlass. He did not fire the gun but beat it with the cutlass to announce the arrival of the party.

Each *abusua* (clan) has its own section of the cemetery. This is simply a part of the encircling forest. When a new grave is made the undergrowth soon grows up again and nothing remains for a stranger to notice except pottery. On every grave is laid the remains of the dead person's bathing utensils—sponge, towel, soap, and bucket—three earthen fireplace globes for cooking, the bowls, dishes, and drinking vessels of his last meal, and a pot for washing-water. Nowadays, if the deceased was the proud possessor of an imported white enamel chamber-pot, this also is put on the grave and shines forth startlingly among the subdued dark native pottery in the shadowy forest.

As soon as the party with the food had left for the cemetery the company at the house dispersed. The food-bearers went and returned in breathless haste, but no sign of the gathering remained by the time they reached home.

Forty days after a death the inheritor of the dead person's farm visits this farm, taking such relatives and friends as care to come. During the forty days nobody has been into the farm. The inheritor walks through the farm pouring rum, and then prays to his predecessor, saying, 'Stand behind this your brother and make the farm prosperous so that he may have food to nourish the children you have left.' The other visitors weep and wail, and, after finishing the rum, return home. The farm may now be used in a normal way.

While I was in Abenase the *Krontihene* visited his dead wife's farm in this way. He was a lonely old man who had been much attached to his wife, and his sincerity made this simple ceremony most impressive. He fasted for a whole day before going, and said that the farm was the place where he would always weep for his wife, for it was there that he and she had so often worked together.

Forty-eight days after an important death, a grand remembrance-day is held, with drumming, drinking, and gunfire ; but this is not essential for poor or humble people. On this occasion a time is fixed for the most elaborate celebration of all, the *Eyigo* or *Gyianotia*. The successor of the dead man is responsible

11. The men sat outside the yard. (*See* page 143.)

12. The women dished up the food to take to the grave. (*See* page 144.)

for the expense of this costly festivity. He will perhaps say, 'Six years hence I will hold the *Eyigo* for my uncle.' And then, if it never comes off, no one remembers that it is due. One informant said, 'My uncle, whom I succeeded, died about ten years ago, but I have not yet done the *Eyigo*, and nobody laughs at me. My uncle did not leave me any money, so how can he expect me to do it ?'

If the successor unexpectedly gets rich and attributes this to the blessing of his dead relative, he will celebrate a grand festival, even if he did not originally intend to do so.

When the *Eyigo* does come off, the survivors may have forgotten what the departed looked like. They have therefore to be reminded. For this purpose an earthenware image is prepared and is made a part of the *abusua kruwa* in which the clansmen put scraps of their own hair. The image is afterwards put on the grave. Nowadays these images are seldom made, but I have found them in old forest cemeteries and have one in my possession.

The Asafo at Funerals

Nowadays the *asafo* as a military body has, naturally, little importance, but it is still immensely important on account of its power to affect a person's status in the next world by honouring him at his funeral.

The dead are laid in state in this world in the grandest possible clothes, jewels, and trappings, because they are held to be entering the next world with these trappings, even though the things are not buried with them. The stuff buried with them is simply equipment *for the journey*. The arrival is in the spirit and the ghostly counterpart of the clothes and jewels arrives too.[1] The signal that the ghost of the dead man is ready for arrival is the commencement of wailing and crying. This tells the long-departed that someone is coming and they must prepare to receive him. No one is allowed to cry or wail until the body has been washed and suitably decked in its finery, otherwise the spirit would depart and be received unworthily clad.

The drumming, dancing, and singing, collectively called 'play', which is performed while the corpse lies in state, is relayed, as it were, to the friends in the next world, and the thought always present is, 'The play that you are given here is the play that you will be received with in the next world.' *Asafo* calls to *asafo*, and as soon as the long-departed warriors and 'big

[1] The dogma of the dead has plenty of articles which are inconsistent with one another.

men' hear their own old *asafo* songs, the gunfire and the drums, they are alert to welcome one of their own kind.

The *asafo* come and play at the death of any member. It is they who go and fetch his body to the town, should he die in his village, and they also carry it to the grave.

In the old days of warfare, every expeditionary force took many women as camp-followers. A few of these used to go into the fighting-line and now and then one would be seized with a frenzy of hysterical fearlessness and would lead a charge with an insane ferocity and horrible valour that scattered the enemy. There are still women alive who have been to war, and when one of them dies she receives full military honours. From time to time an ordinary woman sends the *asafo* a bottle of rum and requests that when she dies the members may play at her funeral.

Chiefs' Funerals

When a chief dies the *omanhene* is notified and he appoints someone to be the 'father' of the funeral on his own behalf. This 'father' has to notify all the other chiefs of the *oman* and each of them sends a contribution and a representative from his own town. The 'father' is in charge of all ceremonial and appoints other representatives to see that due honour is done to the dead chief. The *krontihene* of the bereaved town, who might have been expected to take charge, is considered to be incapacitated with grief. 'With his eyes full of tears, he cannot see.'

When the Ayiribe chief died the Abenase chief was 'father' of the funeral.

Craftsmen's Funerals

Craftsmen are now few, but when they die special ceremonies are done for them. I happened to see the members of a company of four stool-carvers carrying out the work of 'separating' a dead member from his tools.

This was done on the eighth day after the death. A fowl was slaughtered for the dead man, the blood was sprinkled on the tools and he was bidden to depart from them and not cause them to injure anyone who might subsequently use them. He was also asked to bless them that they might bring prosperity to their new owners. Leaves of *adwira* were then dipped into a basin of water from the stream of which the dead man had daily drunk, and the tools were sprinkled. A little mound of sand from the same stream was laid beside them.

'Bad deaths'

Several kinds of death are regarded as bad, and the dead person is not given a normal funeral.

The *Afahye* festival is a bad time to die, for during that festival the long-dead, who should receive the new-comer, are not able to do so, for they are away paying their annual visit to earth. No one therefore cries for the newly dead man : it is hoped that this will delay his departure. His body is not buried for a week, but is placed outside the town on a little raised platform.

When a pregnant woman dies with her child undelivered, she is considered to have died because of some evil she herself has done. At the same time she has imprisoned and bound the spirit of her child and has murdered its body. It is essential that the child should be released, though the mother can never be freed from her disgrace. The fœtus is therefore removed from the dead woman's body and she is given a 'disgraceful' burial.

Such a death occurred in Abenase during my contact with the town. The woman was a Christian, but this was held to make no difference. An Akwapim medicine-man happened to be visiting the town and he was asked to perform the post-mortem operation. He did this alone behind a screen of cloths held by his frightened assistants, washing his hand with rum before and after the work. He said he was the possessor of a medicine strong enough to protect him from the malicious spirit of the dead woman. He charged the terrified relatives £2 10s., a bottle of rum, and a white fowl to kill for his own 'medicine'.

The two bodies were buried in the Christian cemetery, but there was no mourning or crying.

Had the woman not been a Christian her body would have been either dragged on a mat and flung away in the forest or— a more modern custom—buried in a special cemetery for 'bad deaths'. This cemetery is called the *atofodai*. Here are banished the unhonoured bodies of suicides and those meeting violent accidental death. Violent death is either a punishment for a great sin or is the result of great malice of an ill-wisher. In the first case the deceased is not worthy of an honourable burial ; in the second, he will be full of resentment at being cut off prematurely, and his ghost will be vindictive and dangerous, and will chase and kill people of whose continued existence it is jealous. Such a dangerous ghost is called an *'atofo'*.

Suicides

Suicide is also a disgraceful death. When the Abenase *asafo* went into the forest on a search for a lost man it was thought that he might have committed suicide : the conversation on the march was therefore largely about suicides, and I heard more reminiscences on the subject during that march than at any other time.

When a suicide's body is first discovered, the finder has to 'disgrace' it. If the death is by hanging he must cut the rope 'to release the *susuma*'[1], but he must not cut it gently or the ghost will follow him home. He must flog the hanging body, slap its face or bottom, and call it 'fool' and other abusive epithets. Then, having cut it down, he must lay leaves upon it, saying, 'You are disgraced, I am going home to report you.' He leaves the knife or cutlass used in cutting the rope beside the body, spits on it and then goes home to report.

The body is afterwards buried under the tree on which it was hanged ; the branch is lopped off and put on the grave. There is neither coffin nor 'gifts for the journey'. Nor does anyone wail to announce the arrival to the people of the next world. The dead man is given a hollowed palm-kernel to use as a whistle to announce his own arrival.

If the suicide is committed with a knife, cutlass, or other weapon, this is buried with the body to arm the man so that he may kill whomsoever drove him to his death or by witchcraft put the impulse of suicide into him.

A first suicide in any family is considered to be caused by some living person. Any subsequent suicides are caused by the relatives who died the same death. The reincarnation of a suicide is not desired, for it will again end in suicide. The suicide is therefore not mourned.

All libations for suicides are poured with the left hand.

Drowning

If the body of a person drowned in a river is recovered, this is because the river wishes the relatives to ask it why it killed their kinsman. A river never sends back the corpse of anyone whom it likes. Some clans believe that they began as the offspring of rivers. They are therefore neither surprised nor worried if their children be called back into the river whence their fathers came.

Bodies recovered from a river are not taken home but are buried on the bank. The drowned man is assumed to have done wrong, and an *akomfo* is employed to find out what has displeased the river.

[1] Soul.

Children's Funerals

A still-born child or a child that dies before it is a week old is called a *kukuba*,[1] and is buried in an earthen pot. No one weeps for it and it is unkindly handled to impress it with its ill-behaviour in coming frivolously to earth with no intention of staying. It must learn that it has done wrong or it may repeat the offence. Where there is a children's cemetery—as at Abenase—two women furtively bury the pot there in a round grave apart from the other children's graves. If there is no children's cemetery it is buried in the rubbish heap. The pot is lined and covered in the grave with castor-oil leaves and, before it is buried, a hole is knocked in the bottom to allow the child's spirit to emerge and come again. The burial is done immediately after the death, so that no one, particularly the parents, may see the body and grieve over it. Quite apart from the possibility of encouraging the child in its naughty trick of coming without staying, the grief of the parents may injure their own spirits, and this, in the woman's case, may 'spoil her belly' and cause her to stop child-bearing. Moreover, some other well-disposed spirit-child, willing to be born and to stay, might think that the parents were mourning on account of their own wickedness and would not wish to be born to them.

Immediately after the burial, the bereaved parents are made to bathe and take a good meal, eating together from one dish. This is one of the rare occasions on which a man and woman eat together.[2] The parents eat together for a week, dipping their hands simultaneously into the dish. This is held to encourage births, and sometimes barren couples do it to that end. During the week of shared meals the parents handle neither money, farm tools, nor anything considered valuable. When the week is up, they take a ceremonial bath, and before they resume the handling of ordinary objects they go to their farm, accompanied by a few old wives, and touch the growing plants with their hands that they may capture something of the fruitfulness. Then they return home and bathe again, after which they resume normal life.

Among the funerals which I witnessed in Abenase was that of a boy of about nine, the son of an *asafoakye*.

The boy died in the late afternoon and was at once brought to his father's house. The mother lived elsewhere with her own mother.

The body was washed and laid, not in state on a bed, but on

---

[1] Pot-child.

[2] Only on one occasion in the Gold Coast have I seen a husband and wife eating an ordinary meal together. They were a Christian catechist and his wife.

a mat in the yard as the boy in life had often slept. The women-folk and a few men sat in the yard, the women wailing a little at intervals but very softly, admonishing the mother not to weep, and reminding her that, 'if you cry for people, it means that they have gone away : if you don't cry they haven't gone, and will come again.'

Meanwhile the father, severely hit by the loss of his son, had been taken in hand by his friends 'so that he might not look as if he had suffered death.' He was made to bathe, was given a meal and plenty of alcohol, and was brought by his friends back to his own compound where the body lay.

A few other friends meanwhile were knocking up a rough coffin out of packing cases. As soon as it was finished, they brought it, and no more time was wasted, for 'the mother must not cry long.' In the coffin with the body were put a pillow, a coverlet, an old cloth of the father's, a new cloth from the mother's brother, and another from the clan elder. No money was given, and no speeches were made to the dead boy.

The friends hurried the coffin off to the children's cemetery, the parents staying behind.

The next day the father's friends assembled in his house and sat with him drinking and talking in order to keep him from grieving. The woman's friends did the same for her in her house.

When a child is lost by parents who have never lost one before it is called a *sorie*. A *sorie* is buried with all haste and no mourning, in order to preserve the illusion that dying is a thing which that couple's children never do. The dead child's spirit is given no send-off because it is not admitted to have gone. It is in the position of a boy who has, on the impulse of the moment, run away from home. If his parents accept the fact of his departure and lock the door, he will not return, but if they tactfully pretend that they have no knowledge of his absence and leave the door open, he can sneak back if he thinks better of his rash impulse.

CHAPTER XII

TRADITIONAL RELIGION AND CEREMONIAL

The Archaic Survival

Dr. Rattray [1] has described how every Ashanti person belongs to two social groups—the clan of his mother and the *ntro* of his father. Inheritance, succession, and descent are in the clan ; the individual's name and participation in certain religious ritual—usually that connected with river worship—are in the *ntro*. All people in the same clan have one blood, all people in the same *ntro* have one *kra* or spirit. *Kra* and *ntro* are often used synonymously.

It seems to me probable that the *ntro* is the remnant of the old religio-social organization on a patrilineal basis which existed over most of the Gold Coast before the clan system spread from a point somewhere in the North. The clan system is closely bound up with social organization on a warfare basis, the *ntro* system with the pre-warfare social organization on a religio-agricultural basis. I believe that the Kpeshi people, who preceded the Gã immigrants on the coastal plain and spoke a Twi dialect, were a part of this widespread archaic system. Sufficient of the Kpeshi religion and language is still preserved in Temma [2] and elsewhere on the coastal plain to give a good idea of the outline of their religio-social organization. I have described this elsewhere but may briefly recapitulate it here.

There was no military organization and probably no centralized government. The heads of extended families *in the male line* were the only rulers and also performed the ritual for the family gods. The gods were mainly works of nature—trees, lagoons, rivers, hills, pools, the principal ones being rivers and lagoons.

A similar system still exists among the Voltaside Ewe people, and their word for a deity is *tron*, which I suspect to be a variation of *ntro*. These people told me that a 'big *tron* is nearly always a river.'

To return to the *ntro* of the Twi-speaking people, inquiry concerning a man's *ntro* is always put in the form 'What *ntro* do you

---

[1] *Ashanti*, Chap. I.
[2] Since writing this I have found as far West as Axim unmistakable *Kpeshi* rites surviving. These include the Kpeshi agricultural anthem, slightly mispronounced but clearly recognizable. The officiating priest is succeeded in the male line though other inheritance and succession is in the female line.

wash ?' In other words, 'What river-water do you use for ceremonial ?' or 'What river do you worship ?' [1]

Social organization round river worship in Ashanti and Denchera was probably well on the way to break-up before the Denchera-Ashanti war, and this gave the finishing blow to it. The people who fled from Denchera and settled in Akim after that war were the remnant of a military force and they reorganized themselves in their new home on a military basis. They made their war-stools virtually gods, preserving practically nothing of their old religious worship.

There is one exception. The people now in Assene appear to have brought with them a priest of *Bosum* [2] Pra, which river they had worshipped in Denchera. They settled first by an upper reach of the same Pra—near the present Prasukuma—and continued their old worship there. Later they moved to their present site and, though it is not on the Pra itself but on a tributary, they continue their old worship unchanged, and there is to-day in Assene a great annual ritual festival of *Bosum* Pra. All Assene people now observe the *Bosum* Pra food taboos just as if they all belonged to the same *ntro* family group—which of course they all do not. They never eat water yam—not only not on Tuesdays—and they never eat the cat-fish called *Adzwen* that is caught in the rivers, smoked and marketed in large quantities. The priesthood of *Bosum* Pra in Assene is no longer held in the male line but goes from uncle to nephew like most other posts.

The Assene festival is very similar to the old Kpeshi festivals still held in Temma and elsewhere on the coastal plain. Moreover it is celebrated with an enthusiasm unknown elsewhere in Akim-Kotoku. In this festival the chief of Assene, whose position belongs to the later organization on a military basis, participates only as a 'small boy' and an ordinary worshipper.

The Assene Festival

The Assene festival is held in October at the time of the new yam. No one may dig new yam till the *Bosum* Pra priest has dug the first.

Every evening for three weeks before the festival the old priest of *Bosum* Pra beats a gong-gong round the town in the evening telling the people that the festival is approaching and

---

[1] An old man of Abenase whose *ntro* was Poakwa (the sea) said that if I wished to bring him a present from the coast he would like a bottle of sea-water so that if he ever wanted to wash his *ntro* again he would have some of the right water.

[2] *Bosum*—deity.

13. The party halted under a *wawa* tree. (*See* page 153.)

14. Washing the *asipim* chairs for *Kwesidae*. (*See* page 159.)

announcing various public works which the populace must carry out. He tells them, for instance, that they must clear the paths into the town, they must lay in firewood, they must clean up their houses, compounds, clothes, and furniture, for '*Bosum* Pra does not like dirt'.

At the end of the three weeks, on a Monday evening, the rites of *Tekyi Aboagye* are celebrated, together with those of *Bosum* Pra himself. *Tekyi Aboagye* is an ancient deity, but no one remembers anything about him except that his rites must be celebrated. They cannot, however, isolate his rites from those of *Bosum* Pra.

On this Monday, about four in the afternoon, the priest places a pot of foaming palm-wine, a bundle of firewood, a gong-gong, and the priest's antelope-skin hat outside his compound beside a lump of sacred ironstone. A little later he comes out, dons the hat, and parades up and down the street beating the gong-gong and shouting '*Bosome ko sareso, Ei !*'

Then a party of drummers and others assemble in the priest's yard and emerge in procession. Small boys carry firewood, two pots of palm-wine, two stools, a bundle of faggots and creeper-twine. The old priest himself wears white calico and his antelope hat and a small boy holds an umbrella over him. Immediately after him follows a white-clad male *akomfo* (medium). When I saw the festival, a female *akomfo* of *Bosum* Tano (another river), who happened to be in the town on a visit, followed the *Bosum* Pra *akomfo*.

The procession left the town and made for the forest. When it reached a stream someone carried the priest over on his back. In a cleared grove on the edge of the forest the party halted beneath a great *wawa* tree beside which was a tiny fenced enclosure. Under the tree stood a black water-pot of an ancient pattern no longer in common use. The priest's stool and the whitened stools of the two mediums were set under the tree and opposite them the drummers arranged themselves. The drums were of the small under-arm kind and the kind consisting of a leather stretched over the mouth of a large round calabash.

After a little drumming and singing the chief and his elders arrived, bringing not their elders' *asipim* chairs but common chairs. There was no royal grandeur. The chief had no umbrella, no gorgeous cloth or chief's sandals, but wore a dingy cloth and old gym-shoes. The chief and every stool-holder was accompanied by a bearer with a bundle of firewood on a tray and a pot of palm-wine. Each *akomfo* and then the chief and elders offered their palm-wine one by one to the priest. Each gift of palm-wine was poured into the big pot at the foot of the tree to the accompaniment of a prayer by the priest—inaudible in all the drumming and cries of approval.

The attendants meanwhile had been using their sticks and twine to make supports for a tall firewood stack. The gifts of firewood were then offered one by one to the priest and were stacked on the pile. Firewood is the symbol of submission.

Then the priest's party came and bowed their thanks to the donors of palm-wine. The priest prayed again and the whole company returned home. The priest was again carried over the stream, but the chief and elders had to wade.

The next day everyone in the town rose early to mourn for the dead. The women cried and wailed aloud, the men sat mourning and weeping quietly. Later in the morning there was a session of drumming in the chief's yard. Talking-drums recited the exploits of the dead and the leopard-drum snarled its praise of their valour. Ordinary people all went to their farms to fetch enough food for the following day when no one might go to his farm. Women and children took stools, wooden mortars, and clothes down to the stream to wash. The old priest's gong-gong and antelope hat lay all day in the street beside the lump of ironstone.

In the afternoon, mourning gave place to 'play'—drinking, clowning-processions, and scurrilous songs. At nightfall the priest emerged again, donned his hat, took his gong-gong and paraded the street four times. On his fourth journey he ordered silence in the town : there was to be no sound of drums, bells, or *fu-fu* beating, shouting, or singing. Then he came back into his compound accompanied by a crowd of young men and their drums. There they had a short final burst of drumming, and then all noise miraculously subsided and everyone went home in silence.

After dark the priest in his yard kindled a new fire of three logs laid radiating from a point. All the townspeople quenched the fires in their own yards, swept the hearths, and threw the ashes out at the end of the town. Then they flocked to the priest's yard, each bearing a log or stout spar of wood. Each man laid his wood in the priest's fire till it was well alight, the massed wood making a splendid bonfire. Then everyone dragged out his own flaming brand and ran home with it, bringing 'the new fire' to his own compound. Those unable to come to the bonfire secured new fire from their neighbours, but none of the old year's fires was allowed to stay unquenched.

Then an impressive silence settled on the dark town. The

next morning all was quite still. No one went to farm, no one shouted or sang. There was plenty of eating but no drinking.

In the afternoon there was another assembly in the priest's yard and another procession to the edge of the forest. The priest's party sat in the grove and was joined by the elders. Then a messenger with a decorated hatchet was sent 'to tell the river' what the town was doing. After he had returned there was a short 'palaver' of elders so that all the old year's affairs might be settled before the new year began. The palaver in question was a small matter of the resignation of an official and the appointment of his successor, already arranged but not finally announced. This announcement was made and followed by another one declaring that all the old year's palavers were now over.

Then the elders gave presents of rum. The priest took this rum by himself down to the river and poured it on the ground. No one else was allowed to go to the river on that day.

Then the priest's party, including several washers of the priest's and *akomfos' kra*, wearing large gold sun-medallions on white lanyards, filed past the elders and thanked them for the rum.

The company returned to a town still in silence. The next morning silence still prevailed. Any townspeople wanting to pound *fufu* for their meals pounded it as quietly as possible and outside their yards, because 'on that day the *abosum* is in people's houses'. In the morning people went round visiting their friends, exchanging new-year greetings and congratulating one another on having survived to see another year.

In the afternoon the procession to the forest was repeated and, on returning, the whole company halted just inside the town. There they waited, masses of silent people lining the streets. Then the old priest went off by himself to the forest to fetch the yam which he had secretly dug by night and hidden in the forest. Meanwhile the attendants fetched the priest's processional chair—a wooden chair on poles. Everyone stood waiting in silence, backs turned to the direction whence the priest would come, all in a bowed position with covered eyes or clothes over their faces, for no one might behold the new yam till the priest gave the signal.

At last the priest approached, and approaching gave a warning shout, whereupon all eyes were still more tightly closed till he had seated himself in the waiting chair and been raised by the bearers. The bearers gave three rousing yells, and eyes were uncovered to behold the priest seated above the heads of the crowd and holding aloft two new yams fixed in a bent cane. The crowd burst into a frenzy of cheering, the drums crashed into life and the crowd went mad, surging round the uplifted chair. Slowly the chair was borne through the mass of dancing, waving and cheering people. The spirit came on all the *akomfos* and they too were carried shoulder-high, trembling, struggling, and prophesying. On reaching the street outside the priest's house the *krontihene* appeared, carried in another shouldered chair which was brought alongside the priest's. Amid renewed cheers the priest handed over the yam and the *krontihene* received it on behalf of the townspeople. The *krontihene* handed the yam to another old man, also held shoulder-high. This old man broke an egg over the yam and then carried it into the priest's yard, wrapped it in white calico and hid it. The *krontihene* was then carried back into his own yard and the priest into his. The festival was ended.

For some reason which I have been unable to discover, Assene differs from most of the neighbouring towns in having an air of prosperity, energy, enterprise, health, and interest in life. The people themselves attribute this to the blessing of *Bosum* Pra and they keep the festival enthusiastically and carefully, all absentees flocking joyfully home for it. Like most other towns, they have a shrine of *Kupo* [1] but, unlike the others, they take little notice of it. 'It is only a small boy,' they say. 'We don't really need it, for we have a bigger and better god of our own, and he protects us from all the evils that trouble other towns.'

Other Survivals of Ntro Ceremonial

A certain amount of other *ntro* ceremonial fragmentarily survives, detached from the paternal kinship grouping.

For instance, the *Dabenhene* has in his stool-room a basin-shrine of the River *Akom* and performs for it an annual ritual at the time of his stool festival. He said '*Akom* is washed by some people as an *ntro*, or it can be worshipped as an *abosum*.'

Again, one town has in its stool-room a shrine which they said was of the 'River *Tweneboa*'. The caretaker said 'We worship it every year. It is the same *Tweneboa* that some people wash as an *ntro*. We have no people of the *ntro* Tweneboa in this town, but we worship it as an *abosum*.'

[1] See Chap. XIII.

Surviving Lore of the Ntro Paternal Groups

I have said that the *ntro* as an organized and exogamous group is now extinct, and that many people do not even know to which *ntro* they belong. Many, however, do know, and remember assisting in ceremonies of washing the *ntro*, but they say it is seldom done now. I gathered that occasionally in times of desperation—for instance, if a miscarriage is threatened—it may occur to someone that an *ntro* washing might be beneficial and then, if anyone remembers how to officiate, it is done. No one nowadays cherishes a brass basin [1] for washing his *ntro*. The Abenase *krontihene* had one but could hardly be said to cherish it, for when I asked to see it he found it in a corner of the yard, battered and half full of dirt.

But all the people who remembered anything about their *ntro* were quite willing to tell me all they knew and seemed rather amused that I should be interested in this obsolete lore. Many of them were confused between their venerated animal and their tabooed animal, though a few knew enough to be quite clear about the distinction. The venerated animal, they said, 'is the animal that we respect like our grandfather. If we find it lying dead we wrap it in white calico and bury it with rum and with weeping as if it were our father.' Of the tabooed animal they said, 'We don't touch it. It is unclean. If we find it caught in one of our traps we turn our backs and go away, leaving the trap for ever. We never eat it because it is unclean. Our white calico animal we never eat because it is our father.'

They also told me that there was an ancient custom of giving a special greeting to people who belonged to a particular *ntro*. Some of these greetings are still in daily use but often seem to be given indiscriminately.

I give a summary (Chart C[3]) of the *ntro* details which I collected, as some of them do not seem to have been recorded before. I do not consider them important, for the *ntro* has now no social significance. I give them simply as antiquarian's lore which might possibly have some future usefulness in mapping the migrations of peoples or the spread of cults. It is noticeable that the information given in this district does not always agree with that given to Dr. Rattray in Ashanti.[2]

General Veneration of Rivers

Although the systematic ceremonial for most rivers is now so fragmentary and in the hands of such small groups that it

---

[1] Rattray describes these cherished basins of Ashanti. *Ashanti*, Chap. II.
[2] *Ashanti*, Chap. II.   [3] See pp. 202–204.

may be regarded as a survival hardly related to the present day, the general day-by-day veneration of rivers by the populace is unabated.

Every stream has one day in the week on which no one draws water from it and no stream or river is ever used as a rubbish-tip or polluted in any way. Menstruous women may not enter streams but must hand their water-pots to others for filling. Should such a woman enter a stream secretly, it is believed that the water would rise angrily in an unusual flood. An *Akomfo* would then be consulted, become possessed and announce the cause of the river's displeasure. The town gong-gong would then be beaten, warning all women against the offence, and reminding them that further annoyance of the river would cause it to drown someone.

A story is told of an Abenase woman who quite recently was dipping water from one of the neighbouring brooks when she suddenly felt an invisible hand give her a blow on the head. She fell down unconscious and lay till someone found her and took her home. She recovered consciousness and told her story, but died the following day. There was no *akomfo* available for consultation, but the chief sent round his gong-gong beater, saying that probably someone had polluted the stream and that it must not happen again.

When in the normal flood season the stream rises so high that it prevents people from crossing to their farms, the town sub-scribes to give it a sheep, for it is clearly angry and, if not appeased with a voluntary sacrifice, will take one for itself by drowning somebody.

Where a river has an annual ceremonial this is always in the charge of the local *asasewura*, and is thought of as connected with the land. 'The river is the land's husband, and the river is related to the rain,' said one informant. 'The land cannot bring forth without the river just as you cannot make writing unless you have pencil as well as paper.'

The same informant added, 'The rivers all get big, strong, and active at the time of the big rains, so we know that the rivers are the children of the rain.'

Onyame, the so-called 'Sky-God' or 'Supreme God', would, I believe, be more correctly called the rain god and is supreme only because the rivers are the 'children' of the rain and because rain is of supreme importance to life. '*Nyame* is coming' (*Nyame oreba*) is often said when rain is falling, and a stranger whose arrival coincides with a needed shower of rain is called '*Nyame ba*'—a child of *Onyame*. If rain falls on the day of a death or

immediately after a burial it is said that *Onyame* has blest the
spirit of the departed.

Town and Stool Festivals

Kwesidae in Abenase

As all readers of Rattray know, the stool festival of *Kwesidae* [1]
is held every six weeks on a Sunday.

In Abenase it is not so grand as are, we read, the Ashanti
festivals, but it is an occasion on which anyone who has an
important position in the town must leave his village—or any
other place he may be visiting—and come home. No one may
work on his farm on this day.

The *Ohene's* stool is not the only one in the town which
celebrates *Kwesidae*. Every *asafohene* has a right to hold a *Kwesidae*
for his own ancestors' stool and to sacrifice a sheep just as does
the *ohene*. As a rule, however, the smaller stools are content
with rum and a brief prayer and receive a sheep only at the time
of *Afahye*.

While I was in Abenase, however, not even the *ohene's* stool
received a sheep at *Kweisidae* festivals, for it was said that the
Omanhene's funeral had made sheep too scarce and costly.

Preparations for the festival were begun on the Saturday when
the stool-carriers brought out all the *asipim* chairs and all stools
other than the blackened ones.[2] These were washed, rubbed
with cut limes, and set outside to dry.

Early the next morning the *Katamanton* drum was beaten to
bid the elders prepare to assemble. For the next few hours
small boys enjoyed their feast-day licence to beat all the drums
which ordinarily stand in an alcove of the chief's courtyard.
'That is how we find out which boys are going to grow into
good drummers and that is how the young drummers get
practice.'

Then the official drummers appeared, drove off the youngsters,
beat the *Katamanton* to tell the elders the assembly was beginning,
tapped out the stock recitations diligently on the talking drums
and set the whole building vibrating to the deep bass boom of
the great *fontomfrom* drums.

Then the *asafohene* and the other elders appeared, one by one,
accompanied by their *asipim* chairs, and sat in their customary
places in the court. Later the *ohene* and the queen-mother
appeared. With the *ohene* came the horn-blower blowing the
horn decorated with human jawbones ; the ancient drum of

---

[1] *Ashanti*, Chap. VII.   [2] See Rattray, *Ashanti*, Chap. V.

Otu Ayipe Frimpong, hung around with human thighbones, also appeared, and the talking drums greeted it with the lament for the 'old man'.

'*Otu Ayipe Firimpong, Damirifa, damirifa. Due, due.*'

The drums continued beating. No one danced except the old man who sits on the steps of the chief's dais waving an elephant's tail switch as he has done at all assemblies since he was a small boy some eighty years ago. His sense of importance has waxed as his agility has waned, and when he returns his stiff old limbs to his seat after each dance there is ironical applause.

After more drumming the assembly rose and the *ohene* and 'big people' retired to the private part of the building where is the stool-room. On presentation of rum I was allowed to see the stools in their own room.

It was a tiny room : the three black stools, each on a little low table, nearly filled it. In the centre stood *Otu Ayipe's* war-stool on which every Abenase *ohene* is enstooled. To the left was the *Gyasehene's* stool and to the right the queen-mother's. Ordinarily they lie on their sides, but on festival days the dead are 'called' by standing the stools upright. On one stool lay a corroded short sword and a worn hand-brush. In a corner of the room near the stools lay the 'war-medicine' brought from the old home in Denchera. This war-medicine is called *Penyina* and looked to me like a lump of the ironstone conglomerate often used for altars, but of course it was thickly varnished with dried blood.

The story of *Penyina* is that while the people were still in Denchera and at war with Ashanti a man named *Kweku Bronsam* went into the forest one day and suddenly came upon a beautiful little clearing. Feeling certain that it had been supernaturally cleared and swept, he went home and told the chief—*Ayipe Panyim*—and his elders. They took a brass pan and a sheep, visited the clearing with great reverence, sacrificed the sheep, put the blood into the pan and left it. The next day they went again and were astonished to find that the blood had gathered itself into a hard round ball which lay in the centre of the pan. Then *Kweku Bronsam* became possessed like an *akomfo* and announced that the spirit of the thing in the pan had come upon him. The spirit spoke through the tongue of *Kweku Bronsam,* saying, 'My name is *Penyina.* I will be yours and I will be with you in battle.' When they reached home the spirit of the thing in the pan again came upon *Kweku Bronsam* and lashed him into a frenzy of supernatural bravery. In this state he seized a gun and set off for Ashanti in order to 'kill the *Ashantihene*'. He brought home a head, which head was sent to the *Omanhene*—then at Miriem in Denchera—and the skull was hung on his drum. It remained there during all the migrations of the Denchera refugees and is still on the *Omanhene's* drum in Oda to-day.

In earlier days the *Penyina* war-medicine had a male *akomfo* who used to become possessed when he carried it on his head, and while possessed uttered prophesies about warfare. When the stool went to war the stone went too, on the *akomfo's* head, and gave instructions during the battle. Since the last *akomfo*, whom the older people all remember, died, no other has been appointed.

When rum, prayers, drumming, and horn-blowing had been offered to the stools a tray of food arrived from the queen-mother who does the stool cooking. After speeches to the stools, egg-and-yam food was sprinkled on and in front of the stools and other food was set in bowls in front of each. When it had stood there for an hour or so the ghosts were assumed to have eaten such of its invisible essence as they desired and the visible remainder was taken by the *okyeame* and given to the chief's *kra*-washers, and, after bathing themselves and donning all their insignia, they ate it.

Here I may digress into a few remarks on these *kra*-washers, and must preface them with a short account of the dogma of human personality.

A person is believed to be compounded of two entities, the *sunsum* and the *kra*. The *sunsum* is a kind of twin, of which one component is good and the other bad. If the bad one gets in control it leads the person into all sorts of sin and trouble. In dreams and mind-wandering the *sunsum* can leave the body.[1]

The *kra* is that spirit which makes the difference between a dead body and a live body. Animals have *kra*, germinating eggs have *kra*. When the *kra* is enfeebled or injured ill-health results. If witches prey on it the victim pines: if they eat its arm or leg the victim loses the use of the corresponding physical limb. If they eat the *kra* completely the victim dies. Ordinary death corresponds with the departure of the *kra* from the body and the person then becomes a *saman*, or ghost.

The material substance of body and blood is held to be supplied

---

[1] This differs somewhat from the Gã conception of a person's make-up. According to the Gã a person has a *kla*, one *susuma*, and a *gbeft*. The *kla* is identical with the Akan *kra*, the *susuma* is of neutral quality and can be acted upon by various influences, good or bad; it appears to be in many ways the equivalent of the 'unconscious' of the new European thought. The *gbeft* can be either a good destiny or a bad parasitic, preying thing which must be detached and driven away if possible, It has some correspondence with the European 'complex'.

by the mother, the quickening *kra* by the father. Children of the same father have the same *kra* and perform the ceremonial for the welfare of that *kra*, which welfare used to be closely bound up with the worship of the paternal *Obosum*.[1]

An ordinary person is supposed to be able to look after his own *kra* and that of his children, but the *kra* of a chief is said to be exposed to greater dangers than that of an ordinary person. His enemies are more numerous and more powerful. Special officials are therefore appointed to look after his *kra*, to wash it, feed it and revive it should it show signs of flagging. Those officers, who are sometimes spoken of as the 'washers' of the chief's *kra* and sometimes as if they themselves were identical with that *kra*, are of both sexes, and on ceremonial occasions wear a uniform of white calico [2] and a gold disc [3] on the chest hung round the neck on a whitened lanyard.

Nowadays a chief is inclined to rely on imported medicines and magics for the protection of his life and health, so the washers of his *kra* are seldom called into action. Though I have often seen them in their ceremonial garb I have not seen them at their special work.

To return to the festival: though I did not see a sheep slaughtered for *Kwesidae* I was told that the ritual was exactly the same as the *Afahye*, so I may describe that here.

A libation is first poured for the stool and then the sheep is lifted and lowered three times before the stool with an invitation to the dead to come and receive it. Then its throat is cut and the spurting blood is sprinkled on the stools and medicines.

When the carcase is cut up, the shares are always distributed in the same way.

The *okyeame* receives t' e thorax and windpipe 'to help him to make talk'.

The stool-carrier receives the head, all except the lower jaw, 'to strengthen his head for carrying the stool'.

The horn-blower receives the lower jaw.

The heralds receive the heart and lungs.

The chief's sons receive the neck.

The *krontihene* and all the other *asafohenes* receive the upper part of a hind leg between them, because 'the *ohene* is the head and they are the legs'.

The chief's nephews receive the upper part of one front leg.

---

[1] See p. 151.

[2] White calico is, I suspect, always a sign of derivation from the pre-military or pre-stool system of worship.

[3] These discs are some four inches in diameter, are often beautifully decorated, and are reminiscent of the brass discs worn by shire horses at English horse shows.

The queen-mother receives the upper part of the other front leg. Out of this she must cook a meal for the stools.

Bearers of the *afra* symbols receive the lower parts of all the legs.

The chief receives the haunches 'because he sits'. This share is laid for a time in front of the stool before the chief receives it.

The bearers of the cow-tail and elephant-tail switches receive the centre of the back.

The drummer of the war-drum (*odom-bebabetomi*) receives the hide.

The carriers of the chief's palanquin receive the strip of flesh from the back of the neck.

An interesting innovation at the Abenase *Kwesidae* is the giving of food and rum to the chief's new 'medicine-stool'. Of this new stool I shall have more to say later.

Another innovation was the extension of the *Kwesidae* festival to the new deity, *Kupo*, of which again I shall have much to say. The *krontihene* and his assistants dressed up in their new Northern Territory tunics and gave rum to *Kupo*. They did not kill a sheep, but they said they would have done so if sheep had not been so scarce. A little crowd of people, all of whom were under the protection of *Kupo*, came and sat in the enclosure in front of the shrine. Many of them brought small gifts of pennies and kola-nuts. So far as the populace was concerned there was more enthusiasm for *Kupo* than for the stool.

Ahahye and Odwira in Abenase

In the middle of December the towns all celebrate their annual *Odwira* and *Afahye* festivals.

The observer's difficulty about a general festival is that he can be in only one place at a time. I chose to see Abenase's festival though I had been told that it was much more elaborate than most [1] and therefore not typical. Nkwanta, however, held its festival on a different day, and I was able to see this too. I was told that most festivals were like that of Nkwanta.

Early on Odwira morning in Abenase the *Katamanton* drum is beaten in the manner that denotes 'something unusual', and the talking drums call the name of the present chief, adding '*Damirifa, damirifa, due, due.*' This means 'I am sorry for you,'

---

[1] This may be because it contains more of the aboriginal element than most, Abenase being composed of both aborigines and immigrants. The Abanese festival has a few points of resemblance to the *Bosum* Pra festival at Assene. See p. 152.

and offers commiseration to the present chief on the loss of his ancestors.[1]

As soon as the populace hear this call to mourning, the women start to weep and wail for the dead, particularly for those only lately dead.

This weeping is brief and then the women go to their farms to fetch food, but nobody does any work there. Produce is fetched from the farms of the newly dead, and it is gathered and carried home amid loud crying and wailing.

The food is kept for the following day—which is *Afahye* day. *Odwira* is a day of fasting. No fufu may be pounded, and if the people eat at all it must be plain dry food and eaten in private. The day is often known as a *Boada* day. It is held that no one can sleep soundly on an empty stomach, and *boada* means to pretend to sleep.

During the morning of *Adwira* day, the chairs and stools of the chief and elders are washed. In the afternoon and evening there is an assembly in the chief's yard where the drums are all beaten and the talking-drums recite praises of the dead and affirm the sorrow of the living. On this occasion the chief himself dances a solo dance of mourning, and so does the queen-mother. Various dances of pantomime sorrow are performed by people who have lost friends during the year.

In the evening people bring disputes and other cases to the chief or to elders. These cases are heard without fee and 'peace is set' between adversaries so that everyone may enter the new year without strife or anger in his heart. Kinsmen in particular must be in harmony with one another when they give food to the dead. As one man put it, 'Our ancestors will not eat the food if we are not of one mind when we give it. And if they do not eat it they will bring ill upon us.'

All these peace-making 'cases' are heard in secret: in fact, the courts on that day are confessionals to purify the hearts and consciences of the worshippers in readiness for the next day's ceremony.

On the last *Odwira* day in Abenase the chief's uncle (to whom I referred in Chap. II) called the elders together in private and asked if they had received any offence from the chief during the year, urging them, if they had, to speak of it and not harbour it in resentment. My informant added, 'We all looked through

---

[1] Rattray translates '*Damirifa, damirifa, due, due*' as 'Alas, alas: woe, woe.' The phrase is, however, not a mere cry of anguish but of condolence and compassion for another. '*Due, due*' is said soothingly to children who have hurt themselves, while Mr. Ribeiro Ayeh tells me that '*Damirifa*' means 'The wild dog has got you,' death being here pictured as a kind of hound of heaven.

our heads, but found no offence. So the chief's uncle gave us a bottle of rum.'

The next day was *Afahye* day. Early in the morning the gong-gong was beaten round the town telling the women to prepare food to take to the *ebem* grove and the men to go and prepare tables for it.

While they are doing this the important women of the town go round 'playing *Adowa*'. The leader of the *Adowa* company told me, '*Adowa* is the chief of all town playing. We believe that all the dead who played it in the past come and join whenever it is played. It calls them to come and play, and they always long to join in their own play. If we leave out *Adowa* we are not inviting the dead to the festival. We never play *Adowa* frivolously, only to call the dead. At any time other than *Afahye* you may not play *Adowa* unless you sacrifice about ten sheep. We start the playing in the town, but we always finish on the outskirts, believing that next year the town will have grown and there will be a new house where we stop.

'Every house should have an *Adowa* player and every *asafohene*, *okyeame*, and big man must have an *adowa*-player among his relatives. The chief's drum must always come with the *adowa* company.

'It is the women who sing and dance *Adowa*, but the men also belong to the company. They help to drum, but it is not their play. It was the ancient play attached to the women's stools.

'On *Afahye* day we *Adowa* players go first to the queen-mother's house and she gives us rum. Then we go to the elders' houses and they give us money. Nowadays we use the money for rum, but in the ancient days it was salt. We that live eat salt : the dead do not. We never put salt in food for the dead. When the *Adowa* play is over and the women go home the first thing they do is to taste salt. This is what we call "tasting the year". The men do not taste the year. In the olden days salt was too valuable to give to women and they never ate it except when they tasted the year. In those days we valued salt above gold dust, for we could dig gold dust out of the ground.'

Later in the morning the chief's drums were beaten and any young people's musical club might go round singing, dancing, and collecting contributions. For instance, there is a young people's society—I believe of recent origin—called *Ayika*, which specializes in new songs and scurrilous songs, and is essentially a society for 'bright young things'. *Ayika* means 'You are in debt'—for, as my informant put it, 'they all buy fancy things for their play—grand clothes, perfume, and comic drums.'

About noon the carpenter, who had made most of the town's coffins during the year, came and called on me. I was just about to greet him when he burst into floods of such violent tears that I thought he had come to break some appalling news. However, the tears were purely ceremonial, and on account of the town's dead whose coffins he had made. His own family had suffered no bereavement during the year.

In the early afternoon the *ohene* and every *asafohene* killed a sheep for his stool, rolled three balls of new yam and placed them upon the stool. There was no other 'yam custom' than this though the festival is ostensibly a yam festival. On this day people send the *ohene* and the *asafohenes* sixpences and ask to have their names mentioned for blessing when rum is given to the stools.

I did not see any of the ceremonial for the *asafohenes'* stools, as I chose to attend the *asasewura's* ceremony at the riverside, which took place at the same time as the stool ceremonies.

The *asasewura's* ceremony was performed, not by that elder himself, lest he should make some small mistake in the ritual and die in consequence, but by a younger relative.

It was very simple with no pomp. The only people who went were two representatives of the *Asasewura*, a woman carrying a fowl and food, and myself.

We reached a bamboo grove beside the river Esu Kese, and there the worshippers hunted about for the brass pan which is left there from year to year. The ground was soft, had been flooded, and was covered with bamboo driftwood and river debris. I thought the pan must surely have been washed away, but when I said so they told me that the river knew all about the pan and made a point of looking after it. And, sure enough, it turned up about 20 yards from its right place, embedded in the ground and filled with dried mud.

They cleaned it and filled it with river-water, poured rum into it and prayed :

'*Esu kese Afua, bra be gye nsa yi nom. Afe aso, wonsa ni, be gye nom, wo duan ni, wo koko nso ni, ma ye nkwa ni ahua den. Maye ahua den na afi drua ye tumi ye abe ma wo aduan. Kwesi Enim nkwaso, Obloni nkwaso, Ohene nkwaso, Abraseman nkwaso.*'[1]

Then the fowl's head was cut off and blood was made to drip into the pan and on the ground but not into the river. The carcase of the fowl was then bisected lengthways so that each

[1] Esu kese Afua, come and take your wine. We have reached the end of the year, here is your wine, come and take it, here is your food, here also is your fowl, give us life and strength. Give us strength so that at the end of next year we may be able to give you food. Life to Kwesi Enim, Life to the European, Life to the Chief, Life to Abenase.

half included a leg and a wing. Half of it was laid beside the pan 'for the river' with the words, '*Wo koko ni, Esu kese Afua*'— Here is your fowl, Oh great river Afua. The cooked food was sprinkled in the river and on the banks with furthur prayer.

Then the party returned home to the *Asasewura's* house. The *Ohene* was not allowed to proceed with the rest of the town ceremonial till he had the *Asasewura's* message that the river had received its dues. The *Asasewura* appeared to take pleasure in keeping the *Ohene* waiting, and took his bath and decked himself in a leisurely manner before he sent his message.

Meanwhile all the women in the town had been cooking meat stew and pounding yam fufu, and the men had erected tables of trimmed boughs in the *ebem* grove—one table for each *asafohene's* group, and a few extra ones for 'big people' who had a table apiece.

In the chief's house some curious old war equipment was brought out—silver-mounted cartridge belts and knives, bandoliers with silver bells, elephant-tail switches with silver wire instead of elephant-hair. The *ohene's* attendants adorned themselves with these, and everyone entitled to any sort of ceremonial garb or insignia appeared with it. Twins wore their white calico, the *kra*-washers their sun-medallions of silver or gold. The *ohene* dressed in a velvet cloth and a velvet cap with gold decorations, and was heavily festooned with various medicines and amulets, most of them recent acquisitions from Dahomey and elsewhere. He had iron bracelets, leather armlets, and three leather necklaces all from the Northern Territories, a medicine cow-tail switch in one hand and a swinging arrangement of cowries in the other. He was carried sitting in a boat-shaped palanquin of cane covered with coloured cloth. In front of him went a junior stool-bearer with his ordinary traditional white stool, but to the head stool-bearer was entrusted the new-fangled medicine-stool. This stool[1] is a fantastic object hung all over with folded paper charms written in Hausa script, a multitude of tiny mirrors, squares of red and green felt, little leather-covered packages of medicine and a cow-tail decoration.

The procession to the *ebem* grove was headed by a multitude of women carrying dishes of food on their heads. In all processions the lowliest members lead and the seniors are at the tail. After the women came a batch of stools and then more women with the queen-mother and more stools and chairs. Then came the *asafohenes* and the *okyeames* with their gold-headed staves. Next came the *gyasehene*, carried on bearers' shoulders. After him came the *ohene*, carried in his palanquin, and, last of all, the *asasewura*, carried on the shoulders of his kinsmen. The *asasewura's*

[1] See p. 176.

part of the procession was strikingly lacking in grandeur
and had no war equipment. He afterwards explained, 'We were
here before the others came. We were quiet people and we did
not know war'. He carried only a small cow-tail switch with
cowries on the handle. Surrounding him danced and cheered
not only his own *abusua* but all the townsmen of slave origin.
I afterwards asked why, for the *asasewura's* blood is accounted
as noble as any. I was told, 'He was here so early that he does
not know whence he came. The "strangers" also do not know
their origin, so they go with him.'

On reaching the grave the chief sat on his *asipim* chair and the
other elders on theirs. Each *asafohene* offered rum and a prayer
inviting his dead kinsmen to come and eat. A vessel of water
was given before each dish of food was laid on the table so
that the invisible eater might first wash his hands. Those of the
dead whose names were remembered, whether by virtue of their
being ancient and famous or recent and familiar, were given a
dish apiece and called by name to come and eat it. Those not
remembered by name were assumed to be invited by the others
to come and share. 'The big ones will themselves call their
small boys to come and join them in eating.' When an *asafohene*
poured his libations he said : 'Grandfather So-and-so, this is
your food. Wash your hands, come and eat, and give us strength
so that we can wait upon you another year.'

Each *asafohene's* group had its own table : departed chiefs
and queen-mothers had a separate one. Strangers of no pedigree
who had died after long residence in the town were given food
by other 'strangers', but had their own table apart from the clan
tables.

Then a sheep was slaughtered and the blood was sprinkled on
the royal table.

The procession then formed again and left the grove. By
this time it was nearly dark and the sky was ink-black with an
approaching storm. Everyone was excited and deeply moved
by the ceremony. One of the older *okyeames*—normally the most
self-possessed of people—broke down and sobbed loudly on the
way back. Two of the stool-carriers were possessed like *akomfos*
and charged madly back and forth. Even the chief, whom I
had thought nothing could energize, rocked in his palanquin
and slashed about with his two switches. When the palanquin
reached the gate of his yard he performed the difficult feat of
standing up in it while it was still held shoulder-high and dancing
to 'show his strength'. I was told that 'chiefs who are not
powerful fall out when they try to do that.'

16. One of the new shrines. (*See* page 179.)

15. The drums which stand in an alcove of the chief's compound. (*See* page 159.)

The people were now free to eat the new yam, drink, and dance. The next day 'play' societies, such as *Ayika*, paraded the town and collected contributions.

The dishes of food were left on the tables in the *ebem* grove for seven days, at the end of which time vultures had overturned all the dishes and finished the food. The dishes were then washed, smoked in the fire, and stored in the rafters of the houses for the next year.

Here, as elsewhere in the Gold Coast, it is regarded as a great misfortune for anyone to die during the festival. Such a dead person is not buried till afterwards, but his body is laid over his open grave on a raised platform of boughs, and there is no crying for him.

The theory of death during the festival is somewhat different from that held elsewhere. It is not that the death spoils the festival but that the festival spoils the dead man's chances of being suitably received in the next world. During a festival the stools of the ancient and eminent dead, which normally are laid on their sides, are set upon their bases. This calls the dead to come and sit upon them. When anyone dies at an ordinary time, as soon as the body is washed and dressed his relatives cry loudly, as already explained. This crying informs the long dead that a new-comer is approaching and they prepare to receive him. On his arrival he goes first to pay his respects to his *asafohene* and other elders, and these give orders for his comfort and proper installation in his new home. But if he should arrive while the big men and their retinues are all away on earth, there is no one to receive him and he is lost and stranded, until they return from earth at the end of the festival.

Odwira and Afahye in Nkwanta

The gay part of the Abenase festival is the procession to the *ebem*. Everyone in the town goes and no one wishes to be outdone by his neighbour in grandeur. The other towns, however, do not have such a procession. The people feed their dead in their own houses and no one sees if they do it perfunctorily. Nkwanta festival, which I saw, is, I am told, a typical one, and it well illustrates the decay of interest in ancient festivals. People of the coastal plain, whose annual festival is the pivot of the year's activity, would have poured scorn on the proceedings and declared them unworthy of the name of festival.

Early in the morning of *odwira* day at Nkwanta the chief's drums were beaten and women wailed briefly for their dead. This stopped about six in the morning, and for the rest of the day people sat about, ostensibly fasting and remembering their dead. Any small shrines and medicines in private houses were given rum and thanks. The chief should have sat in the open all day, but actually he sat only from about four in the afternoon onwards and then only in his own yard. He said, 'If I sat in the open the people would all have to come, and they don't want to very much.' In the yard the chief's drums were beaten and any youths and boys who felt like dancing came and did so.

The next day—*Afahye* day—the drums were beaten again in the morning and people gave one another New Year greetings. In the afternoon mashed yam mixed with palm-oil was brought to the chief's yard and daubed on the drums, the walls, the stools, and stool-room shrines. Then a sheep was slaughtered for the stool, after which those who liked joined the dancing in the chief's yard.

Everyone who could afford a sheep should have killed one in his own house, but most people said they were too poor.

CHAPTER XIII

THE NEW CULTS

Decline of the Traditional Cults

The special veneration of stools appears to be bound up with social organization on a warfare basis, for the stool was taken to war as a special 'medicine'[1] for bringing victory. The person of the 'Chief' also acquired from the stool magical victory-bringing properties and the worship of dead-and-gone 'chiefs' became a part of stool worship. These dead chiefs and the departed ancestors of the common people are virtually gods and receive prayers for general blessing, life, and fertility.

The stool cult is recent compared with the land and river cults, but as warfare was for several centuries the main pre-occupation of the people, the stool cult almost obliterated the earlier cults in so far as these were organized cults bound up with government and social organization.

The earlier cults, however, survive everywhere disconnectedly. For a long time they survived on an organized basis in the cult of the *ntro*—a cult now virtually extinct in Akim-Kotoku—and in the annual *Afahye* agricultural festival, though the latter became merged in the stool festival of *Odwira*. Fragmentarily the earlier cults still survive in the shape of river and forest worship carried on by small groups detached from the main system of social organization. The largest of these detached fragments is the Assene festival of *Bosum* Pra, and nearly every stream which is a village water supply has someone to give it a small annual sacrifice. The general attitude of the populace to all streams is that they are sacred : no stream is ever polluted and each has a weekly sabbath on which no one may go to it to draw water, to wash, or to fish.

[1] I do not wish to imply that the original and primary significance of the stool among the Akan peoples was that of a war medicine. It was probably first venerated because of its close association with the dead ancestor who had sat on it. That ancestor was asked to confer general blessing on his living descendants, but when warfare became their chief concern victory in warfare became the chief blessing which the ancestor was asked to confer.

However, the Gã, Adangme, and certain Ewe peoples, who adopted war-stools and 'chiefs' much later than did the Akan, adopted them deliberately and primarily as war-medicines and as an essential part of their new and deliberate military organization.

Priests [1] (*Abosomfo*) are now conspicuously absent. In the whole of Akim-Kotoku I met but four who could properly be called priests. One was the priest of *Bosum* Pra at Assene, another was the descendant of the slave who was left behind at Akrofonsu to look after the rites of the Pra when the *Omanhene's* party left to look for a new site. In many towns, chiefs act as occasional priests of those rivers which demand an annual ritual : they also act as the occasional priests of a few ancient river-shrines now kept in stool-rooms as a part of the stool regalia. In towns where the *asasewura* is other than the chief, it is he who acts as priest of the land and local river.

Mediums (*akomfo*) whose work is to be 'possessed' by the spirits of shrines, rivers, stools, the dead and other deities, and to act while so possessed as mouthpieces of these deities, are also few and are becoming fewer. Where any are found in Akim-Kotoku they are usually very old people, and of most deities and old shrines I was told 'The old *akomfo* died a few years ago and the deity has not married a new one.' That is to say, no one has since been possessed by a spirit believed to be that of the deity in question. It has been pointed out by several anthropologists that the utterances of possessed mediums are a valuable condensation of public opinion and an index to the trends of public interest. Where a deity fails to possess a medium at all, it is a clear indication that no one is interested in that deity.

We may say, then, that interest in the archaic, nature-worshipping religion is now disorganized, fragmentary and not bound up with the social organization. We may attribute its decline during two centuries mainly to the swinging over of interest to stool worship and the organization of the community on a military and matrilineal basis round the stool as a centre.

But we now also find considerable decline of interest in stool ritual and such associated festivals as *odwira*. This is partly to be expected, for the stools were mainly concerned with warfare, and the *pax Britannica* has wiped this out. But both stools and departed chiefs are still virtually gods, and at *Odwira* and *Addae* festivals are supplicated as givers of fertility and general blessing. Why then have they so declined ?

Is the reason for this decline Christianity and education ? I think certainly not. Apathy towards traditional ceremonial is

---

[1] Rattray translated the word *akomfo* as 'priest' or priestess, but I think this term is properly confined to the passive medium or mouthpiece whom the spirit possesses in the course of what Europeans would call an hysterical fit. The true priest who is never so possessed, but takes charge of a deity and its worship, is correctly termed *abosomfo*.

even more noticeable in remote places, where even catechists never go, than in the busier centres where there are both churches and schools. The reason is, I think, that new needs have grown up which the people feel are not met by either the old religion or by Christianity.

And to meet these new needs an entirely new and growing system has appeared within the last twenty years. This I shall now describe.

The New Needs

In the last twenty years there has been in the forest country an enormous increase in preoccupation with witchcraft. On the coastal plains where the ancient gods have not greatly declined, the question asked whenever anyone either dies, is sick, or unfortunate, is, 'What has he done to offend his gods and be so punished?' In Akim the question asked is, 'What envious witch has done this?' The main causes of the increased pre-occupation with witchcraft in Akim are, I think, two : firstly, venereal disease ; and secondly, the cocoa industry. It is my personal opinion that the former, in mining districts and some others, is almost universal, and over most of Akim is alarmingly prevalent. It is responsible for most of the sterility, still-births, and sickly, short-lived infants. It is also responsible for melancholia, marital misery, an embittered outlook on life, and, in general, for most of the neurosis which is the solid substratum of witchcraft. The chief crimes traditionally attributed to witches are the killing of children, the causing of sterility, and the conversion of other people into witches (i.e. neurotics) against their knowledge and will ; it was therefore inevitable that witchcraft should be blamed when first these ills unmistakably increased. The secondary activities attributed to witches include the power to spoil crops, to spoil cocoa fermentations, and to become rich by 'sucking away' the invisible essence of money so that the victim meets financial losses and the spoiler financial windfalls. Witches are some-times even blamed for spoiling the thoughts of prospective European mining companies and causing them to go away and take their money with them. They are also accused of maliciously causing gold and diamonds to retreat so deeply into the earth that prospectors cannot find them. A neurotic and ne'er-do-weel school-boy who failed in his examination told me that envious, illiterate relatives had by witchcraft spoiled his brain. The difference between witchcraft [1] and mere 'bad medicine' is that

---

[1] I have already described Gold Coast witchcraft, as such, in *Religion and Medicine of the Gã People*, and I shall not do so again here. I am here concerned with some recent movements associated with it.

the latter requires palpable apparatus, *suman*, herbs, incantations, and ceremonies : the former works simply by the silent, invisible projection of will by the witch. The power of a bad medicine worker can be destroyed, either by himself or by others, simply by flinging his box-of-tricks into the latrine, but the power of a witch is insidiously seated within himself, works often against his own will, and defies his most earnest and piteous efforts to be rid of it.

The mental effects of venereal disease on the highly-strung African are not sufficiently appreciated. When so afflicted as to be unable to beget children or to persuade a wife to stay with him, he usually turns sour and begrudges other people their children and wives. But wheth... ... becomes neurotic enough to believe himself a destructive witch, ...ng others by wishing, whether he becomes actively malicious enough to purchase bad *suman*,[1] or whether he becomes, as sometimes happens, so desperate that he runs amok with a cutlass, his jealous envy of others is always warring with his better nature, and he is the wretched battle-ground of conflicting emotions.

Not only did the cocoa industry bring an increase in witch-craft but also an increase in plain, ordinary stealing. Both cocoa and the money paid out by the cocoa-buyers to the small farmers are often stolen. The police and all the tribunals know well that the cocoa season is the season of maximum crime. Though a part of this crime can be laid at the door of the liquor on which much of the money is spent, a great part of it is simple theft.

The influx of strangers for cocoa-trading and mining has also increased the tendency of women to be unfaithful to their husbands. New safeguards against adultery and marital infidelity are therefore sought.

Another feature of modern times which is often cited by the people themselves as creating a need for new and supernatural protection is—paradoxically enough—education.

A youth who is selected by an uncle or other relative to be sent to school becomes the object of jealousy and spite, for education is regarded (by those who have it not) chiefly as a means to wealth and advancement in the world of European activities, the African members of which world are frequently thought of as the natural enemies of the illiterate community. Many a literate youth who has failed to do well at school or who at the end of his schooling has failed to make good, attributes his failure to the activities of envious witches in his family.

---

[1] *Suman* have been thoroughly described by Rattray. They are palpable charms and talismans.

Among the patients I have met undergoing treatment by native practitioners have been a number of literates with a paranoic conviction that their relations had spoilt their careers.

The mental troubles of young literates often go much deeper and lie in the inability to reconcile conflicting standards, and consequent feelings of guilt when actions committed under one standard are referred to judgment under the other. The most gravely unbalanced of all the mental patients of native practitioners I have met have been young literates whose histories, when gleaned and unravelled, have disclosed a sense of guilt at the bottom of the whole trouble. One distraught patient, on seeing me for the first time, stared and then screamed out, 'You are white, like god! You have come to judge me, like God. Go away. I fear you. Go away and do not judge me, oh, I beg you, do not judge me!' The warfare between conflicting demands and the discovery that the literate life is exacting and not what it seemed, readily accounts for the special proneness of young literates to become unbalanced. Venereal disease, as a source of neurosis, afflicts literate and illiterate alike.

Privately Owned Medicines to meet the New Needs

The movement to find new supernatural safeguards first took the form of private enterprise. There has since grown up—as I shall later describe—a strong movement for the tribalization of the new safeguards and their establishment under public ownership and official patronage.

A few examples of privately owned medicines [1] and the uses to which they are put may here be given.

In one compound in Abenase was a little fenced enclosure not unlike a pig-sty. In a small curtained space inside this was a medicine. It belonged to a woman who had bought it from some medicine men in Akwapim, and when I first saw it these men were paying it an annual visit in order to test whether its power was still in it or whether any mischance had 'spoilt' it.

The woman told me why she had bought this medicine. A dozen years or so earlier, when her parents were alive, the mother

---

[1] A 'medicine' is controlled by means of magic, a god is moved by means of worship. A medicine is limited in its application but is reliable in its responses within those limits. It is also impartial. Thus far, it is akin to natural phenomena and its practitioners are akin to scientists. The difference between magic and science is that the responses which are believed to be called forth by various manipulations and actions are based, in the one case, on imagination and in the other on observation and experiment.

A god, unlike a medicine, is not automatically or reliably responsive. It has a will and a judgment of its own. It is capricious. It is not limited in its scope.

found that her husband suffered from venereal disease, so she refused to sleep with him. He agreed that this was reasonable and abstained from intercourse with her for ten years. At the end of this time, having taken various remedies, he declared himself cured. The wife was sceptical of the cure and still refused him. Shortly after, the man died. After his death the woman performed the widow's *Boada* ceremony of mourning and separation, and then, unexpectedly, herself died. Shortly afterwards her brother also died and her daughter (my informant) fell sick. Afraid that she also might die, she consulted an *akomfo* to find out the reason for the deaths. She was told that her dead father considered that her mother, having failed to fulfil a wife's rôle for many years, had no right to perform a widow's ceremonial. He had therefore brought a 'case' against her in a court of justice in the world of the dead (*samade*) and she had died in response to a 'summons' to appear as defendant. Her brother also was required as a witness, so he too was summoned. Further evidence was required, so a summons was served on the daughter in the shape of a mortal illness. However, the dead, like the living, cannot penetrate the barrier of a really strong protective medicine, so the daughter hastily procured such a medicine.

The medicine-men told me that this medicine came from Dahomey, and the two tests which they performed on it were also products of Dahomey. One of the tests consisted in the holding aloft of a stick on which were nailed, like two flags or two leaves of a book, a pair of small mats woven of flexible cane. To any leading questions put to this oracle the two leaves swung open to indicate yes and remained closed to indicate no. The other testing apparatus was a small wooden image from which the manipulator, in some obscure manner, produced a squeaking noise, intelligible, he said, to himself. It conveyed nothing to the audience.

Another important modern medicine belonged to the Abenase chief. It consisted of a stool which, unlike the traditional stools, was covered all over with little mirrors and charms. It stood in a room of its own and the chief sat on it for a few minutes daily to absorb its good influence and so be protected from any evil magically projected by enemies. It was also believed to help the sitter to long life, prosperity, and greater strength. 'In these days,' I was told, 'there is much bad influence trying to break down a chief, and he needs more strength to repel it.'

This medicine of the chief's was bought, about fourteen years ago, from the Northern Territories. The chief consulted the elders before buying it and the town contributed towards its purchase. He did not tell me its price, but said it was very expensive. He himself went to fetch it, accompanied by eleven attendants, six of whom he sent back, half-way, because of heavy travelling expenses. He tells me that his successors will inherit this stool and sit on it daily as he does.

This medicine may be said to have usurped the position formerly occupied by the washers of the chief's *kra*.

Few if any chiefs at the present day now consider their stools, their ancestors and their traditional ceremonial sufficient security against the dangers of modern times. One wealthy chief, a literate, told me that he had just returned from a visit to Dahomey in his own car. I did not ask him his mission, but guessed that it was to buy powerful 'medicine'. His subjects afterwards confirmed this guess. It was an open secret that he was a sufferer from venereal disease : he had many young wives but no children. He required magical talismans to cure his barrenness, and to protect him against bad magic, witchcraft, political intrigue and annoyance by the police. He was sent to all the most expensive medicine-men in Dahomey, and the total expenses of the expedition were about a thousand pounds. His subjects sanctioned this expenditure far more readily than they would have sanctioned a much smaller one on roads or water supply. Many other Gold Coast chiefs, including some of the best-educated literates, have protected themselves by similar pilgrimages.

During my stay in Abenase the chief purchased another medicine regarded as important. It had long been known that diamonds could be dug from the ground beside the stream near the town, and the exploitation of these diamonds by a European mining company would have brought the town money. But no such company had come, though several had come prospecting. A medicine was therefore purchased to bring the diamonds to the surface, to influence the will of the prospectors and to frustrate the evil intentions of town enemies who, by magic, might cause the diamonds to recede deep into the earth and the minds of prospectors to be turned elsewhere. This medicine was buried by night in the street outside the chief's house and a sheep was killed over it.[1]

Another example of the awe which new and foreign medicines can command occurred when I had been only a few days in Abenase. Someone had a new umbrella stolen. He reported the theft to the chief and asked the chief to announce by gong-

---

[1] According to the latest news I had from Abenase the medicine had been effective and a European Company had taken up a mining concession and had begun making payments.

gong that if the umbrella was not returned the owner would travel to Lateh in Akwapim and call upon a foreign deity called *Akonodi* of that place and ask him to kill the thief. The announcement was made and the next morning the owner woke to find the umbrella had been put inside the gate of his yard.

Another private medicine was owned by an *asafohene* of Abenase. Its shrine stood behind a kind of hurdle in his yard. He told me all about it. This is what he said :

'About four years ago I was lean and sick and was not prospering. A stranger told me about the god in his country and said that it could cure me. So I travelled there. It was a town called Growi, eleven days' walk from Bontuku, where the French Commissioner is. The god was called *Mesi* and there were hundreds of iron rings on it. The first time I went, they charged me nothing but kola-nuts. They prayed for me and said "You are now blest. Go." So I went home and was no longer sick. The next year I went again and took with me another *asafohene* and my nephew, and together we brought home a shrine to set up here. I took five shillings to thank the god for curing me. When I brought away my own shrine I gave two dogs, one fowl, salt, and tobacco, but no money. I had first to cut the head off the fowl before the god to see if he liked me. The fowl died on its back and not on its breast, so I knew I was accepted. I became the priest of my shrine and the other *asafohene* became its *okyeame*.

'The rules that you must keep if you drink [1] this god's medicine are these : you must not smoke a pipe, you must not go to your wife on the day that you go to the shrine ; you must not steal, practise witchcraft or curse anybody else to death. If you are a witch and you drink the medicine you will die without a warning illness. If you have taken the medicine and your wife is unfaithful to you she will die unless she confesses. The man, her partner in adultery, will not die unless he tells lies about it.

'If anyone else wants to take this medicine, he comes here, splits a kola-nut, and gives sixpence. I then tell the god what he wants. He cuts the throat of a fowl to see if the god agrees and, if so, that is all.

'All my own children have taken the medicine and so have about twenty other people. They are now safe from witchcraft, and if a witch attempts against them, she will die. If she kills their children she will die, but it will not save the children.

'The medicine also puts me in a garden' (i.e. brings me pros-

[1] See p. 182.

perity). 'If an unknown thief steals from me and I call on the medicine to catch the thief it will make him sick, but it will not kill him.'

I saw this private shrine in action only once. One of the nephews who had drunk the medicine robbed another man's game-trap of an antelope. Shortly afterwards he 'got sick in the lungs' and, fearing that further punishment was approaching, he quickly came to the shrine and confessed with a kola-nut and a fowl. He soon recovered.

Publicly Owned Medicines

I have just described a shrine imported by a man for his own benefit and later thrown open to a few of his relatives and friends. So eager are the public to share in the benefits of any new shrine or medicine that promises protection from thieves, illness, loss of children, barrenness and neurosis—most of which evils are attributed to witchcraft—that many an enter-prizing man has recognized such shrines as sound commercial propositions, has set one up, and allows the public to come and partake of its blessing on payment of a fee.

Most of the shrine owners, like my friend who owns the *Mesi* shrine, had no professional interest in medicine before acquiring a shrine. A few of them, however, were already professional practitioners of ordinary herbal-cum-magical medicine. Such professionals were, however, very few in Akim-Kotoku before the shrine fashion set in. Although this older type of medicine-man is so common in other parts of the Gold Coast that I was thoroughly familiar with his kind, I met only one in the whole of Akim-Kotoku—the one whose photograph is facing p. 168. But of the new type of shrine, privately owned but open to the public for a fee, there are now dozens.

When anyone wishes to set up a new shrine, he usually travels to the distant home of one of the gods of the Northern Territory strangers whose reports of their own country first awakened the interest of Akim-Kotoku people in their gods. These strangers are mostly labourers who left their homes in the spirit of adven-turous enterprise, strong vigorous men free from the afflictions weighing so heavily on Akim-Kotoku people to-day. These strangers reported, in particular, that witchcraft was unknown in their country, for their gods protected them against it.

Nature of New Deities

The nature of the new gods in their own home was a matter which seemed worth examining, so I chose two gods whose

shrines were most common in Akim—namely, *Nana Tongo* and
Senya Kupo—and travelled to the Northern Territories to visit
them. *Nana Tongo* I had known in the Gold Coast since 1932,
and knew, even then, that many Gold Coast pilgrims visited his
home. *Senya Kupo* was unknown to me till I worked in Akim-
Kotoku.

The home of *Senya Kupo* is at Senyon, near Bole, that of *Nana
Tongo* in the Tong Hills near Zuarungu. Dr. Rattray [1] has
already described that aspect of *Nana Tongo* which is presented
to most visitors, and Dr. Fortes will no doubt in due time
describe the position of this god and its priest in the social
organization of the tribe. I therefore need only say of *Nana
Tongo* that he seemed to me to be a 'place god' or the *genius loci*
of a hill (or, as the Gã would say, the *dzenmawon* of a hill) and had
long been worshipped as a tribal deity whose work was the same
as the work of a Gã *dzenmawon*—namely, to make the crops grow,
rain to fall, hunger to retreat, and both man and cattle to beget
offspring. Witchcraft, Dr. Fortes assures me, is unknown in
that district.

I visited *Kupo* at Senyon in the company of the god's own
medium (or *akomfo* as Twi-speaking people would describe her).
She was a relative of the Kupo priest and had been staying in
Bole, where I succeeded in making friends with her. She could
speak Twi, and kindly acted as my interpreter at Senyon.

Kupo appeared to be an old tribal deity who had seen better
days. I was told that he was once the head of seven villages
which, because of depletion by an epidemic, had amalgamated
into the one which I visited at Senyon. This consisted of two
blocks of compounds, the people orientated according to what
seemed to be a dual organization. There were two heads, one
apparently more priestly than the other. Each carried a staff,
one carved with a bird, the other with a hyæna. The more
priestly of the two wore white like the priests of the coastal
plains, and did not shake hands. The village was apparently
very old, for the kitchen midden had grown enormous. This
midden was kept beautifully conical and resembled a small
Silbury Hill. Between the two blocks of dwellings was a
simple shrine on the end of the bounding wall of one block, and
nearby grew a sacred tree. Close to the shrine stood a short
clay pillar with a rain-pot in the top. This, they said, was
'for the sun, to make it rain, and to make the crops grow.'
The two priests sat on stone blocks and other people sat on
logs highly polished by many sitters. Fifty yards or so outside

[1] *Tribes of The Ashanti Hinterland.*

the town was a cleared round grove of a type familiar
on the coastal plain. In it were two ironstone fireplaces,
a few heaps of cowries, and some big stones for the priests'
seats. 'Here,' they said, 'we kill and cook cows for *Kupo*.'
Nearby was a huge cairn of wild animals' bones—including
buffaloes' skulls and elephants' jaws—collected by a famous
hunter 'whom *Kupo* used to help to hunt.'

We all sat near the shrine—I well under the tree, for it was
noon and hats were not allowed there. They told me very
little till I had presented a fowl and they had used it to ascertain
whether the god liked me. The priest took the fowl in his
hand, explaining to the god why I had come, then he cut its
throat, sprinkled the blood around and flung the dying bird
before the shrine. Luckily the god expressed approval by
accepting the fowl—that is, the fowl died on its back and not on
its breast—whereupon the whole company became more friendly
and showed me the other grove and answered all my questions.
They said, '*Kupo* has no house except the Earth. He lives inside
the earth and helps the earth to grow crops. No one has ever
seen him, but he goes everywhere. He is a god of the soil and
we give him of our crops for his food. If you belong to him
you must not lie or steal or he will kill you.' *Kupo's* festival,
they told me, was in March, and it appeared to be the important
agricultural event of the year.

A man who had travelled with me from Akim-Kotoku wished
to crave the protection and help of *Kupo*, for he was worried
about enemies who, he thought, were using supernatural means
to injure him. He whispered his troubles to the priest, quite
probably telling him more than he told me, a fowl was slain
on his behalf and his request was laid before *Kupo*. The fowl
indicated *Kupo's* approval and the priest told him that *Kupo*
would now stand by him and prosper him. If satisfied with
Kupo's aid at the end of the year he should return, they told him,
bringing a thank-offering. He gave *Kupo* a small gift then and
there, and departed much happier.

Pilgrims who wish to set up shrines for themselves usually
give the god a bigger gift, but no exorbitant demands are made.

The essential insignia taken away is a pot.

Practitioners who set up shrines in Akim—whether shrines
of *Kupo*, *Tongo*, or any of the other Northern Territory gods—
usually lay out a good deal of money on Northern Territory
robes, spears, gong-gongs, talismans, and other trappings to
impress their customers.

When shrine-keepers subsequently return to the Northern

Territories on pilgrimages of thanksgiving after making money
out of their shrines, they usually bring handsome gifts to the
original priests. *Nana Tongo's* priest has plainly become very
wealthy, and gives more active encouragement to his clients to
return substantial thanks than does *Kupo's* priest. The latter
does not appear to be either wealthy or grasping.

Other very common shrines in Akim are those of *Tigari* and
Asasi. The former comes from the Wa district of the Northern
Territories and the latter from Kontrobo, in the French Ivory
Coast. I have not visited these in their own homes, but from
pilgrims' accounts they appear to be similar to *Tongo* and *Kupo*.

It is thus clear that in their old homes, newly exported deities
are tribal gods with a long-established priesthood and that their
festivals are a tribal affair. They are mainly concerned with
agriculture and fertility, and they know nothing of witchcraft.

But as soon as they are established in Akim they are supposed
to be specially competent to deal with witchcraft, and they
furthermore occupy a curious position between gods and
medicines (*Abosum* and *adru*). In their old homes they act as
gods, that is, as intelligent, reflecting beings who exercise both
caprice and judgment and listen to prayer and to reason. In
their new shrines they act as gods only when they are accepting
or rejecting new adherents, exercising in this both knowledge and
judgment. On all other occasions they act as medicines and
their responses to their adherents' actions are as automatic and
inexorable as the action of a fire in burning the hand put into it.

The new gods are usually called *adru* (medicine) and new
adherents are said to 'drink the medicine' even though no
physical drinking takes place.

I asked what was the difference between what the *adru*, *Kupo*,
could do and what the *abosum*, *Anokyi*, could do, and why they
did not set up shrines of *Anokyi*. I was told 'If you call upon
Anokyi to help you, you must call upon him every time you
want him and tell him what you want. Once you have drunk
Kupo he will protect you from theft, witchcraft, and adultery
without your thinking any more about it. If you have drunk
Kupo and your wife is unfaithful, the medicine will catch her.
Anokyi will catch her only if you make her stand up and swear
by *Anokyi* that she is innocent, saying may he kill her if she be
not. Then, if she is lying, she will die.'

The new shrines therefore are something really new. They
are unlike anything known in Akim before, they are equally
unlike that which they themselves were before they were brought
to Akim.

Tribalization of New Supernatural Safeguards

Many of the new shrines are owned, as I have said, by private practitioners, but a much more interesting development has taken place. This may be called re-tribalization.

In nearly every town in Akim-Kotoku [1] a communally owned shrine has been set up under the ægis of the chief and elders. The elders have first met and decided that the townspeople urgently needed protection from the rapidly growing ills of witchcraft, bad medicine, stealing, and marital infidelity. In Abenase, for instance, the elders decided that too many people were dying because of witchcraft or were troubled by witchcraft, and many nephews were conspiring to kill their uncles so that they might have their cocoa. 'Men still have too much pity to kill their fathers, but cocoa makes them kill their uncles.'

And in nearly every town the chief and elders have resolved to collect enough money to set up a shrine. The people have most willingly subscribed, and sums varying from £40 to £80 have been collected.

As soon as the money is ready, several officials are deputed to travel to the Northern Territories and acquire a shrine for the town. These officials usually include the *krontihene*, and he is made the priest of the new shrine.

The priesthood of the *krontihene* is interesting when we consider the towns of the coastal plains which still retain the essentials of an earlier social organization. To this organization it seems that the Akim towns are now showing some tendency to revert. The coastal towns, up to about one hundred and fifty years ago, had neither stools nor war-chiefs, but had vigorous tribal gods and were ruled by the priests of these gods. Under stress of war they deliberately created war stools, war chiefs and *krontihenes*. Invariably they chose as *krontihene* one of their priests. We now find that Akim towns, which cannot recall a time when they had no stools or no *krontihene*, or when they had a governmental priesthood, are deliberately converting their *krontihenes* into priests.

Some observers of the Gold Coast believe that chiefs and stools have had their day. As the centres of military organization they certainly have, and perhaps they have lost other attributes as well. Some observers also describe new and 'advanced' systems which they hope will appear in place of the declining one. Be this as it may, it is quite certain that a vigorous counter-tide is surging through the great mass of the population and its

[1] Also in Akim-Abuakwa, Akim-Bosome, and elsewhere in the Gold Coast for aught I know.

chiefs. Spontaneously, inarticulately, and without knowledge of what they are doing, they are re-establishing many features of a long-abandoned type of organization.

·The Shrines at Work

When a shrine has been set up, whether it be a town shrine or a shrine owned by a private practitioner, people come to join its fellowship and be taken under its protection. This is called 'drinking the medicine'. The 'drinkers' are charged about a shilling a head and as many fowls as need be. The candidate for protection must cut the throat of a fowl and fling the dying bird before the shrine. If the bird dies breast upwards, the gift is accepted by the god : if the back is upwards the gift is rejected and the candidate is not approved by the god. The rejected suppliant then publicly confesses a few sins and tries again. He repeats this till his gift is accepted. He then drinks the 'medicine'. This may consist of either real water, ceremonially treated by the priest, a herbal bath, the eating of a kola-nut, or being marked on the face with spots of white clay. He is then secure against witchcraft, bad medicine, theft, and adulterous intrigue for the rest of his life, provided he keeps the rules. Anyone who tries to bewitch him, harm him magically, rob him, or entice away his wife, will be 'caught by the medicine'. He himself must practice neither witchcraft, bad medicine, theft, nor adultery, or he will be 'caught' too. Anyone so 'caught' is smitten with sickness : if he confesses quickly and is taken to the shrine and cleansed, he recovers ; if not, he dies.

Many a morning does the word go round the town, 'The medicine has caught somebody,' and the victim is carried to the shrine. Often this victim is a thorough-going neurotic : more often than not he has a rankling guilt complex, and is greatly benefited, if not cured, by confession. Often an astonishing tale of misdemeanours emerges. Nearly always venereal disease is at the bottom of the tales of marital unhappiness, envy, and neurosis.

Workers of 'bad medicine' are often 'caught by the medicine'. I have seen at the shrines amazing collections of apparatus (*suman*) handed over by the penitents. These include *suman* designed to cause other people's death,[1] to cause accidents with

---

[1] In particular, people who wish to kill others often used a 'bad medicine' called '*Ogbaniba*', involving the construction of an elaborate *suman*. This was so frequently used that the *Omanhene* issued a special proclamation concerning the punishment of anyone caught with this *suman* in his possession. An *Ogbaniba suman* was found in the house of a Fanti labourer while I was in Abenase, and, though it was not proved that he had used it locally, he was handcuffed and taken to the *Omanhene*. He never returned to Abenase and I do not know how he was dealt with.

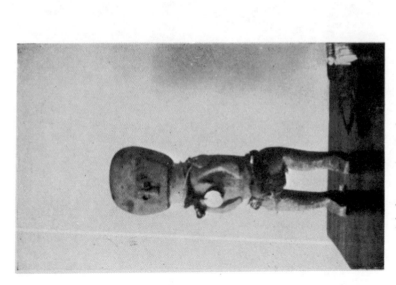

18. One father brought a day-old child.
(*See* page 191.)

17. A bad *suman* given up by a penitent.
(*See* page 184.)

cutlasses, hoes, and motor-lorries, to 'suck away' others' money
and enrich the *suman-owner*, to cause others' wives to leave them,
and to make others unsuccessful in obtaining wives.

Here I may give an example of two of the actual cases brought
before the shrine of *Kupo* in Abenase while I was there.

A woman, quite clearly a 'nerve case', gradually grew more
and more ailing and unbalanced. She became deaf, then she
became unable to stand. At length she called her mother and
confessed that she was a witch (*obeyefo*). She said she had
caused thirteen deaths in her own *abusua*, five in her husband's,[1]
and was planning to kill him also. She belonged, she said, to
a company of witches, some members of her own town, some
of Oda. Their meeting-place was in Accra, whither she was in
the habit of travelling in the spirit in a big touring car—a modern
variation of the witch's 'flying-dream' and the animal-riding
dream. She said it was she who had caused the *okyeame's* wife
to have a long and difficult accouchement, not in order to injure
the wife but in order to make the husband call in expensive
medicine-men and become impoverished. It was she who was
'holding the wombs' of all the barren women in the town so
that they could not conceive children. She had offered to sell
her own child's leg to another witch, but the other had refused
it. The offer was both made and refused in the spirit, without
any physical communication between the two witches. But had
the offer been accepted material money would have come to the

---

[1] It is not now generally believed that witches can kill only members of their
own *abusua*, though some of the older people still propound the theory that it is
necessary for someone of the victim's *abusua* to connive at the deed. This older
theory was given to me as follows :

'The right of killing, both visible and invisible killing, is on the mother's side.
In the olden days a man would call a conditional curse (*hyira*) on a chief, saying
that the chief must die if he did not hear the man's case against another man.
Then when the case was over the loser would be killed. Also his mother and
her brothers and sisters and their children would be killed and the mother's mother
as well if she was not too old for child-bearing. This was to prevent them from
begetting any more children of wicked blood. So also in the invisible killing (witchcraft) the reason of killing is on the mother's side. In the old days too the right
of selling the children into slavery was on the mother's side. So also in witchcraft
the right of selling the children's *kra* is on the mother's side. The father's *kra* is
the head of the house. If you offend your father and he does not speak it out his
kra may avenge itself on the children by making them sick, but the mother's *kra*,
if angry, can take revenge and kill the children. The father trains the children's
kra and builds it up, but the mother has the right to sell it. Therefore it needs
someone on your mother's side to sell your *kra* to the witches.'

Many anthropologists believe that witchcraft is mainly an expression of kinship jealousies. Personally I believe this explanation usually puts the cart before
the horse. Witches are primarily neurotics, and it is always a neurotic's unfortunate
relatives who have to bear the main brunt of his daily ill-humours. For instance,
if he be a paranoic it is the people living close around him whom he believes to be
plotting against him.

13

seller, as an apparent windfall, and, as the purchaser invisibly removed the spiritual counterpart of the child's leg, the child would have lost the use of the material limb. The woman was further planning, she said, that her husband should be killed by a log while helping to load a timber-lorry. Her husband, however, had drunk of the medicine of *Kupo*, so the medicine had 'caught' the plotting wife on the eve of the day she had marked for his death, and made her mortally sick and forced her to confess.

She was carried at once to *Kupo's* shrine, where she repeated her confession and added that she was not on good terms with her husband as he kept her short of money and clothing. She said that she had had her witch's dæmon (*obeye*) from her birth, and its seat was in her head. The priest said, this being so, the dæmon could not be entirely removed from her as could the acquired demons which people kept in their clothes, their waist-beads or their armpits. But its power to do harm could be destroyed if she drank *Kupo's* medicine : the medicine would 'block her way' to do harm. Her power of flying to witches' meetings, however, was an acquired power, seated in her waist-beads. This could be destroyed by giving up the beads. She would still be able to see the other witches going to their meetings, but she would be unable to join them and would die if she tried.

After her confession she gave up her waist-beads, which were then hung on *Kupo's* wall alongside a large collection of similar trophies. She then cut the head off a fowl, but, as the fowl died breast downwards, the priest said that *Kupo* was unsatisfied, and she had not told all. She then added that her own baby gave her no pleasure as it cried without ceasing, so she had been planning to kill it by her witchcraft. The next fowl indicated that *Kupo* was satisfied. The woman immediately recovered sufficiently to be able to walk home, and she and her relatives were all considerably happier.

For this purification *Kupo* charged a goat and £4, £1 18*s.* of which was paid then and there.

Such moneys are kept in a special treasury for *Kupo's* expenses, which include a cow at the annual festival and the heavy outlay of the priests and attendants on their occasional pilgrimages to the Northern Territories to return thanks. This treasury may also be broached if the town is 'in trouble'.

Another case of witchcraft was interesting because the neurotic woman blamed herself not only for her children's deaths but for the general poverty and wretchedness of the whole town.

The case began shortly after the death of the woman's two-month-old child, when she fell ill and said that it was she who had killed by witchcraft not only this child but four earlier ones. She asked to be taken to *Kupo's* shrine to complete her confession and to be freed from her demon which she said had tormented her for years.

At the shrine she said that her demon's name was *Ekua Eniedin ba* and that it abode under her eyelids in the form of an invisible centipede. She said she had a secret song which she silently sang to it:

> *Atufo gyengyen' beye wo mu*
> *Ekua Dansowa atufo gyengyen beye wo mu.*
>
> (*A bulging bussel has a demon inside it*
> *Ekua Dansowa's bulging bussel has a demon in it.*)

When she sang, she said, her demon became active and did all the deeds she had set it. It had killed her five children, her sister's four children and her sister. At this point she got highly excited, danced and sang her song aloud to the assembled company. She said that it was by her will that her parents, brothers, and sisters were in poverty and could not prosper. She had also turned the main street of the town into an invisible river called *Kwesiko*, and everyone who crossed it lost three-pence for each crossing, with the result that everyone in the town remained poor. The river, she said, would depart if the *ohene* offered it a sheep and an egg.

At this point she asked to be allowed to cut off a fowl's head, but, as the fowl died breast downwards, she was told to continue her confession. She did, saying that her husband had never pleased her and that one day, when he had given her only six-pence for housekeeping, she went to her farm and there cursed him to God (*Onyame*). Such a curse, I was told, is harmless when uttered indoors in the presence of others, but uttered when alone in the bush it is damaging.

Here she slaughtered another fowl, which again indicated incomplete confession. She then said that it was she who, in the spirit, had 'dug up' all the diamonds and hidden them in the river, and had also taken away the courage of those who would otherwise have had the enterprise to start the diamond industry. She added that if the *ohene* took a sheep, a piece of calico and some eggs and gave to the river, the diamonds would come back.

Then she slaughtered another fowl, which showed her to have confessed all.

Her head was then shaved and she 'drank' *Kupo's* medicine. A goat was killed at her expense and was cooked in *Kupo's* grove. Neither her husband nor any of the relatives she had injured was allowed to assist her in the expenses of her purification or to stand as her guarantors 'for the medicine would then have been offended and would have said "I am helping you against this woman, but you are helping *her*." '

This was the end of her dealings with *Kupo*, but the mood of confession was still on her and the next day she declared that she had been unable to sleep all night because of a weight still on her mind. She said that some years before, in another district, she had offended an Ashanti deity named *Anokyi*. She had quarrelled with her husband and said that if he did not send her back to her parents *Anokyi* must kill her. The husband prepared to send her back, but she changed her mind and refused to go. This was making a fool of *Anokyi*, for which she ought to have pacified him with rum. So she performed the tardy pacification and then felt that she had a clean sheet. She quickly became better. Her husband prepared to divorce her, which they both appeared to have long desired, and both were obviously much happier.

Another case which I witnessed in Abenase concerned the violation of an important rule laid down for *Kupo's* adherents, namely, that they must not cherish malice and spite against others, must not speak ill of others, and must not secretly nurse rancour in their hearts. In every community all over the Gold Coast such feelings are held to produce ill-health, and they are undoubtedly responsible for a great deal of 'nerves'.

The woman in question quarrelled bitterly with her sister and refused to make up the quarrel. She also hated her husband's other wife. She became very thin, irritable, and ailing, and at length fell ill of what appeared to me to be probably pneumonia. Her father, who had himself had some training as a medicine-man elsewhere early in life, consulted an oracle of his own and announced that she had offended some medicine. She was asked if this was true. She said it was. She was ostensibly a Christian, but, against the rules of the church, had secretly drunk of *Kupo's* medicine and had violated the rules of *Kupo* by cherishing bitterness and hate in her heart. Possibly the secret disobedience to her church rules contributed to her anxieties.

The father-in-law, an honest, earnest little man, went straight to *Kupo's* shrine on her behalf, as she was too ill to go. He stood before the shrine and gave an impressively simple account of his daughter-in-law's illness and confession, and then slaughtered a fowl on her behalf. The fowl indicated that *Kupo* was unsatisfied, so he went home again and told her. She said it was true that she had more to confess and told of an occasion on which her husband had given his other wife palm-oil for her cooking and had given her nothing, causing her inside to swell with hatred of the other.

Another fowl and this new confession were brought back to the shrine, and this time *Kupo* showed himself satisfied. The father-in-law then paid a guinea and went home.

The woman was now free of the displeasure of *Kupo* and her illness was ready to be treated by ordinary remedies. However, about an hour afterwards she died. Later I enquired why *Kupo* had allowed her to die after pronouncing her cleansed of her sin, and was told that she had left the confession too late and was 'already dead' when she made it.

There was some controversy about her burial. She was nominally a Christian, and those of her relatives who were also Christians wished her to be buried with Christian rites in the Christian cemetery. The catechist, however, heard about her confession and said that if she had 'drunk fetish' she was no Christian and must have heathen burial. The corpse lay for two days while the dispute was settled.

The Prasu Festival

Here I may give an account of the *Omanhene's* annual visit to Afosu, as it is a striking example of the way the new medicine is encroaching upon the old ancestor-worship.

When the Akim-Kotoku *Omanhene's* stool first fled from Denchera-Miriem, its owners settled on the east bank of the Pra near what is now the village of Prasu Kuma. They stayed there about one generation and then, when the Ashanti made another attack on them, their chief *Ampim Otioda* and some of his followers were seized by despair, and drowned themselves in the Pra after flinging in most of their heirlooms. Their survivors therefore regarded the district as 'bad land', and left it. A slave was left behind in charge of the weekly worship of the Pra, but annually the *Omanhene* still visits the place to worship the spirit of his drowned ancestor, to thank the Pra for guarding his bones, and to perform the ritual for the other ancestors in the deserted cemetery not far away.

On these annual visits the *Omanhene* and his retinue stay at Afosu within easy reach of the old sites. At Afosu there is one of the new imported shrines of the *Kupo* type, that of a deity

called *Nangro*. Its annual festival is held during the *Omanhene's*
stay in Afosu. A crowd of visitors come at the same time, but it
is *Nangro's* celebrations in which they take most interest, and it
is unlikely that they would come were *Nangro* not there.

On the first day the *Omanhene's* visit to the riverside took
place. There was no grandeur. The *Omanhene* wore no rich
clothing, had no umbrella, and went on foot through the few
miles of forest from Prasukuma to the riverside. The *Kyidomhene*,
who was with him, also made no display.

On the way through the forest the party stopped beside two
huge stones shaped like tree-trunks—connected in the old days,
I believe, with the worship of the land. Here the *Omanhene*
poured a libation and offered a prayer.

Reaching the river bank, some sand was scooped out of the
river and made into a mound on which was set a basin of river
water. The horn-blowers blew on their horns and the drummers
beat their drums to call the attention of the dead in the river.
These dead, say the Prasukuma people, can sometimes be heard
beating their own drums under the water. The *Omanhene* poured
rum on the ground and called upon both the river and the dead
ancestors. Then an elder poured rum into the basin, added an
egg and then sprinkled cooked yam-and-egg food in the river,
on the bank, and on the mound of sand. Then a sheep was
slaughtered, its blood was sprinkled in the basin and on the
mound, the feet and ears were laid on the mound, the entrails
were rolled in the hide and flung into the stream. Then every
one was sprinkled with river water for blessing, and, after singing
a few songs, they walked home again.

Two days later the *Omanhene*, this time carried in his palanquin
and accompanied only by two or three officials, paid a visit to
the deserted cemetery. This was his first such visit, and he was
said to be very nervous lest he should perform the rites incor-
rectly and die. He was also said to be uncertain whether his
ancestors approved of his election to the stool. He did not
allow me to witness the ceremony, lest this should give offence
to the ancestors, and on the eve of the occasion he took special
precautions to protect himself from harm with a modern imported
medicine.

In the morning, before the visit to the cemetery, another
expensive medicine (*suman*) which the *Omanhene* had recently
purchased, was laid in the yard of his quarters and a sacrifice
was made to it.

To the festival of *Nangro* three days were devoted, and great
interest was taken in it.

The *Nangro* shrine is owned by the whole town, and of the £100 collected for its setting-up the *Omanhene*, I am told, paid a part. The annual profits from the shrine are 'shown to him' and he is given a share.

On the first day of *Nangro's* festival the *Omanhene*, accompanied by his official horn-blowers and retinue, attended the dance. Rum was poured before the shrine on his behalf and the god was asked to bless him and to prosper the whole *oman*. The priests of the shrine sat and shook their calabash rattles and sang songs of praise and thanksgiving. A great variety of people brought free-will offerings and many new worshippers came for the first time to 'drink the medicine' and receive protection. These initiates paid two shillings each, and spots of white clay were put on their foreheads, arms, and tongues. A young wife of the *Omanhene*, believed to be pregnant, came and was blest. She was brushed all over with *Nangro's* broom to sweep away evil, and was given two strands of the broom to take with her for the daily repetition of the treatment. Several people, who had already 'drunk the medicine', brought their infants to be blest. One father brought a day-old child. The whole celebration was charged with enthusiasm, spontaneity, and genuine gaiety.

I also had the opportunity later of seeing *Nangro* at his everyday work, and was there when he dealt with two people 'caught by the medicine'.

The first of these was a young woman who fell sick and said that the medicine which she had previously drunk had caught her for wrong-doing. The rules of *Nangro* forbid quarrelling and malicious feelings, and if rancour is concealed in a worshipper's heart he will fall sick. The woman said her heart was full of bitterness against her husband, so she had come to speak it out and be cleansed and cured of her sickness. She said that her husband never gave her a cloth, never made her a farm, and never fulfilled any of a husband's obligations. Her mother had advised her to divorce him. The husband, who was present, certainly appeared to be a lazy good-for-nothing, but the wife evidently felt that the blame was partly hers. She killed several fowls before *Nangro* indicated satisfaction, and each time produced a further confession of her own shortcomings.

Another woman 'caught' by the medicine, and made sick, came to the shrine and confessed to having committed adultery. The ordeal of the fowl showed her confession complete, and her cleansing was undertaken. Her head was shaved and the hair thrown on the town rubbish heap, and then she herself was thrown on the rubbish heap. Then she was brought back, bathed in *Nangro's* cleansing water, rubbed with white clay and made to dance before *Nangro's* shrine to the sound of his rattles. On three separate days she danced and then was pronounced cleansed of her sin. She said that her sickness had completely left her.

The townsmen told me that they first decided to have a shrine at a time when about forty young children had died, they thought at the hands of witches. They were also suffering from a great nuisance of cocoa-stealing and palm-wine robbing. The £100 was easily raised and several officials were deputed to set off in search of a protective medicine. They travelled to Kumasi, where they met the stranger who told them about *Nangro*, and they went with him to a Northern place called Lobi. A representative from Lobi came with them and set up their shrine. It consists of two altars and two pots inside a concrete wall. One set is male and the other is female, and both have to be served equally.

They said that the partakers of the medicine must neither steal, commit adultery, quarrel, lie, nor secretly cherish animosity. Anyone who plans to harm them magically or by witchcraft, steals from them, or seduces their wives, is 'caught' by the medicine and made sick. The medicine also brings fertility, and many barren couples come and ask to be enabled to bring forth children. Such children are often named *Nangro*.

They added that the stealing of cocoa and palm-wine had stopped.

Asasi [1] and some other New Shrines

The shrines of *Asasi*, another imported deity from the French Ivory Coast, are similar to the others in their functions, rules, and regulations, but the essential insignia includes a pair of earthen leopards standing at right-angles to one another inside a low-walled enclosure. Outside is a pot of watery 'medicine' which accepted candidates actually drink after being taken by the hand through the leopards' house.

Tuntumerim has a shrine of *Asasi* owned by the whole town ; the elders sent a deputation to the French Ivory Coast to fetch it.

Asasi's shrines, being of rather gaudy and spectacular appearance, attract more strangers than most of the others. In particular a great many strangers visit an *Asasi* shrine at Benim. This is not a Kotoku town, but, as a great many Kotoku people visit it, it may be described here.

---

[1] Not to be confused with the earth-goddess *Asase*.

19. Presenting thank-offerings at the Nangro shrine. (*See* page 191.)

20. Beheaded fowls lying before Nangro's shrine. (*See* page 192.)

The Benim shrine was established under the ægis of the town elders, but they appointed as chief priest a medicine-man who had been previously living in the town as a private practitioner of ordinary medical lore. This priest has several assistants, including diviners, and, when *Asasi* shows dissatisfaction with a client, the diviners find out the reason for it.

Many of the Benim clients are from Fanti country, and often one of them still worships the *obosum* of his own *ntro*. Anyone coming to join the *Asasi* fraternity must, if he knows to what *ntro* he belongs, bring a sheep and slaughter it, not for *Asasi* but for his old *obosum*, and must explain that in joining the company of the new god he means no disrespect to the old.[1]

One man whom I saw come to drink the medicine for the first time brought fowls and a goat for *Asasi*, but *Asasi* rejected them. He went to the diviners to enquire why ; they told him that *Bosum* Pra, the *obosum* of his *ntro*, had been very good to him and had given him children by each of his four wives, and that he had come to *Asasi* mainly because he wanted further prosperity. He must go home again, they said, and ask *Bosum* Pra's permission to drink Asasi. He said it was too far to go home, but he would implore *Bosum* Pra at Benim. He did so, but again Asasi rejected his fowl. He went to the diviners again and they told him that he had helped a man to kill another by lending him money with which to buy an expensive bad medicine. He admitted this, killed another fowl, but *Asasi* rejected it.

He then made six other minor confessions, killing a fowl between each, but *Asasi* rejected them all. He then said he had no more confessions to make, so the diviners advised him to give *Bosum* Pra pacification on behalf of each of his wives, as they had all received great blessing from that *obosum*.

Another case which I witnessed at Benim is worth mentioning in view of the statement sometimes made that only adults can be witches. This may be true in some parts of the Gold Coast, but I have not found it so in Akim.

The child in question, aged about two, was suffering from diarrhœa, which in itself is common enough and causes little comment even when fatal. But the child was held to be behaving abnormally.[2] For instance, she refused to sit down. The

---

[1] The ceremony of apologetically slaughtering a sheep for family deities is often performed by converts to Christianity.

[2] Modern psychology has shown that many psychological disorders do start in early childhood. Africans, who are very acute observers of human behaviour, know this. They have long known, for instance, that a young child, displaced from the affections of its mother by the birth of a second child, may be seriously upset.

parents were both already members of *Asasi's* fraternity, so they brought her to the shrine. The diviner said she had been born a witch and travelled in the spirit to witch's meetings but was not yet old enough to kill other people or to eat human flesh. She was charged twenty-five shillings—half the sum charged to any adult who comes and asks to be cured of witch-craft—was given a drink of *Asasi's* medicine and was hooted at. Then a fowl was slaughtered on her behalf and was accepted by the deity. The parents, who had been looking miserably anxious, were immediately wreathed in smiles, and, curiously enough, the child itself, which had been grizzling incessantly and refusing to sit down, caught something of its parents' new satisfaction, suddenly stopped whining, sat on its mother's knee, and snuggled contentedly.

On another occasion the Benim shrine was consulted by the Abenase chief on behalf of his daughter in somewhat interesting circumstances.

The girl in question was an unusually bonny specimen of about fifteen, and her mother's relatives had betrothed her to a wealthy but elderly man of Akwapim and had accepted the marriage fee. The girl had never seen her bridegroom, and when he came to claim her she disliked him and declined to go. Now, it is emphatically not the custom to force a girl to marry a man whom she dislikes. Her step-mother, in whose compound at Abenase she lived, was definitely on her side, and her father, the chief, who was very fond of her, was plainly much worried. He was anxious, however, not to offend the suitor, who was not only wealthy but was a medicine-man of Akwapim and might be expected to take supernatural revenge. The suitor considered that, left to herself, the girl would have liked him, so he sued the parents for defamation of character and breach of contract. They paid him £15. But the chief still thought his daughter had missed a good marriage, so he employed a second Akwapim medicine-man, not to persuade the girl against her will, but to change her affections so that she might welcome the marriage. But the girl sulked, and then one day said that she was sick. It was then decided to send her to the shrine at Benim, first to find out, by slaughtering a fowl, whether her sickness was genuine, and second, to find out from the diviner whether the sickness was 'because her spirit disagreed with the marriage'.

The fowl ordeal pronounced her quite sincere, and the diviner announced that the sickness was the manifestation of the dis-agreement of her spirit with the prospect of the marriage. The diviner also censured and warned her father, reminding him that he had earlier allowed an older daughter to be married to a rich man against the wishes of her spirit and that the daughter had since died. Her death, he declared, was not due to any sickness, but was simply the protest of her spirit against the marriage. The father should have known, even before the first incident, that no good ever came of an unwilling marriage, and should at any rate have learnt a lesson from his first daughter's death.

Public opinion unanimously upheld the diviner's censure of the father. However, still avaricious, he caused his daughter to be given another medicine 'to change her spirit'. But with the moral support of *Asasi* her spirit remained recalcitrant, and the last I heard of her was that she had married another and younger man entirely pleasing to her spirit.

I should add that I have never met another case of attempted forced marriage in illiterate communities. But in more sophisticated circles there is a tendency among those literate fathers who have renounced 'native custom' to sell—or virtually to sell—their daughters to wealthy men, not only for the ready money but in the hope of continued financial benefit. And it would not be surprising if the tendency were to spread to illiterate parents. It is clear, however, that the tendency may be placed among those money-bred modern evils which the people quite clearly recognize as evils and which are being so strikingly resisted by the vigorous growth of the new shrines.

To return to *Asasi's* shrine at Benim; this is placed by the roadside and made arresting by a good deal of coloured paint, garish decoration, and gun-firing 'to call the god', so it attracts more clients than the more secluded shrines. On fairly average days I have counted twenty or more supplicants in one morning. Other private practitioners' shrines are not quite so flourishing, but most of them receive several new clients every day.

Asasi at Benim has two special departments, one for Mahomedans and another for Christians. The Mahomedans have an umbrella under which they kill sheep in the Mahomedan fashion : if *Asasi* accepts their sacrifice the dying animal jerks its legs in vigorous spasms but if it dies limply the sacrifice is held to be rejected.

Christians are forbidden by their churches to 'drink fetish', but in Abenase most of them have taken *Kupo's* medicine secretly by night.[1] *Asasi* at Benim has a hidden grove where

[1] The Presbyterian catechist himself told me that he knew they did this, but he could not prevent it.

Christians drink the medicine. Some of them salve their consciences by refraining from the slaughter of the fowl, saying,
'if you don't sacrifice an animal there is no offence if you take
communion in church afterwards,' but they hope that by paying
Asasi's fee and allowing the priest to commend them to *Asasi's*
care they will be protected, not only from witchcraft but from
lorry accidents, falling trees, and cutlass accidents.

At *Asasi's* Benim shrine there are eight priests including the
diviner, eight priestly attendants, and eight wives of the chief
priests. Daily the wives cook a good meal for the deity and place
it on a table under an umbrella. A chair spread with a velvet
cover is placed for the deity to sit upon, and, as soon as the food
is placed on the table, all business is suspended till the invisible
diner is held to have finished his meal and the dishes are removed.

The people of Ayiribe have a shrine of *Kupo* for which they
paid nothing, but as people are prone to believe that greater
costliness denotes greater value, Ayiribe has set up, at a cost of
about £20, a second shrine, that of a deity called *Wirika*. Three
messengers were appointed by the town to travel to the Northern
Territories and seek for a suitable shrine. They hit upon *Wirika*,
of which I know nothing except that its rules and regulations are
like those of the others.

Nyankumasi people have a shrine of *Kupo* and another of a
deity called *Cheriya*, which they say came from the Wa district
of the Northern Territories. They say it is advisable to have
two deities in case one should wish to go to sleep or temporarily
to leave the town. Membership of the *Cheriya* fraternity is
sealed by the eating of one of the deity's kola-nuts. Most people
pay half a crown to join, but poor people are admitted for sixpence. Rich people—who have more to be protected by the
deity—make larger voluntary contributions when they join.

Cheriya protects its members from false witness, theft, con-
spiracy, and adultery, and smites down perjurers, thieves, con-
spirators, and adulterers. It is said to be specially vigilant in
protecting uncles from the machinations of nephews who seek
their uncles' deaths. *Cheriya* also makes the claim—a unique
one I believe—that its members are immune from death by snake-
bite. A snake which bites a member promptly dies, but its
victim takes no harm.

I saw two Nyankumasi women who had fallen sick and who
came and declared themselves witches. One said she had killed five
of her own relatives, the other said she had killed fourteen. Each
of them after confession was prayed for and heartily booed.
Each presented *Cheriya* with £2 10s. and two bottles of rum

22. Type of medicine-man common in other parts of the Gold Coast. In Akim-Kotoku this one only was found. (*See* page 197.)

21. Spots of white clay were put on their foreheads, arms and tongues. (*See* page 191.)

and was promptly cured. The money and rum, the priest said, were not essential to the cure, for '*Cheriya* only wants Truth. If you confess all, you are cured.'

Annual Festivals of the New Shrines

I have already described the annual festival of Nangro at Afosu and have mentioned that the *Omanhene* attended it.

I was not at Abenase at the time of *Kupo's* annual festival, but I saw a good many of the visitors who had come for it, and the *Krontihene*, *Kupo's* priest, gave me an account of it. The whole town contributed to buy a cow—a more expensive sacrifice than any of the older festivals can command—and there was certainly great enthusiasm. Several old elders, who might have been expected to disparage the new and eulogize the old, said, 'The medicine is doing its work well, so we must do all we can to thank it. It has helped many people who were in trouble and danger. It has taken away our fear. And it has stopped a lot of stealing and bad deeds.'

I did attend the shrine festival at Edzubea—Abenase's sister town—and was told that it was typical of the new shrine festivals. It far surpassed in heartiness and festiveness any of the older town festivals except that of Assene. Everyone, including the chief and elders, attended, and everyone was gay and interested. Besides the priest and his assistants, all in spectacular Northern Territory robes and trappings, there were about six women *akomfo*, all in costume, all dancing, and all possessed. The frequency and vigour with which a deity possesses mediums is a reliable index to the general interest taken in its worship. A deity appoints its own *akomfo* by the process of possessing her, and, whilst most of the older deities of the district have not, for many years, appointed even one new *akomfo*, the new deity in Edzubea alone has appointed six.

In Nyankumasi, where there are two new shrines, these take it in turns to receive the cow annually presented by the grateful townsmen.

In general it may be said that the annual festivals of the new shrines are comparable in gaiety and zest with the ancient festivals of the cults of pre-stool days, which survive in some districts outside Akim and in Assene and are in sharp contrast to the *Afahye* and *Odwira* festivals of most towns in which nobody bestirs himself to take much interest.

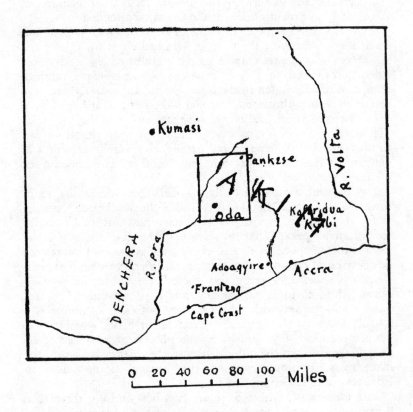

The area in the small square is the area enlarged in the map opposite.

CHART A.—CONDITIONS OF OCCUPATION OF LAND BY THE TOWNS OF THE AKIM-KOTOKU STATE

Town.	Clan.	Place of Origin.	Time of Foundation of Present Town.	Landowner of Present Site.	Disposal of Proceeds of Land Sales, Timber and Mines.
Aberem	Toa	Claim to be Aborigines	No tradition	Aberem	1/3 to *Omanbene*, rest to landowner.
Kwisi	,,	,,	,,	Kwisi	1/3 to *Omanbene*, rest shared by joint landowners.
Manso	,,	,,	,,	Manso-Toa group	,, ,,
Akroso	,,	,,	,,	,,	,, ,,
Ashantimang	,,	,,	,,	,,	,, ,,
Suponsu	,,	,,	,,	,,	1/3 to *Omanbene*, rest to landowner.
Adjuafo	,,	,,	,,	Adjuafo	,, ,,
Akinkase	Asenie	,,	,,	Dabenhene's stool	1/3 to *Omanbene*, rest shared by joint landowners.
Pankese	Asuna	Akwamu	Early 17th century?	Pankese-Nyafamang	
Nyafamang	Aduana	,,	,,		*Omanbene* claims whole (highly anomalous).
Adausena	,,	,,	,,	Adausena ,,	,, ,,
Ntronang	,,	,,	,,	Ntronang or Adausena (disputed)	,, ,,
Akokoaso	Koana	Adanse-Fomena	Before B. of Feyase	Akokoaso	1/3 to *Omanbene*, rest to landowner.
Abontodiase	Bretu	,,	,,	Abontodiase	,, ,,
Ayiribe	,,	Ashanti-Ofuase	,,	Ayiribe	1/3 to *Omanbene*, rest shared by joint landowners.
Anyinam	,,	,,	,,	Anyinam-Bieni	,, ,,
Bieni	,,	,,	,,		,, ,,
Apaso	Oyeko	Adanse Ayiase	,,	Apaso ,,	1/3 to *Omanbene*, rest to landowner.
Kotokuom	,,	Adanse Kontrase	,,	Kotokuom	,, ,,
Nkwateng	,,	Adanse	,,	Nkwateng	,, ,,
Anyinase	Agona	Denchera	After B. of Feyase	Apoli (Abuakwa) Rent £50 p.a.	1/3 to *Abuakwabene*, rest to landowner.

CHART A.—*continued.*

Town.	Clan.	Place of Origin.	Time of Foundation of Present Town.	Landowner of Present Site.	Disposal of Proceeds of Land Sales, Timber and Miens.
Abenase	Agona	Part Denchera, part Aborigines	,, ,,	Abenase	1/3 to *Omanbene*, rest to landowner.
Edzubea	,,	,, ,, ,,	,, ,, ,,	Edzubea	,, ,, ,, ,,
Awisa	,,	,, ,, ,,	,, ,, ,,	Awisa	,, ,, ,, ,,
Akrofonso	,,	Denchera ,, ,,	,, ,, ,,	Oda (Akrofonso is caretaker)	Whole to *Omanbene*.
Prasukuma	,,	,,	,, ,, ,,	Oda (Prasukuma is caretaker)	,, ,,
Oda	,,	Denchera via Akrofonsu and Jyadem	19th century	Oda: by recent purchase from Wenchi	,, ,,
Assene	,,	Denchera via Assene and Manso	Time of Oda foundation	,, ,, ,,	,, ,,
Aboabo. Hwekwae	,,	Denchera via Manso / Denchera via Akrofonsu and Jyadem	,, ,, ,,	,, ,, ,,	1/3 to *Omanbene*, rest to landowner.
Tuntumerim	Aduana	Adausena	,, ,, ,,	Adausena: 1 sheep p.a. Awisa: 1 sheep p.a.	Whole to landowner if land were sold.
Nkwanta	Agona	Denchera via Manso	,, ,, ,,	Nkwanta: by recent purchase from Apoli	If mines were established, 1/3 of income would go to *Omanbene*, rest to landowner.
Afosu	,,	Agogo	After Yaa Asantewa War	Oda: 1 sheep p.a.	Whole to *Omanbene*.
Mamanso	,,	Ashanti Denchera	,, ,, ,,	Aberem: 1 sheep and £4 p.a.	1/3 to *Omanbene*, rest to landowner.
Abodom	Asuna	Konongo Ashanti Kokofu	Reign of Osei Bonso 1888	Oda: 1 sheep p.a.	Whole to *Omanbene*.
Asuosu	Oyeko			Manso Toa group: £5 and 1 sheep p.a.	1/3 to *Omanbene*, rest shared by joint landowners.
Anamase	,,	Ashanti Bankame	End 19th century	Adekuma-Anamase aborigines. Rent £55 p.a.	1/3 shared Bosomehene and Abuakwahene. 1/3 Adekuma, 1/3 Anamase aborigines of Bosome.

CHART A.—*continued.*

Town.	Clan.	Place of Origin.	Time of Foundation of Present Town.	Landowner of Present Site.	Disposal of Proceeds of Land Sales, Timber and Mines.
Esuboi N. .	Asenie	Ashanti Akyim	,, ,,	Abontodiase. £10 and 1 sheep p.a.	1/3 to *Omanhene*, rest to landowner.
Esuboi S. .	,,	,, ,,	,, ,,	Manso-Toa group. £10 and 1 sheep p.a.	1/3 to *Omanhene*, rest shared by joint landowners.
Mpintimpi .	Bretu	,, ,,	,, ,,	Assene	1/3 to *Omanhene*, rest to landowner.
Eshiem . .	Asuna	Fanti Aberekum	1900–1910	Manso-Toa group. £5 and 1 sheep p.a.	1/3 to *Omanhene*, rest shared by joint landowners.
Prasu-Amuena	Bretu	Juaben	End 19th century	Assene	1/3 to *Omanhene*, rest to landowner.
Akoase . .	Agona	,,	,, ,,	Oda	Whole to *Omanhene*.
Amua . .	Asona	,,	,, ,,	Assene	1/3 to *Omanhene*, rest to landowner.
Chenchenku .	Bretu	,,	,, ,,		
Nwiesu . .	Aduana	,,	,, ,,	Part ,, Assene, part Dabenhene's stool	1/3 ,, *Omanhene*, 1/3 to members of Dabenhene's stool.
Odmasua .	Asuna	,,	,, ,,	Oda	Whole to *Omanhene*.
Noem . .	,,	,,	,, ,,	,,	,, ,,

14

CHART C

Abosum.	Day of Worship.	Venerated Animal.	Tabooed Food or Animal.	Greeting.	Herb used in Washing.	Remarks on the Abosum, etc.
Bosum Pra .	Wednesday		Cat-fish Hornbill White fowl Water-yam on Wednesdays Palm-wine on Wednesdays	'Ya Ahinewa !'	egoro adwira	River. To worshippers of Bosum Pra who do not eat water-yam at all the greeting 'Ya Obiri !' is given.
Bosum Twi .	Sunday	Wild dog odompo			Ssnne adwira	Lake in Ashanti.
Bosum Muru .	Tuesday	Dog, Crocodile ?	Dog, Crocodile ?		adwira	River in Ashanti.
Bosum Akora .	Friday Monday	Wild dog	Crab		adwira	River in Ashanti.
Bosum Muram .						
Bosum Nketia .				'Anyado !'	adwira	The Gã expression for circumcision is to 'cut nketia'. The high priest of a Gã Fraternity originating in Akwapim is called the 'Nyado'.
Bosum Poakwa .	Tuesday			'Ya, Ahinewa!'		Poakwa is the Sea. Along the entire coast sea-fishing on Tuesdays is prohibited even where ntro cult is unknown.

CHART C   203

	Day		Black Monkey / Tortoise		adwira / adwira sunme	
Bosum Esum .	Sunday		Black Monkey			
Bosum Aboadi .	Friday / Sunday	*Nsansai* antelope Leopard	Tortoise			
Bosum Ankamadi						
Bosum Akom .		Dog ?	Snail			'The dog is our sheep. We eat it for sacrifice.'
Bosum Boni .		Dog *odompo*	Pumpkin *efre*	'Ya, Ahinewa!'		River near Krachyi, rising near the source of the R. Afram.
Bosum Dwirebi .	Wednesday Monday	*Otrom* antelope	*Mampam* lizard. Animals with striped skins. Spotted black-and-white fowls		*adwira*	"This *'bosum* is a rock called *Kwabu Boo*. A river arises out of this rock. In olden days the rock could talk.
Bosum Densu .		Wild dog ?	Green snail *temriwa*. Wild dog ?			River. No dog may be kept as a pet.
Bosum Adom .	Friday Wednesday	Leopard	*Anwa* snail. Dog. Any partially eaten animal found dead	'Ya Emu !'		
Bosum Nyankamadie			Leopard			Is not a river.
Bosum Fe .			*Akam* gourd			
Bosum Eyisu .						
Bosum Koinsi .	Tuesday	Dog Tortoise	No food taboos			
Bosum Nse .						From Akwapim. Dogs prohibited as pets.

14*

CHART C.—*continued.*

Abosum.	Day of Worship.	Venerated Animal.	Tabooed Food or Animal.	Greeting.	Herb used in Washing.	Remarks on the Abosum, etc.
Bosum Dwurumprem	Friday	Crocodile	Dog Goat		*adwira sunme*	A river near Tafo.
Bosum Tua						From Akwapim.
Bosum Ayensu		Wild pig *kotoke*				
Bosum Tano						River in Ashanti.
Bosum Dinyira	Tuesday Wednesday	None	Dog Tortoise			
Bosum Tweneboa		Crocodile			*sunme adwira*	A river near Achiase. Surasie people also have a shrine of Tweneboa with ritual divorced from the paternal group.
Bosum Kyremadie	Thursday					A sub-division of Tweneboa ?
Bosum Abeka		None	*Mampam* lizard	'Ya, Abrao !'	*sunme adwira nyranyra*	This abosum is a Fanti hill.
Bosum Emise		None	White fowl	'Anyado !'		
Bosum Budu			Crab *temriwa* snail	'Ya, Abrao !'		A Fanti hill.
Bosum Abaka			Snail Lizard	'Ya, Ahinewa!'		
Bosum Amisakyi		Crocodile	*Mampam* lizard Rat	'Ya, Anyado !'		A Fanti river.
Bosum Epo						Of Fanti origin.

INDEX

Mother, Queen, 21, 26, 28, 29, 39, 52, 116
—, wife's, 90, 91
Mourning clothes, 41

Nana Tongo, 180, 182
Nangro, 105, 190
— festival, 135, 190–192, 197
Native Administration Ordinance, 126, 129, 131, 133
— state, 1
Nentwi, 121
Nephew, as successor, 82–84
—, father's, 82–84
— inheritance system, 117
Nifa, 6, 47
Nifahene, 6, 48, 50
— definition of, 14
Nkwanta, 48, 64, 163, 169
Noboa system, 73
Northern Territory, 123, 176, 180, 181–183, 196
Nsawabodie, 87
Nsawam, 2, 48
Nsiye, 87
Nsuabode, 142
Ntra dwom, 130
Ntro, 96, 104, 116, 151, 156, 157, 171, 193
— ceremonial, 156
— paternal group, 157
Ntronang, 4, 45
Ntam kese, 22, 23
Ntama po, 87
Nwiesu, 62
Nyafamang, 116
Nyame, 158
Nyankumasi, 10, 37, 58, 63, 196, 197
Nyanyao, 2, 3

Obeaberema, 116
Obeye, 186
Obeyefo, 185
Obligations, funeral, 95
Obosum, 21, 162, 193
Ocheroso, 4, 5, 48
Oda, 3, 4, 25, 39, 48, 49, 62, 63, 116
—, *gyashene* of, 38
Odikro, 17, 21, 25, 49, 50, 57, 122
—, definition of, 13
—'s, stool, 57, 61
—, woman as, 116

Odisiso, 105
Odom-bebabetomi, 163
Odumase, 5
Odwira ceremony, 62
— festival, 171, 197
— — in Abenase, 163–169
— — in Nkwanta, 169, 170
Ofuasi, 3, 65
Ogbaniba, 184 n.
Ogobra custom (see *Bradwu*), 137, 138
Ohene, 14, 21, 23, 24, 31, 48, 60, 62, 63, 122
—, definition of, 13
—, 'father' of, 18
—, marriage of, 108–109
— of Anyinase, 50
—'s stool, 17, 25, 57, 61
Ohenebea, 21
Okyeame, 21, 22, 31, 32, 66, 75, 143
—, duties of, 28
Oman, 1, 4, 36, 131–134, 138
—, allegiance, 37
—, control, 11
— council, 120
—, finances of, 47–56
—, gathering of, 39 *et seq.*
—, land litigation and, 53
—, land ownership and, 49
—, management of, 6, 7
—, organization of, 6, 47
—, preservation of, 132, 134
—, relationship to land ownership, 7, 8
—, transference of towns to, 5
Omanhene, 4–14, 39–58, 60, 67, 80, 109, 120, 121, 131–133, 189–191
—, definition of, 14
—, financial duties of, 6–8
—, funeral of, 39–46, 142
—'s, stool, 12
—, woman as, 116
Onyame, 158, 159, 187
Opanyim, 13
Opoku Ware, 3
Ordinance, Native Administration, 129, 131, 133
Oreko, 4, 37
— clan, 1, 2, 8, 9
Osei Tutu, 3
— — Agyeman, 39
Osina, 3
Oto, 138
Otu Ayipe Firimpong, 15, 160
— —'s war stool, 160